SO-AWG-846

Microsoft® Office Word 2003
ILLUSTRATED, CourseCard Edition

INTRODUCTORY

Microsoft Office Specialist Program

WHAT DOES THIS LOGO MEAN?

It means this courseware has been approved by the Microsoft® Office Specialist Program to be among the finest available for learning one or more of the applications of the Microsoft Office 2003 Suite. It also means that upon completion of this courseware, you may be prepared to take an exam for Microsoft Office Specialist qualification. If "1 of 2" or "2 of 2" appears below the logo on the cover, this indicates this courseware has been approved as part of a sequence of texts for preparation to become a Microsoft Office Specialist. See the table below for more information.

WHAT IS A MICROSOFT OFFICE SPECIALIST?

A Microsoft Office Specialist is an individual who has passed exams for certifying his or her skills in one or more of the Microsoft Office desktop applications such as Microsoft Word, Microsoft Excel, Microsoft PowerPoint®, Microsoft Outlook®, Microsoft Access, or Microsoft Project. The Microsoft Office Specialist Program is the only program in the world approved by Microsoft for testing proficiency in Microsoft Office desktop applications and Microsoft Project. This testing program can be a valuable asset in any job search or career advancement.

ILLUSTRATED TITLES FOR OFFICE 2003 MICROSOFT OFFICE SPECIALIST CERTIFICATION

The Illustrated Series offers a growing number of Microsoft-approved courseware products that cover the objectives required to pass a Microsoft Office Specialist exam. After studying with any of the books listed below, you should be prepared to take the Microsoft office Specialist Program exam indicated. The following titles have certification approval as courseware for the Microsoft Office Specialist program:

Exam	Course Technology Illustrated Series Textbook
Microsoft Office Access 2003	Microsoft Office Access 2003 – Illustrated Introductory, CourseCard Edition (1-4188-4298-2) or Microsoft Office Access 2003 – Illustrated Complete, CourseCard Edition (1-4188-4299-0)
Microsoft Office Excel 2003	Microsoft Office Excel 2003 – Illustrated Introductory, CourseCard Edition (1-4188-4295-8)
Microsoft Office Excel 2003 Expert	Microsoft Office Excel 2003 – Illustrated Complete, CourseCard Edition (1-4188-4296-6)
Microsoft Office PowerPoint 2003	Microsoft Office PowerPoint 2003 – Illustrated Introductory, CourseCard Edition (1-4188-4304-0)
Microsoft Office Word 2003	Microsoft Office Word 2003 – Illustrated Introductory, CourseCard Edition (1-4188-4301-6)
Microsoft Office Word 2003 Expert	Microsoft Office Word 2003 – Illustrated Complete, CourseCard Edition (1-4188-4302-4)
Microsoft Office 2003 (separate exams for Word, Excel, Access and PowerPoint)	Microsoft Office 2003 – Illustrated Introductory (0-619-05789-0) and Microsoft Office 2003 – Illustrated Second Course (0-619-18826-X) when used in a sequence, meet the requirements for Microsoft Office Specialist for Word, Excel, Access, and PowerPoint.

MORE INFORMATION:

To learn more about becoming a Microsoft Office Specialist, visit www.microsoft.com/officespecialist.

To learn about other Microsoft Office Specialist approved courseware from Course Technology, visit www.course.com.

The availability of Microsoft Office Specialist certification exams varies by application, application version, and language. Visit www.microsoft.com/officespecialist for exam availability.

Microsoft, the Microsoft Office Logo, PowerPoint, and Outlook are trademarks or registered trademarks of Microsoft Corporation in the United States and/or other countries, and the Microsoft Office Specialist Logo is used under license from owner.

Microsoft® Office Word 2003
ILLUSTRATED, CourseCard Edition

INTRODUCTORY

Jennifer A. Duffy

THOMSON
COURSE TECHNOLOGY

Australia • Canada • Mexico • Singapore • Spain • United Kingdom • United States

Microsoft® Office Word 2003—Illustrated Introductory, CourseCard Edition

Jennifer A. Duffy

Managing Editor:
Marjorie Hunt

Senior Product Manager:
Christina Kling Garrett

Associate Product Manager:
Emilie Perreault

Production Editors:
Melissa Panagos, Summer Hughes

Product Manager:
Jane Hosie-Bounar

Editorial Assistant:
Shana Rosenthal

QA Manuscript Reviewers:
John Freitas,
Holly Schabowski

Developmental Editor:
Pamela Conrad

Composition House:
GEX Publishing Services

Text Designer:
Joseph Lee, Black Fish Design

COPYRIGHT © 2006 Thomson Course Technology, a division of Thomson Learning™. Thomson Learning™ is a trademark used herein under license.

Printed in the United States of America

5 6 7 8 9 BM 09 08 07 06

For more information, contact Thomson Course Technology, 25 Thomson Place, Boston, Massachusetts, 02210.

Or you can visit us on the World Wide Web at www.course.com

ALL RIGHTS RESERVED. No part of this work covered by the copyright hereon may be reproduced or used in any form or by any means—graphic, electronic, or mechanical, including photocopying, recording, taping, Web distribution, or information storage and retrieval systems—without the written permission of the publisher.

For permission to use material from this text or product, submit a request online at www.thomsonrights.com

Any additional questions about permissions can be submitted by e-mail to thomsonrights@thomson.com

Trademarks
Some of the product names and company names used in this book have been used for identification purposes only and may be trademarks or registered trademarks of their respective manufacturers and sellers.

Microsoft and the Office logo are either registered trademarks or trademarks of Microsoft Corporation in the United States and/or other countries. Thomson Course Technology is an independent entity from Microsoft Corporation, and not affiliated with Microsoft in any manner.

This text may be used in assisting students to prepare for a Microsoft Office Specialist Exam. Neither Microsoft Corporation, its designated review company, nor Thomson Course Technology warrants that use of this text will ensure passing the relevant exam.

Use of the Microsoft Office Specialist Approved Courseware Logo on this product signifies that it has been independently reviewed and approved in complying with the following standards: "Includes acceptable coverage of all content related to the Microsoft Office Exam entitled Microsoft Office Word 2003 and sufficient performance-based exercises that relate closely to all required content, based on sampling of text."

ISBN-13: 978-1-4188-4301-4
ISBN-10: 1-4188-4301-6

The Illustrated Series Vision

Teaching and writing about computer applications can be extremely rewarding and challenging. How do we engage students and keep their interest? How do we teach them skills that they can easily apply on the job? As we set out to write this book, our goals were to develop a textbook that:

- works for a beginning student

- provides varied, flexible, and meaningful exercises and projects to reinforce skills

- serves as a reference tool

- makes your job as an educator easier, by providing resources above and beyond the textbook to help you teach your course

Our popular, streamlined format is based on advice from instructional designers and customers. This flexible design presents each lesson on a two-page spread, with step-by-step instructions on the left, and screen illustrations on the right. This signature style, coupled with high-caliber content, provides a comprehensive yet manageable introduction to Microsoft Office Word 2003—it is a teaching package for the instructor and a learning experience for the student.

About This Edition

New to this edition is a free, tear-off Word 2003 CourseCard that provides students with a great way to have Word skills at their fingertips.

Acknowledgments

Many talented people at Course Technology helped to shape this book — thank you all. I am especially indebted to Pam Conrad for her precision editing and endless good cheer throughout the many months of writing. On the home front, I am ever grateful to my family for their patience, and to Nancy Macalaster, who so lovingly cared for my babies when I needed to be at my desk.

Jennifer A. Duffy
and the Illustrated Team

Preface

Welcome to *Microsoft® Office Word 2003—Illustrated Introductory, CourseCard Edition*. Each lesson in this book contains elements pictured to the right.

How is the book organized?

The book is organized into eight units and an appendix on Word, covering creating, editing, and formatting text and documents. Students also learn how to create and format tables and Web sites, add graphics, and merge Word documents.

What kinds of assignments are included in the book? At what level of difficulty?

The lessons use MediaLoft, a fictional chain of bookstores, as the case study. The assignments on the light purple pages at the end of each unit increase in difficulty. Data Files and case studies, with many international examples, provide a great variety of interesting and relevant business applications. Assignments include:

- **Concepts Reviews** include multiple choice, matching, and screen identification questions.

- **Skills Reviews** provide additional hands-on, step-by-step reinforcement.

- **Independent Challenges** are case projects requiring critical thinking and application of the unit skills. The Independent Challenges increase in difficulty, with the first one in each unit being the easiest (most step-by-step with detailed instructions). Independent Challenges 2 and 3 become increasingly more open-ended, requiring more independent problem solving.

- **E-Quest Independent Challenges** are case projects with a Web focus. E-Quests require the use of the World Wide Web to conduct research to complete the project.

- **Advanced Challenge Exercises** set within the Independent Challenges provide optional steps for more advanced students.

- **Visual Workshops** are practical, self-graded capstone projects that require independent problem solving.

Each 2-page spread focuses on a single skill.

Concise text introduces the basic principles in the lesson and integrates a real-world case study.

UNIT A
Word 2003

Saving a Document

To store a document permanently so you can open it and edit it in the future, you must save it as a **file**. When you **save** a document you give it a name, called a **filename**, and indicate the location where you want to store the file. Files can be saved to your computer's internal hard disk, to a floppy disk, or to a variety of other locations. You can save a document using the Save button on the Standard toolbar or the Save command on the File menu. Once you have saved a document for the first time, you should save it again every few minutes and always before printing so that the saved file is updated to reflect your latest changes. You save your memo with the filename Marketing Memo.

STEPS

> **TROUBLE**
> If you don't see the extension .doc on the filename in the Save As dialog box, don't worry. Windows can be set to display or not to display the file extensions.

1. **Click the** Save button **on the Standard toolbar**

   The first time you save a document, the Save As dialog box opens, as shown in Figure A-7. The default filename, Memorandum, appears in the File name text box. The default filename is based on the first few words of the document. The .doc extension is assigned automatically to all Word documents to distinguish them from files created in other software programs. To save the document with a different filename, type a new filename in the File name text box, and use the Save in list arrow to select where you want to store the document file. You do not need to type .doc when you type a new filename. Table A-3 describes the functions of the buttons in the Save As dialog box.

2. **Type** Marketing Memo **in the File name text box**

   The new filename replaces the default filename. It's a good idea to give your documents brief filenames that describe the contents.

> **TROUBLE**
> This book assumes your Data Files for Unit A are stored in a folder titled UnitA. Substitute the correct drive or folder if this is not the case.

3. **Click the** Save in list arrow, **then navigate to the drive or folder where your Data Files are located**

   The drive or folder where your Data Files are located appears in the Save in list box. Your Save As dialog box should resemble Figure A-8.

4. **Click** Save

   The document is saved to the location you specified in the Save As dialog box, and the title bar displays the new filename, "Marketing Memo.doc."

5. **Place the insertion point before** August **in the second sentence, type** early, **then press** [Spacebar]

   You can continue to work on a document after you have saved it with a new filename.

6. **Click**

   Your change to the memo is saved. Saving a document after you give it a filename saves the changes you make to the document. You also can click File on the menu bar, and then click Save to save a document.

Clues to Use

Recovering lost document files

Sometimes while you are working on a document, Word might freeze, making it impossible to continue working, or you might experience a power failure that shuts down your computer. Should this occur, Word has a built-in recovery feature that allows you to open and save the files that were open at the time of the interruption. When you restart Word after an interruption, the Document Recovery task pane opens on the left side of your screen and lists both the original and the recovered versions of the Word files. If you're not sure which file to open (original or recovered), it's usually better to open the recovered file because it includes your latest changes to the document. You can, however, open and review all the versions of the file that were recovered and select the best one to save. Each file listed in the Document Recovery task pane has a list arrow with options that allow you to open the file, save the file, delete the file, or show repairs made to the file.

WORD A-10 GETTING STARTED WITH WORD 2003   OFFICE-102

Tips, as well as troubleshooting advice, are located right where you need them—next to the step itself.

Clues to Use boxes provide concise information that either expands on the major lesson skill or describes an independent task that in some way relates to the major lesson skill.

Every lesson features large, full-color representations of what the screen should look like as students complete the numbered steps.

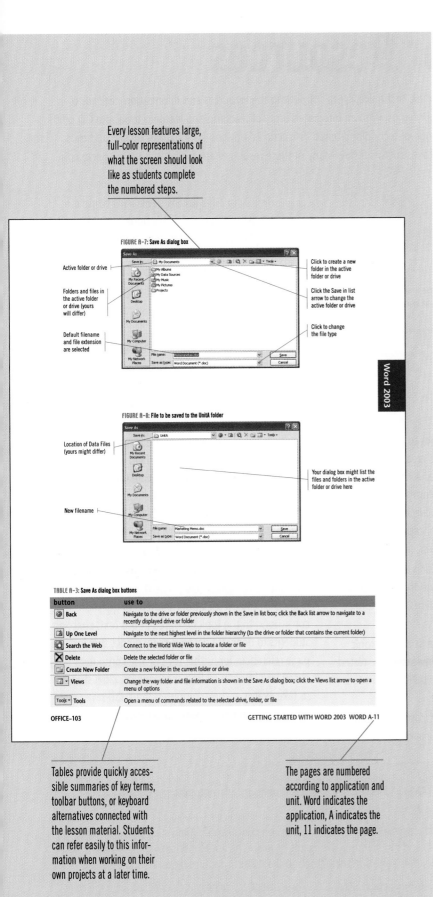

FIGURE A-7: Save As dialog box

Active folder or drive

Folders and files in the active folder or drive (yours will differ)

Default filename and file extension are selected

Click to create a new folder in the active folder or drive

Click the Save in list arrow to change the active folder or drive

Click to change the file type

FIGURE A-8: File to be saved to the UnitA folder

Location of Data Files (yours might differ)

New filename

Your dialog box might list the files and folders in the active folder or drive here

TABLE A-3: Save As dialog box buttons

button	use to
Back	Navigate to the drive or folder previously shown in the Save in list box; click the Back list arrow to navigate to a recently displayed drive or folder
Up One Level	Navigate to the next highest level in the folder hierarchy (to the drive or folder that contains the current folder)
Search the Web	Connect to the World Wide Web to locate a folder or file
Delete	Delete the selected folder or file
Create New Folder	Create a new folder in the current folder or drive
Views	Change the way folder and file information is shown in the Save As dialog box; click the Views list arrow to open a menu of options
Tools	Open a menu of commands related to the selected drive, folder, or file

OFFICE-103

GETTING STARTED WITH WORD 2003 WORD A-11

Tables provide quickly accessible summaries of key terms, toolbar buttons, or keyboard alternatives connected with the lesson material. Students can refer easily to this information when working on their own projects at a later time.

The pages are numbered according to application and unit. Word indicates the application, A indicates the unit, 11 indicates the page.

Word 2003

What online content solutions are available to accompany this book?

Visit www.course.com for more information on our online content for Illustrated titles. Options include:

MyCourse 2.0

Need a quick, simple tool to help you manage your course? Try MyCourse 2.0, the most flexible syllabus and content management tool available. MyCourse 2.0 offers you brand new content, including Topic Reviews, Extra Case Projects, and Quizzes to accompany this book.

WebCT

Course Technology and WebCT have partnered to provide you with the highest quality online resources and Web-based tools for your class. Course Technology offers content for this book to help you create your WebCT class, such as a suggested Syllabus, Lecture Notes, Practice Test questions, and more.

Blackboard

Course Technology and Blackboard have also partnered to provide you with the highest quality online resources and Web-based tools for your class. Course Technology offers content for this book to help you create your Blackboard class, such as a suggested Syllabus, Lecture Notes, Practice Test questions, and more.

Is this book Microsoft Office Specialist Certified?
Microsoft Office Word 2003—Illustrated Introductory, CourseCard Edition covers the objectives for Microsoft Office Word 2003 and has received certification approval as courseware for the Microsoft Office Specialist program. See page ii (the back of the title page) for more information on other Illustrated titles meeting Microsoft Office Specialist certification.

The first page of each unit indicates which objectives in the unit are Microsoft Office Specialist skills. If an objective is set in red, it meets a Microsoft Office Specialist skill. A document in the Review Pack cross-references the skills with the lessons and exercises.

Instructor Resources

The Instructor Resources CD is Course Technology's way of putting the resources and information needed to teach and learn effectively into your hands. With an integrated array of teaching and learning tools, the CD offers you and your students a broad range of technology-based instructional options—the highest quality and most cutting–edge resources available to instructors today. Many of these resources are available at www.course.com. The resources available with this book are:

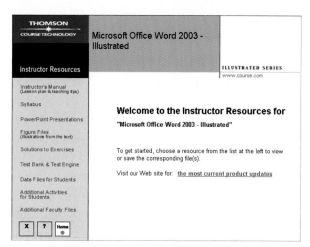

- **Data Files for Students**—To complete most of the units in this book, your students will need Data Files, which you can put on a file server for students to copy. The Data Files are available on the Instructor Resources CD-ROM and in the Review Pack, and can also be downloaded from www.course.com.

  Direct students to use the **Data Files List** located in the Review Pack and on the Instructor Resources CD. This list provides instructions on copying and organizing files.

- **Solutions to Exercises**—Solutions to Exercises contains every file students are asked to create or modify in the lessons and End-of-Unit material. A Help file on the Instructor Resources CD includes information for using the Solution Files. There is also a document outlining the solutions for the End-of-Unit Concepts Review, Skills Review, and Independent Challenges.

- **PowerPoint Presentations**—Each unit has a corresponding PowerPoint presentation that you can use in a lecture, distribute to your students, or customize to suit your course.

- **Instructor's Manual**—Available as an electronic file, the Instructor's Manual is quality-assurance tested and includes unit overviews and detailed lecture topics with teaching tips for each unit.

- **Sample Syllabus**—Prepare and customize your course easily using this sample course outline.

- Figure Files—The figures in the text are provided on the Instructor Resources CD to help you illustrate key topics or concepts. You can create traditional overhead transparencies by printing the figure files, or you can create electronic slide shows by using the figures in a presentation program such as PowerPoint.

- ExamView—ExamView is a powerful testing software package that allows you to create and administer printed, computer (LAN-based), and Internet exams. ExamView includes hundreds of questions that correspond to the topics covered in this text, enabling students to generate detailed study guides that include page references for further review. The computer-based and Internet testing components allow students to take exams at their computers, and also save you time by grading each exam automatically.

SAM 2003 Assessment & Training

SAM 2003 helps you energize your class exams and training assignments by allowing students to learn and test important computer skills in an active, hands-on environment.

With SAM 2003 Assessment, you create powerful interactive exams on critical applications such as Word, Outlook, PowerPoint, Windows, the Internet, and much more. The exams simulate the application environment, allowing your students to demonstrate their knowledge and think through the skills by performing real-world tasks.

Designed to be used with the Illustrated series, SAM 2003 Assessment & Training includes built-in page references so students can create study guides that match the Illustrated textbooks you use in class. Powerful administrative options allow you to schedule exams and assignments, secure your tests, and run reports with almost limitless flexibility.

Brief Contents

Contents

WORD 2003   **Formatting Text and Paragraphs**   **C-1**

Formatting Documents

Creating and Formatting Tables

WORD 2003

Illustrating Documents with Graphics

F-1

Creating a Web Page G-1

Merging Word Documents H-1

WORD 2003

Collaborating on Documents   APP-1

Glossary   1

Index   5

Read This Before You Begin

Software Information and Required Installation

This book was written and tested using Microsoft Office 2003—Professional Edition (which includes Microsoft Office Word 2003), with a typical installation on Microsoft Windows XP, including installation of the most recent Windows XP Service Pack, and with Internet Explorer 6.0 or higher. Some of the exercises in this book assume that your computer is connected to the Internet. If you are not connected to the Internet, see your instructor.

Tips for Students

What are Data Files?

To complete many of the units in this book, you need to use Data Files. A Data File contains a partially completed document, so that you don't have to type all the information in the document yourself. Your instructor will either provide you with copies of the Data Files or ask you to make your own copies. Your instructor can also give you instructions on how to organize your files, as well as a complete file listing, or you can find the list and the instructions for organizing your files in the Review Pack. In addition, because Unit A does not have supplied Data Files, you will need to create a Unit A directory at the same level as all of the other unit directories in order to save the files you create in Unit A.

Why is my screen different from the book?

Your desktop components and some dialog box options might be different if you are using an operating system other than Windows XP.

Depending on your computer hardware and the Display settings on your computer, you may notice the following differences:

- Your screen may look larger or smaller because of your screen resolution (the height and width of your screen).

- Your title bars and dialog boxes may not display file extensions. To display file extensions, click Start on the taskbar, click Control Panel, click Appearance and Themes, then click Folder Options. Click the View tab if necessary, click Hide extensions for known file types to deselect it, then click OK. Your Office dialog boxes and title bars should now display file extensions.

- Depending on your Office settings, your Standard and Formatting toolbars may be displayed on a single row and your menus may display a shortened list of frequently used commands. Office menus and toolbars can modify themselves to your working style by displaying only the most frequently used buttons and menu commands. To view buttons not currently displayed, click a Toolbar Options button at the right end of either the Standard or Formatting toolbar. To view the full list of menu commands, click the double arrow at the bottom of the menu.

TOOLBARS IN ONE ROW

TOOLBARS IN TWO ROWS

This book assumes you are displaying toolbars in two rows and displaying full menus. In order to have your toolbars displayed on two rows, showing all buttons, and to have the full menus displayed, you must turn off the personalized menus and toolbars feature. Click Tools on the menu bar, click Customize, select the show Standard and Formatting toolbars on two rows and Always show full menus check boxes on the Options tab, and then click Close.

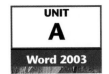

Getting Started with Word 2003

OBJECTIVES

Understand word processing software
Start Word 2003
Explore the Word program window
Start a document
Save a document
Print a document
Use the Help system
Close a document and exit Word

SAM

If you have a SAM user profile, you may have access to hands-on instruction, practice, and assessment of the skills covered in this unit. Log in to your SAM account and go to your assignments page to see what your instructor has assigned.

Microsoft Office Word 2003 is a word processing program that makes it easy to create a variety of professional-looking documents, from simple letters and memos to newsletters, research papers, Web pages, business cards, resumes, financial reports, and other documents that include multiple pages of text and sophisticated formatting. In this unit, you will explore the editing and formatting features available in Word, learn how to start Word, and create a document. ▰▰▰▰ You have just been hired to work in the Marketing Department at MediaLoft, a chain of bookstore cafés that sells books, music, and videos. Shortly after reporting to your new office, Alice Wegman, the marketing manager, asks you to familiarize yourself with Word and use it to create a memo to the marketing staff.

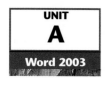

Understanding Word Processing Software

A **word processing program** is a software program that includes tools for entering, editing, and formatting text and graphics. Microsoft Word is a powerful word processing program that allows you to create and enhance a wide range of documents quickly and easily. Figure A-1 shows the first page of a report created using Word and illustrates some of the Word features you can use to enhance your documents. The electronic files you create using Word are called **documents**. One of the benefits of using Word is that document files can be stored on a disk, making them easy to transport, exchange, and revise. You need to write a memo to the marketing staff to inform them of an upcoming meeting. Before beginning your memo, you explore the editing and formatting capabilities available in Word.

DETAILS

You can use Word to accomplish the following tasks:

- **Type and edit text**

  The Word editing tools make it simple to insert and delete text in a document. You can add text to the middle of an existing paragraph, replace text with other text, undo an editing change, and correct typing, spelling, and grammatical errors with ease.

- **Copy and move text from one location to another**

  Using the more advanced editing features of Word, you can copy or move text from one location and insert it in a different location in a document. You also can copy and move text between documents. Being able to copy and move text means you don't have to retype text that is already entered in a document.

- **Format text and paragraphs with fonts, colors, and other elements**

  The sophisticated formatting tools available in Word allow you to make the text in your documents come alive. You can change the size, style, and color of text, add lines and shading to paragraphs, and enhance lists with bullets and numbers. Formatting text creatively helps you highlight important ideas in your documents.

- **Format and design pages**

  The Word page-formatting features give you power to design attractive newsletters, create powerful resumes, and produce documents such as business cards, CD labels, and books. You can change the paper size and orientation of your documents, add headers and footers to pages, organize text in columns, and control the layout of text and graphics on each page of a document.

- **Enhance documents with tables, charts, diagrams, and graphics**

  Using the powerful graphic tools available in Word, you can spice up your documents with pictures, photographs, lines, shapes, and diagrams. You also can illustrate your documents with tables and charts to help convey your message in a visually interesting way.

- **Create Web pages**

  The Word Web page design tools allow you to create documents that others can read over the Internet or an intranet. You can enhance Web pages with themes and graphics, add hyperlinks, create online forms, and preview Web pages in your Web browser.

- **Use Mail Merge to create form letters and mailing labels**

  The Word Mail Merge feature allows you to easily send personalized form letters to many different people. You can also use Mail Merge to create mailing labels, directories, e-mail messages, and many other types of documents.

FIGURE A-1: A report created using Word

Format the size and appearance of text

Insert graphics

Create columns of text

Add bullets to lists

Create tables

Add headers to every page

Align text in paragraphs evenly

Add lines

Create charts

Add page numbers in footers

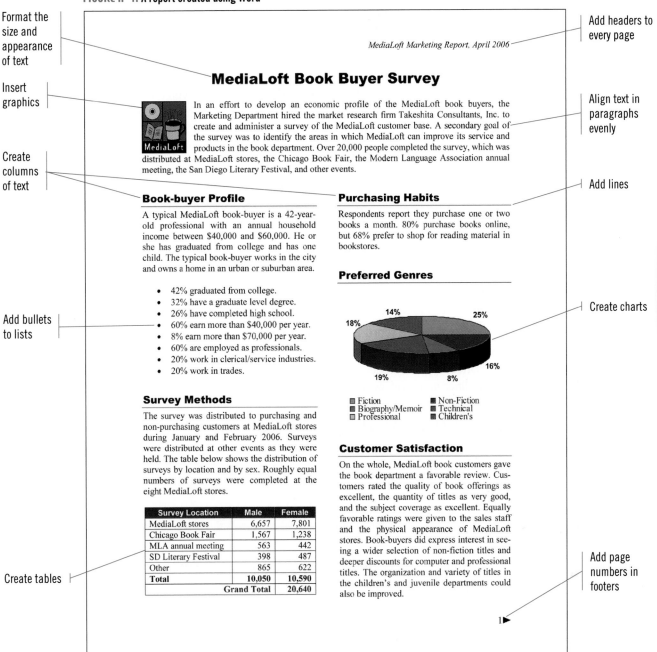

MediaLoft Marketing Report, April 2006

MediaLoft Book Buyer Survey

In an effort to develop an economic profile of the MediaLoft book buyers, the Marketing Department hired the market research firm Takeshita Consultants, Inc. to create and administer a survey of the MediaLoft customer base. A secondary goal of the survey was to identify the areas in which MediaLoft can improve its service and products in the book department. Over 20,000 people completed the survey, which was distributed at MediaLoft stores, the Chicago Book Fair, the Modern Language Association annual meeting, the San Diego Literary Festival, and other events.

Book-buyer Profile

A typical MediaLoft book-buyer is a 42-year-old professional with an annual household income between $40,000 and $60,000. He or she has graduated from college and has one child. The typical book-buyer works in the city and owns a home in an urban or suburban area.

- 42% graduated from college.
- 32% have a graduate level degree.
- 26% have completed high school.
- 60% earn more than $40,000 per year.
- 8% earn more than $70,000 per year.
- 60% are employed as professionals.
- 20% work in clerical/service industries.
- 20% work in trades.

Survey Methods

The survey was distributed to purchasing and non-purchasing customers at MediaLoft stores during January and February 2006. Surveys were distributed at other events as they were held. The table below shows the distribution of surveys by location and by sex. Roughly equal numbers of surveys were completed at the eight MediaLoft stores.

Survey Location	Male	Female
MediaLoft stores	6,657	7,801
Chicago Book Fair	1,567	1,238
MLA annual meeting	563	442
SD Literary Festival	398	487
Other	865	622
Total	**10,050**	**10,590**
	Grand Total	**20,640**

Purchasing Habits

Respondents report they purchase one or two books a month. 80% purchase books online, but 68% prefer to shop for reading material in bookstores.

Preferred Genres

14% 25% 18% 16% 19% 8%

- Fiction
- Biography/Memoir
- Professional
- Non-Fiction
- Technical
- Children's

Customer Satisfaction

On the whole, MediaLoft book customers gave the book department a favorable review. Customers rated the quality of book offerings as excellent, the quantity of titles as very good, and the subject coverage as excellent. Equally favorable ratings were given to the sales staff and the physical appearance of MediaLoft stores. Book-buyers did express interest in seeing a wider selection of non-fiction titles and deeper discounts for computer and professional titles. The organization and variety of titles in the children's and juvenile departments could also be improved.

1►

Clues to Use

Planning a document

Before you create a new document, it's a good idea to spend time planning it. Identify the message you want to convey, the audience for your document, and the elements, such as tables or charts, you want to include. You should also think about the tone and look of your document—is it a business letter, which should be written in a pleasant, but serious tone and have a formal appearance, or are you creating a flyer that must be colorful, eye-catching, and fun to read?

The purpose and audience for your document determines the appropriate design. Planning the layout and design of a document involves deciding how to organize the text, selecting the fonts to use, identifying the graphics to include, and selecting the formatting elements that will enhance the document's message and appeal. For longer documents, such as newsletters, it can be useful to sketch the layout and design of each page before you begin.

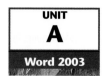

Starting Word 2003

Before starting Word, you must start Windows by turning on your computer. Once Windows is running, you can start Word or any other application by using the Start button on the Windows taskbar. You can also start Word by clicking the Word icon on the Windows desktop or the Word icon on the Microsoft Office Shortcut bar, if those items are available on your computer. ▰▰▰▰ You use the Start button to start Word so you can familiarize yourself with its features.

STEPS

1. **Click the Start button ⊞start on the Windows taskbar**

   The Start menu opens on the desktop. The left pane of the Start menu includes shortcuts to the most frequently used programs on the computer.

2. **Point to All Programs on the Start menu**

   The All Programs menu opens. The All Programs menu displays the list of programs installed on your computer.

> **TROUBLE**
> If Microsoft Office is not on your All Programs menu, ask your technical support person for assistance.

3. **Point to Microsoft Office**

   A menu listing the Office programs installed on your computer opens, as shown in Figure A-2.

4. **Click Microsoft Office Word 2003 on the Microsoft Office menu**

   The **Word program window** opens and displays a blank document in the document window and the Getting Started task pane, as shown in Figure A-3. The blank document opens in the most recently used view. **Views** are different ways of displaying a document in the document window. Figure A-3 shows a blank document in Print Layout view. The lessons in this unit will use Print Layout view.

5. **Click the Print Layout View button ▤ as shown in Figure A-3**

   If your blank document opened in a different view, the view changes to Print Layout view.

> **TROUBLE**
> If your toolbars are on one row, click the Toolbar Options button at the end of the Formatting toolbar, then click Show Buttons on Two Rows.

6. **Click the Zoom list arrow on the Standard toolbar as shown in Figure A-3, then click Page Width**

   The blank document fills the document window. Your screen should now match Figure A-3. The blinking vertical line in the upper-left corner of the document window is the **insertion point**. It indicates where text appears as you type.

7. **Move the mouse pointer around in the Word program window**

   The mouse pointer changes shape depending on where it is in the Word program window. In the document window in Print Layout view, the mouse pointer changes to an **I-beam pointer** I or a **click and type pointer** I ≡. You use these pointers to move the insertion point in the document or to select text to edit. Table A-1 describes common Word pointers.

8. **Place the mouse pointer over a toolbar button**

   When you place the pointer over a button or some other element of the Word program window, a ScreenTip appears. A **ScreenTip** is a label that identifies the name of the button or feature.

TABLE A-1: Common Word pointers

pointer	use to
I	Move the insertion point in a document or to select text
I ≡ or I	Move the insertion point in a blank area of a document in Print Layout or Web Layout view; automatically applies the paragraph formatting required to position text at that location in the document
⟨	Click a button, menu command, or other element of the Word program window; appears when you point to elements of the Word program window
⟨	Select a line or lines of text; appears when you point to the left edge of a line of text in the document window
⟨ᵐⁱ⟩	Open a hyperlink; appears when you point to a hyperlink in the task pane or a document

FIGURE A-2: Starting Word from the All Programs menu

Frequently used programs (your list may differ)

Displays menu of programs installed on your computer

Start button

Click to start Word (the order of the programs listed may differ)

FIGURE A-3: Word program window in Print Layout view

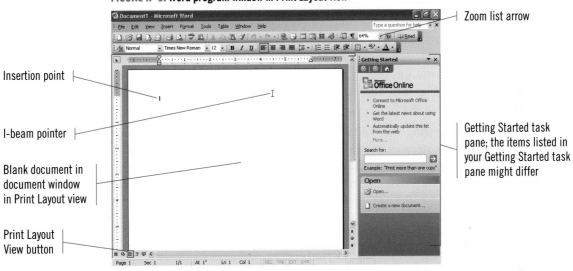

Insertion point

I-beam pointer

Blank document in document window in Print Layout view

Print Layout View button

Zoom list arrow

Getting Started task pane; the items listed in your Getting Started task pane might differ

Clues to Use

Using Word document views

Each Word view provides features that are useful for working on different types of documents. The default view, **Print Layout view**, displays a document as it will look on a printed page. Print Layout view is helpful for formatting text and pages, including adjusting document margins, creating columns of text, inserting graphics, and formatting headers and footers. Also useful is **Normal view**, which shows a simplified layout of a document, without margins, headers and footers, or graphics. When you want to quickly type, edit, and format text, it's often easiest to work in Normal view. **Web Layout view** allows you to accurately format Web pages or documents that will be viewed on a computer screen. In Web Layout view, a document appears just as it will when viewed with a Web browser. **Outline view** is useful for editing and formatting longer documents that include multiple headings. Outline view allows you to reorganize text by moving the headings. You switch between these views by clicking the view buttons to the left of the horizontal scroll bar or by using the commands on the View menu.

Two additional views make it easier to read documents on the screen. **Reading Layout view** displays document text so that it is easy to read and annotate. When you are working with highlighting or comments in a document, it's useful to use Reading Layout view. You switch to Reading Layout view by clicking the Read button on the Standard toolbar or the Reading Layout button to the left of the horizontal scroll bar. You return to the previous view by clicking the Close button on the Reading Layout toolbar. **Full Screen view** displays only the document window on screen. You switch to Full Screen view by using the Full Screen command on the View menu; you return to the previous view by pressing [Esc].

Changing views does not affect how the printed document will appear. It simply changes the way you view the document in the document window.

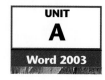
Exploring the Word Program Window

When you start Word, a blank document appears in the document window and the Getting Started task pane appears. You examine the elements of the Word program window.

Using Figure A-4 as a guide, find the elements described below in your program window.

- The **title bar** displays the name of the document and the name of the program. Until you give a new document a different name, its temporary name is Document1. The title bar also contains resizing buttons and the program Close button, buttons that are common to all Windows programs.

- The **menu bar** contains the names of the Word menus. Clicking a menu name opens a list of commands. The menu bar also contains the **Type a question for help box** and the Close Window button. You use the Type a question for help box to access the Word Help system.

- The **toolbars** contain buttons for the most commonly used commands. The **Standard toolbar** contains buttons for frequently used operating and editing commands, such as saving a document, printing a document, and cutting, copying, and pasting text. The **Formatting toolbar** contains buttons for commonly used formatting commands, such as changing font type and size, applying bold to text, and changing paragraph alignment. The Clues to Use in this lesson provides more information about working with toolbars and menus in Word.

- The **Getting Started task pane** contains shortcuts for opening a document, for creating new documents, and for accessing information on the Microsoft Web site. The blue words in the Open section of the task pane are **hyperlinks** that provide quick access to existing documents and the New Document task pane. If your computer is connected to the Internet, you can use the Microsoft Office Online section of the task pane to search the Microsoft Web site for information related to Office programs. As you learn more about Word, you will work with other task panes that provide shortcuts to Word formatting, editing, and research features. Clicking a hyperlink in a task pane can be quicker than using menu commands and toolbar buttons to accomplish a task.

- The **document window** displays the current document. You enter text and format your document in the document window.

- The horizontal and vertical rulers appear in the document window in Print Layout view. The **horizontal ruler** displays left and right document margins as well as the tab settings and paragraph indents, if any, for the paragraph in which the insertion point is located. The **vertical ruler** displays the top and bottom document margins.

- The **vertical and horizontal scroll bars** are used to display different parts of the document in the document window. The scroll bars include **scroll boxes** and **scroll arrows**, which you can use to easily move through a document.

- The **view buttons** to the left of the horizontal scroll bar allow you to display the document in Normal, Web Layout, Print Layout, Outline, or Reading Layout view.

- The **status bar** displays the page number and section number of the current page, the total number of pages in the document, and the position of the insertion point in inches, lines, and characters. The status bar also indicates the on/off status of several Word features, including tracking changes, overtype mode, and spelling and grammar checking.

FIGURE A-4: Elements of the Word program window

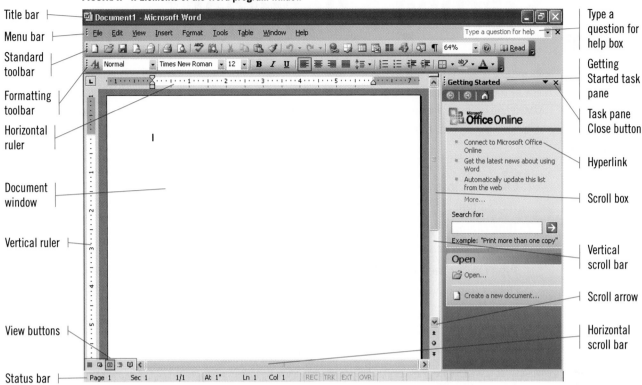

Title bar
Menu bar
Standard toolbar
Formatting toolbar
Horizontal ruler
Document window
Vertical ruler
View buttons
Status bar

Type a question for help box
Getting Started task pane
Task pane Close button
Hyperlink
Scroll box
Vertical scroll bar
Scroll arrow
Horizontal scroll bar

Word 2003

Clues to Use

Working with toolbars and menus in Word 2003

The lessons in this book assume you are working with full menus and toolbars visible, which means the Standard and Formatting toolbars appear on two rows and display all the buttons, and the menus display the complete list of menu commands.

You can also set Word to use personalized toolbars and menus that modify themselves to your working style. When you use personalized toolbars, the Standard and Formatting toolbars appear on the same row and display only the most frequently used buttons. To use a button that is not visible on a toolbar, click the Toolbar Options button at the end of the toolbar, and then click the button you want on the Toolbar Options list. As you work, Word adds the buttons you use to the visible toolbars, and moves the buttons

you haven't used recently to the Toolbar Options list. Similarly, Word menus adjust to your work habits, so that the commands you use most often appear on shortened menus. You double-click the menu name or click the double arrow at the bottom of a menu to view additional menu commands.

To work with full toolbars and menus visible, you must turn off the personalized toolbars and menus features. To turn off personalized toolbars and menus, double-click Tools on the menu bar, click Customize, click the Options tab, select the Show Standard and Formatting toolbars on two rows and Always show full menus check boxes, and then click Close.

Starting a Document

You begin a new document by simply typing text in a blank document in the document window. Word includes a **word-wrap** feature, so that as you type Word automatically moves the insertion point to the next line of the document when you reach the right margin. You only press [Enter] when you want to start a new paragraph or insert a blank line. You can easily edit text in a document by inserting new text or by deleting existing text. ██████ You type a quick memo to the marketing staff to inform them of an upcoming meeting.

STEPS

1. Click the Close button in the Getting Started task pane

The task pane closes and the blank document fills the screen.

QUICK TIP

If you press the wrong key, press [Backspace] to erase the mistake, then try again.

2. Type Memorandum, then press [Enter] four times

Each time you press [Enter] the insertion point moves to the start of the next line.

3. Type DATE:, then press [Tab] twice

Pressing [Tab] moves the insertion point several spaces to the right. You can use the [Tab] key to align the text in a memo header or to indent the first line of a paragraph.

QUICK TIP

Smart tags and other automatic feature markers appear on screen but do not print.

4. Type April 21, 2006, then press [Enter]

When you press [Enter], a purple dotted line appears under the date. This dotted underline is a **smart tag**. It indicates that Word recognizes the text as a date. If you move the mouse pointer over the smart tag, a **Smart Tag Actions button** ⑤ appears above the date. Smart tags are one of the many automatic features you will encounter as you type. Table A-2 describes other automatic features available in Word. You can ignore the smart tags in your memo.

5. Type: TO: [Tab] [Tab] Marketing Staff [Enter]
             FROM: [Tab] Your Name [Enter]
             RE: [Tab] [Tab] Marketing Meeting [Enter] [Enter]

Red or green wavy lines may appear under the words you typed. A red wavy line means the word is not in the Word dictionary and might be misspelled. A green wavy line indicates a possible grammar error. You can correct any typing errors you make later.

QUICK TIP

To reverse an AutoCorrect adjustment, immediately click the Undo button ↶ on the Standard toolbar.

6. Type The next marketing meeting will be held May 6th at 10 a.m. in the Bloomsbury room on the ground floor., then press [Spacebar]

As you type, notice that the insertion point moves automatically to the next line of the document. You also might notice that Word corrects typing errors or makes typographical adjustments as you type. This feature is called **AutoCorrect**. AutoCorrect automatically detects and adjusts typos, certain misspelled words (such as "taht" for "that"), and incorrect capitalization as you type. For example, Word automatically changed "6th" to "6th" in the memo.

QUICK TIP

Type just one space after a period at the end of a sentence when typing with a word processor.

7. Type Heading the agenda will be a discussion of our new cafe music series, scheduled for August. Please bring ideas for promoting this exciting new series to the meeting.

When you type the first few characters of "August," the Word AutoComplete feature displays the complete word in a ScreenTip. **AutoComplete** suggests text to insert quickly into your documents. You can ignore AutoComplete for now. Your memo should resemble Figure A-5.

8. Position the ⊥ pointer after for (but before the space) in the second sentence, then click

Clicking moves the insertion point after "for."

9. Press [Backspace] three times, then type to debut in

Pressing [Backspace] removes the character before the insertion point.

10. Move the insertion point before marketing in the first sentence, then press [Delete] ten times to remove the word marketing and the space after it

Pressing [Delete] removes the character after the insertion point. Figure A-6 shows the revised memo.

Blank lines between paragraphs

Purple dotted underline indicates a smart tag

Green wavy underline indicates a possible grammar error (your memo will show your name)

Text wraps to the next line (yours might wrap differently)

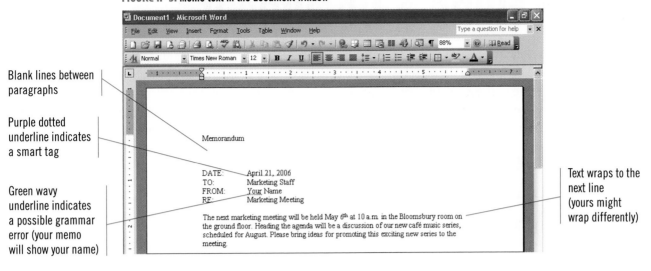

FIGURE A-6: Edited memo text

Text inserted in the memo

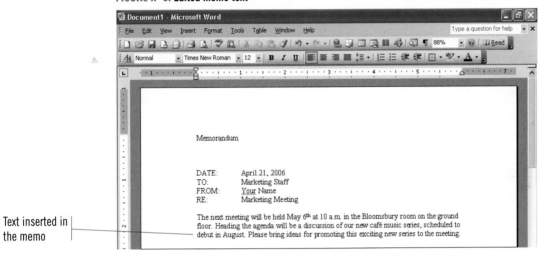

TABLE A-2: Automatic features in Word

feature	what appears	to use
AutoComplete	A ScreenTip suggesting text to insert appears	Press [Enter] to insert the text suggested by the ScreenTip; continue typing to reject the suggestion
Spelling and Grammar	A red wavy line under a word indicates a possible misspelling; a green wavy line under text indicates a possible grammar error	Right-click red- or green-underlined text to display a shortcut menu of correction options; click a correction to accept it and remove the wavy underline
AutoCorrect	A small blue box appears when you place the pointer under text corrected by AutoCorrect; an AutoCorrect Options button ⌐ ▾ appears when you point to the corrected text	Word automatically corrects typos, minor spelling errors, and capital-ization, and adds typographical symbols (such as © and ™) as you type; to reverse an AutoCorrect adjustment, click the AutoCorrect Options button, then click Undo or the option that will undo the action
Smart tag	A purple dotted line appears under text Word recognizes as a date, name, address, or place; a Smart Tag Actions button ⓘ appears when you point to a smart tag	Click the Smart Tag Actions button to display a shortcut menu of options (such as adding a name to your address book in Outlook or opening your Outlook calendar); to remove a smart tag, click Remove this Smart Tag on the shortcut menu

Word 2003

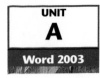
Saving a Document

To store a document permanently so you can open it and edit it in the future, you must save it as a **file**. When you **save** a document you give it a name, called a **filename**, and indicate the location where you want to store the file. Files can be saved to your computer's internal hard disk, to a floppy disk, or to a variety of other locations. You can save a document using the Save button on the Standard toolbar or the Save command on the File menu. Once you have saved a document for the first time, you should save it again every few minutes and always before printing so that the saved file is updated to reflect your latest changes. You save your memo with the filename Marketing Memo.

STEPS

TROUBLE
If you don't see the extension .doc on the filename in the Save As dialog box, don't worry. Windows can be set to display or not to display the file extensions.

1. **Click the Save button on the Standard toolbar**

   The first time you save a document, the Save As dialog box opens, as shown in Figure A-7. The default filename, Memorandum, appears in the File name text box. The default filename is based on the first few words of the document. The .doc extension is assigned automatically to all Word documents to distinguish them from files created in other software programs. To save the document with a different filename, type a new filename in the File name text box, and use the Save in list arrow to select where you want to store the document file. You do not need to type .doc when you type a new filename. Table A-3 describes the functions of the buttons in the Save As dialog box.

2. **Type Marketing Memo in the File name text box**

   The new filename replaces the default filename. It's a good idea to give your documents brief filenames that describe the contents.

TROUBLE
This book assumes your Data Files for Unit A are stored in a folder titled UnitA. Substitute the correct drive or folder if this is not the case.

3. **Click the Save in list arrow, then navigate to the drive or folder where your Data Files are located**

   The drive or folder where your Data Files are located appears in the Save in list box. Your Save As dialog box should resemble Figure A-8.

4. **Click Save**

   The document is saved to the location you specified in the Save As dialog box, and the title bar displays the new filename, "Marketing Memo.doc."

5. **Place the insertion point before August in the second sentence, type early, then press [Spacebar]**

   You can continue to work on a document after you have saved it with a new filename.

6. **Click**

   Your change to the memo is saved. Saving a document after you give it a filename saves the changes you make to the document. You also can click File on the menu bar, and then click Save to save a document.

Clues to Use

Recovering lost document files

Sometimes while you are working on a document, Word might freeze, making it impossible to continue working, or you might experience a power failure that shuts down your computer. Should this occur, Word has a built-in recovery feature that allows you to open and save the files that were open at the time of the interruption. When you restart Word after an interruption, the Document Recovery task pane opens on the left side of your screen and lists both the original and the recovered versions of the Word files. If you're not sure which file to open (original or recovered), it's usually better to open the recovered file because it includes your latest changes to the document. You can, however, open and review all the versions of the file that were recovered and select the best one to save. Each file listed in the Document Recovery task pane has a list arrow with options that allow you to open the file, save the file, delete the file, or show repairs made to the file.

FIGURE A-7: Save As dialog box

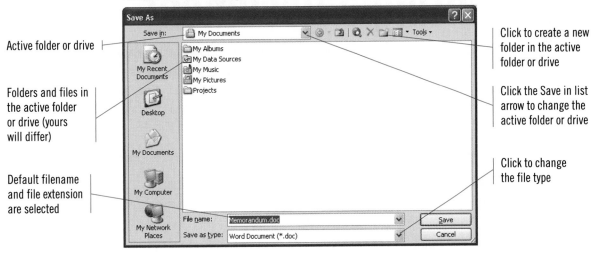

Active folder or drive

Folders and files in the active folder or drive (yours will differ)

Default filename and file extension are selected

Click to create a new folder in the active folder or drive

Click the Save in list arrow to change the active folder or drive

Click to change the file type

FIGURE A-8: File to be saved to the UnitA folder

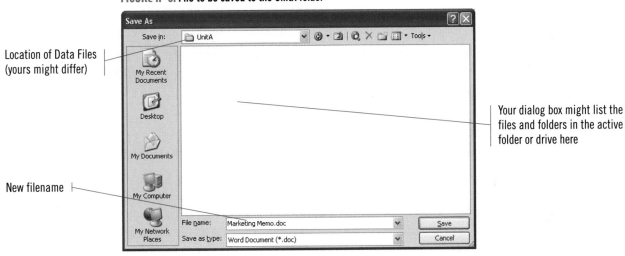

Location of Data Files (yours might differ)

New filename

Your dialog box might list the files and folders in the active folder or drive here

TABLE A-3: Save As dialog box buttons

button	use to
⊙ Back	Navigate to the drive or folder previously shown in the Save in list box; click the Back list arrow to navigate to a recently displayed drive or folder
🔁 Up One Level	Navigate to the next highest level in the folder hierarchy (to the drive or folder that contains the current folder)
🔍 Search the Web	Connect to the World Wide Web to locate a folder or file
✕ Delete	Delete the selected folder or file
🗂 Create New Folder	Create a new folder in the current folder or drive
▦ ▾ Views	Change the way folder and file information is shown in the Save As dialog box; click the Views list arrow to open a menu of options
Tools ▾ Tools	Open a menu of commands related to the selected drive, folder, or file

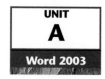

Printing a Document

Before you print a document, it's a good habit to examine it in **Print Preview** to see what it will look like when printed. When a document is ready to print, you can print it using the Print button on the Standard tool-bar or the Print command on the File menu. When you use the Print button, the document prints using the default print settings. If you want to print more than one copy of a document or select other printing options, you must use the Print command. You display your memo in Print Preview and then print a copy.

STEPS

1. **Click the Print Preview button on the Standard toolbar**

   The document appears in Print Preview. It is useful to examine a document carefully in Print Preview so that you can correct any problems before printing it.

2. **Move the pointer over the memo text until it changes to ⊕, then click**

   Clicking with the ⊕ pointer magnifies the document in the Print Preview window and changes the pointer to ⊖. The memo appears in the Print Preview window exactly as it will look when printed, as shown in Figure A-9. Clicking with the ⊖ pointer reduces the size of the document in the Print Preview window.

   QUICK TIP
   You can also use the Zoom list arrow on the Print Preview toolbar to change the magnification in the Print Preview window.

3. **Click the Magnifier button on the Print Preview toolbar**

   Clicking the Magnifier button turns off the magnification feature and allows you to edit the document in Print Preview. In edit mode, the pointer changes to I. The Magnifier button is a **toggle button**, which means you can use it to switch back and forth between magnification mode and edit mode.

4. **Compare the text on your screen with the text in Figure A-9, examine your memo care-fully for typing or spelling errors, correct any mistakes, then click the Close Preview button Close on the Print Preview toolbar**

   Print Preview closes and the memo appears in the document window.

5. **Click the Save button on the Standard toolbar**

   If you made any changes to the document since you last saved it, the changes are saved.

6. **Click File on the menu bar, then click Print**

   The Print dialog box opens, as shown in Figure A-10. Depending on the printer installed on your computer, your print settings might differ slightly from those in the figure. You can use the Print dialog box to change the current printer, change the number of copies to print, select what pages of a document to print, and mod-ify other printing options.

7. **Click OK**

   The dialog box closes and a copy of the memo prints using the default print settings. You can also click the Print button on the Standard toolbar or the Print Preview toolbar to print a document using the default print settings.

FIGURE A-9: Memo in the Print Preview window

Print Preview toolbar

Magnifier button

Close Preview button

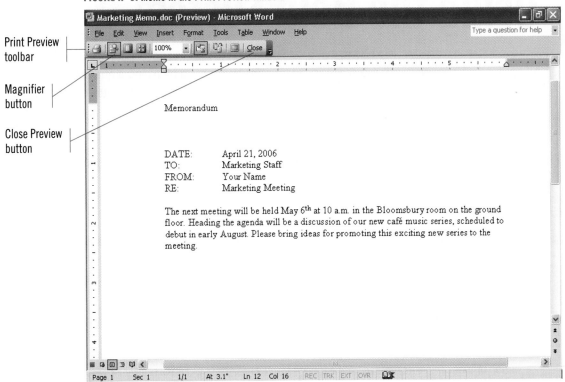

Word 2003

FIGURE A-10: Print dialog box

Default printer (yours might differ)

Select the range of pages to print

Select the special aspects of the document to print

Change document properties for printing, such as orientation, page order, and paper source

Change the number of copies to print

Change the number of pages to print on a sheet of paper

Print using the current settings

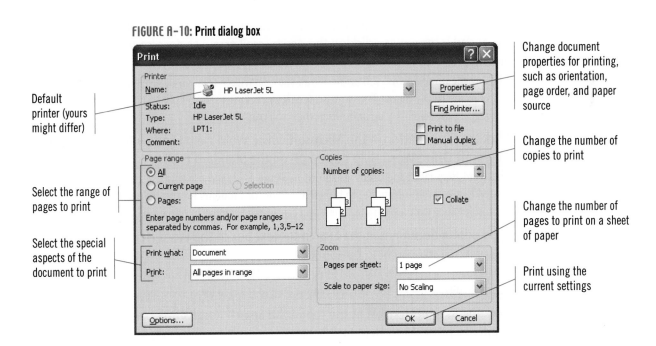

Using the Help System

Word includes an extensive Help system that provides immediate access to definitions, instructions, and useful tips for working with Word. You can quickly access the Help system by typing a question in the Type a question for help box on the menu bar, by clicking the Microsoft Office Word Help button on the Standard toolbar, or by selecting an option from the Help menu. If you are working with an active Internet connection, your queries to the Help system will also return information from the Microsoft Office Online Web site. Table A-4 describes the many ways to get help while using Word. ██████ You are curious to learn more about typing with AutoCorrect and viewing and printing documents. You search the Word Help system to discover more about these features.

STEPS

TROUBLE
The figures in this lesson reflect an active Internet connection. If you are not connected to the Internet, then connect if possible.

1. **Type AutoCorrect in the Type a question for help box on the menu bar, then press [Enter]**

   The Search Results task pane opens. Help topics related to AutoCorrect are listed in blue in the task pane. Notice that the pointer changes to 🖑 when you move it over the blue hyperlink text. If you are working online, it may take a few seconds for information to appear in the task pane.

2. **Click About automatic corrections in the Search Results task pane**

   The Microsoft Office Word Help window opens, as shown in Figure A-11. The Help window displays the "About automatic corrections" Help topic you selected. The colored text in the Help window indicates a link to a definition or to more information about the topic. Like all windows, you can maximize the Help window by clicking the Maximize button on its title bar, or you can resize the window by dragging a top, bottom, or side edge.

TROUBLE
If the hyperlink is not visible in your Help window, click the down scroll arrow until it appears.

3. **Read the information in the Help window, then click the colored text hyperlinks**

   Clicking the link expands the Help topic to display more detailed information. A definition of the word "hyperlink" appears in colored text in the Help window.

4. **Read the definition, then click hyperlinks again to close the definition**

5. **Click Using AutoCorrect to correct errors as you type in the Help window, then read the expanded information, clicking the down scroll arrow as necessary to read the entire Help topic**

   Clicking the up or down scroll arrow allows you to navigate through the Help topic when all the text does not fit in the Help window. You can also **scroll** by clicking the scroll bar above and below the scroll box, or by dragging the scroll box up or down in the scroll bar.

6. **Click the Close button in the Microsoft Office Word Help window title bar, then click the Microsoft Office Word Help button 🔘 on the Standard toolbar**

   The Word Help task pane opens, as shown in Figure A-12. You use this task pane to search for Help topics related to a keyword or phrase, to browse the Table of Contents for the Help system, or to connect to the Microsoft Office Online Web site, where you can search for more information on a topic.

7. **Type print a document in the Search for text box in the Word Help task pane, then click the green Start searching button 🔜**

   When you click the green Start searching button, a list of Help topics related to your query appears in the Search Results task pane. You can also press [Enter] to return a list of Help topics.

8. **Click the Back button 🔙 at the top of the Search Results task pane, then click Table of Contents in the Word Help task pane**

   The table of contents for the Help system appears in the Word Help task pane. To peruse the table of contents, you simply click a category in the list to expand it and see a list of subcategories and Help topics. Categories are listed in black text in the task pane and are preceded by a book icon. Help topics are listed in blue text and are preceded by a question mark icon.

QUICK TIP
Click the Back and Forward buttons on the Word Help window toolbar to navigate between the Help topics you have viewed.

9. **Click Viewing and Navigating Documents, click a blue Help topic, read the information in the Microsoft Office Word Help window, then click the Close button in the Help window**

FIGURE A-11: Microsoft Office Word Help window

Microsoft Office Word Help window

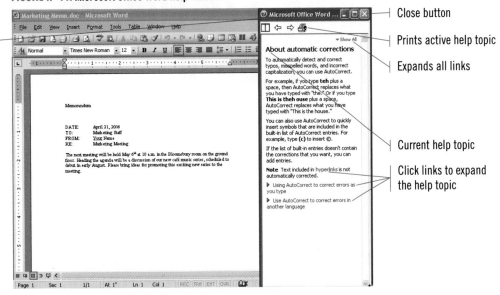

Close button

Prints active help topic

Expands all links

Current help topic

Click links to expand the help topic

FIGURE A-12: Word Help task pane

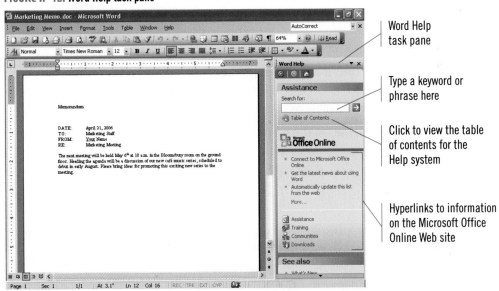

Word Help task pane

Type a keyword or phrase here

Click to view the table of contents for the Help system

Hyperlinks to information on the Microsoft Office Online Web site

TABLE A-4: Word resources for getting Help

resource	function	to use
Type a question for help box	Provides quick access to the Help system	Type a word or question in the Type a question for help box, then press [Enter]
Word Help task pane	Displays the table of contents for the Help system, provides access to a search function, and includes hyperlinks to Help information on the Microsoft Office Online Web site	Press [F1] or click the Microsoft Office Word Help button ⑦ on the Standard toolbar; in the Word Help task pane, type a word or phrase in the Search for text box to return a list of possible Help topics, click Table of Contents to browse the complete list of Help topics, or click a link to access information on the Microsoft Office Online Web site
Microsoft Office Online Web site	Connects to the Microsoft Office Online Web site, where you can search for information on a topic	Click the Microsoft Office Online command on the Help menu, or click a link in the Word Help task pane
Office Assistant	Displays tips related to your current task and provides access to the Help system	Click Show the Office Assistant on the Help menu to display the Office Assistant; click Hide the Office Assistant on the Help menu to hide the Office Assistant

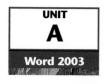

Closing a Document and Exiting Word

When you have finished working on a document and have saved your changes, you can close the document using the Close Window button on the menu bar or the Close command on the File menu. Closing a document closes the document only, it does not close the Word program window. To close the Word program window and exit Word, you can use the Close button on the title bar or the Exit command on the File menu. Using the Exit command closes all open documents. It's good practice to save and close your documents before exiting Word. Figure A-13 shows the Close buttons on the title bar and menu bar. You close the memo and exit Word.

STEPS

1. **Click the Close button on the Word Help task pane**

   The task pane closes. It is not necessary to close the task pane before closing a file or the program, but it can be helpful to reduce the amount of information displayed on the screen. Table A-5 describes the functions of the Word task panes.

2. **Click File on the menu bar, then click Close**

   If you saved your changes to the document before closing it, the document closes. If you did not save your changes, an alert box opens asking if you want to save the changes.

   QUICK TIP
   To create a new blank document, click the New Blank Document button on the Standard toolbar.

3. **Click Yes if the alert box opens**

   The document closes, but the Word program window remains open, as shown in Figure A-14. You can create or open another document, access Help, or close the Word program window.

4. **Click File on the menu bar, then click Exit**

   The Word program window closes. If any Word documents were still open when you exited Word, Word closes all open documents, prompting you to save changes to those documents if necessary.

TABLE A-5: Word task panes

task pane	use to
Getting Started	Open a document, create a new blank document, or search for information on the Microsoft Office Online Web site
Word Help	Access Help topics and connect to Help on the Microsoft Office Online Web site
Search Results	View the results of a search for Help topics and perform a new search
Clip Art	Search for clip art and insert clip art in a document
Research	Search reference books and other sources for information related to a word, such as for synonyms
Clipboard	Cut, copy, and paste items within and between documents
New Document	Create a new blank document, XML document, Web page, or e-mail message, or create a new document using a template
Shared Workspace	Create a Web site (called a document workspace) that allows a group of people to share files, participate in discussions, and work together on a document
Document Updates	View information on a document that is available in a document workspace
Protect Document	Apply formatting and editing restrictions to a shared document
Styles and Formatting	Apply styles to text
Reveal Formatting	Display the formatting applied to text
Mail Merge	Perform a mail merge
XML Structure	Apply XML elements to a Word XML document

FIGURE A-13: Close and Close Window buttons

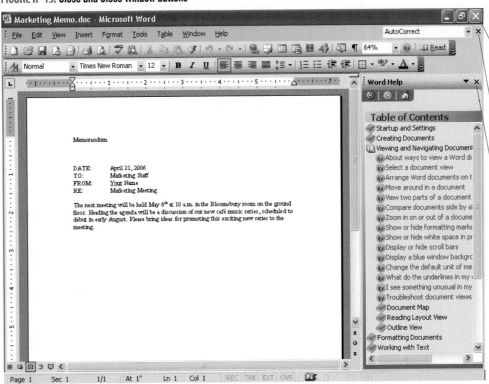

Close button on title bar closes all open documents and exits Word

Close Window button closes the current document

Close button closes the task pane

FIGURE A-14: Word program window with no documents open

Practice

▼ CONCEPTS REVIEW

Label the elements of the Word program window shown in Figure A-15.

FIGURE A-15

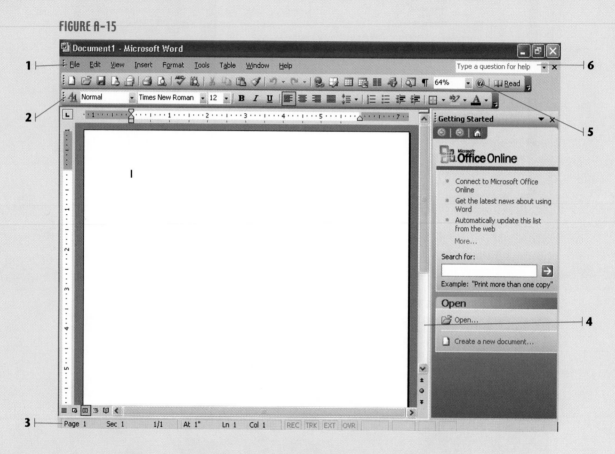

Match each term with the statement that best describes it.

7. **Print Preview**
8. **Office Assistant**
9. **Status bar**
10. **Menu bar**
11. **AutoComplete**
12. **Horizontal ruler**
13. **AutoCorrect**
14. **Normal view**

a. Displays a simple layout view of a document
b. Displays tips on using Word
c. Displays the document exactly as it will look when printed
d. Suggests text to insert into a document
e. Fixes certain errors as you type
f. Displays the number of pages in the current document
g. Displays tab settings and document margins
h. Provides access to Word commands

Select the best answer from the list of choices.

15. **Which task pane opens automatically when you start Word?**
    a. Document Updates
    b. Getting Started
    c. Word Help
    d. New Document

16. **Which element of the Word program window shows the settings for the left and right document margins?**
    a. Formatting toolbar
    b. Status bar
    c. Horizontal ruler
    d. Getting Started task pane

17. **What is the function of the Exit command on the File menu?**
    a. To close the current document without saving changes
    b. To close all open documents and the Word program window
    c. To save changes to and close the current document
    d. To close all open programs

18. **Which view do you use when you want to adjust the margins in a document?**
    a. Outline view
    b. Web Layout view
    c. Normal view
    d. Print Layout view

19. **Which of the following does not appear on the status bar?**
    a. The current page number
    b. The current tab settings
    c. The Overtype mode status
    d. The current line number

20. **Which of the following is not used to access the Help system?**
    a. Type a question for help box
    b. The Office Assistant
    c. Microsoft Office Online
    d. The Research task pane

▼ SKILLS REVIEW

1. **Start Word 2003.**
    a. Start Word.
    b. Switch to Print Layout view if your blank document opened in a different view.
    c. Change the zoom level to Page Width.

2. **Explore the Word program window.**
    a. Identify as many elements of the Word program window as you can without referring to the unit material.
    b. Click each menu name on the menu bar and drag the pointer through the menu commands.
    c. Point to each button on the Standard and Formatting toolbars and read the ScreenTips.
    d. Point to each hyperlink in the Getting Started task pane.

Word 2003

    e. Click the view buttons to view the blank document in Normal, Web Layout, Print Layout, Outline, and Reading Layout view.

    f. Click the Close button in Reading Layout view, then return to Print Layout view.

3. Start a document.

    a. Close the Getting Started task pane.

    b. In a new blank document, type **FAX** at the top of the page, then press [Enter] four times.

    c. Type the following, pressing [Tab] as indicated and pressing [Enter] at the end of each line:

        To: [Tab] **Dr. Beatrice Turcotte**

        From: [Tab] **Your Name**

        Date: [Tab] **Today's date**

        Re: [Tab] **Travel arrangements**

        Pages: [Tab] **1**

        Fax: [Tab] **(514) 555-3948**

    d. Press [Enter], then type **I have reserved a space for you on the March 4-18 Costa Rica Explorer tour. You are scheduled to depart Montreal's Dorval Airport on Plateau Tours and Travel charter flight 234 at 7:45 a.m. on March 4th, arriving in San Jose at 4:30 p.m. local time.**

    e. Press [Enter] twice, then type **Please call me at (514) 555-4983 or stop by our offices on rue St-Denis.**

    f. Insert this sentence at the beginning of the second paragraph: **I must receive full payment within 48 hours to hold your reservation.**

    g. Using the [Backspace] key, delete **Travel** in the Re: line, then type **Costa Rica tour.**

    h. Using the [Delete] key, delete **48** in the last paragraph, then type **72.**

4. Save a document.

    a. Click File on the menu bar, then click Save.

    b. Save the document as **Turcotte Fax** to the drive and folder where your Data Files are located.

    c. After your name, type a comma, press [Spacebar], then type **Plateau Tours and Travel**.

    d. Click the Save button to save your changes to the document.

5. Print a document.

    a. Click the Print Preview button to view the document in Print Preview.

    b. Click the word FAX to zoom in on the document, then proofread the fax.

    c. Click the Magnifier button to switch to edit mode, then correct any typing errors in your document.

    d. Close Print Preview, then save your changes to the document.

    e. Print the fax using the default print settings.

6. Use the Help system.

    a. Click the Microsoft Office Word Help button to open the Word Help task pane.

    b. Type **open a document** in the Search text box, then press [Enter].

    c. Click the topic Open a file.

    d. Read about opening documents in Word by clicking the links to expand the Help topic.

    e. Close the Help window, type **viewing documents** in the Type a question for help box, then press [Enter].

    f. Click the link Zoom in on or out of a document in the Search Results task pane, then read the Help topic.

    g. Close the Help window, then close the Search Results task pane.

7. Close a document and exit Word.

    a. Close the Turcotte Fax document, saving your changes if necessary.

    b. Exit Word.

▼ INDEPENDENT CHALLENGE 1

You are a performance artist, well known for your innovative work with computers. The Missoula Arts Council president, Sam McCrum, has asked you to be the keynote speaker at an upcoming conference in Missoula, Montana, on the role of technology in the arts. You are pleased at the invitation, and write a letter to Mr. McCrum accepting the invitation and confirming the details. Your letter to Mr. McCrum should reference the following information:

- The conference will be held October 10–12, 2006, at the civic center in Missoula.
- You have been asked to speak for one hour on Saturday, October 11, followed by a half hour for questions.
- Mr. McCrum suggested the lecture topic "Technology's Effect on Art and Culture."
- Your talk will include a 20-minute slide presentation.
- The Missoula Arts Council will make your travel arrangements.
- Your preference is to arrive in Missoula on Friday, October 10, and depart on Sunday, October 12.
- You want to fly in and out of the airport closest to your home.

a. Start Word.

b. Save a new blank document as **McCrum Letter** to the drive and folder where your Data Files are located.

c. Model your letter to Mr. McCrum after the sample business letter shown in Figure A-16. Use the following formatting guidelines: 3 blank lines after the date, 1 blank line after the inside address, 1 blank line after the salutation, 1 blank line after each body paragraph, and 3 blank lines between the closing and your typed name.

d. Begin the letter by typing today's date.

e. Type the inside address. Be sure to include Mr. McCrum's title and the name of the organization. Make up a street address and zip code.

f. Type a salutation.

g. Using the information listed above, type the body of the letter:

- In the first paragraph, accept the invitation to speak and confirm the important conference details.
- In the second paragraph, confirm your lecture topic and provide any relevant details.
- In the third paragraph, state your travel preferences.
- Type a short final paragraph.

h. Type a closing, then include your name in the signature block.

Advanced Challenge Exercise

- View the letter in Normal view, then correct your spelling and grammar errors, if any, by right-clicking any red- or green-underlined text and then choosing from the options on the shortcut menu.
- View the letter in Print Layout view, then remove any smart tags.
- View the letter in Reading Layout view, then click the Close button on the Reading Layout toolbar to close Reading Layout view.

i. Proofread your letter, make corrections as needed, then save your changes.

j. Preview the letter, print the letter, close the document, then exit Word.

FIGURE A-16

June 12, 2006

Dr. Leslie Morris
Professor of American Literature
Department of Literature
Manchester State College
Manchester, NH 03258

Dear Dr. Morris:

Thank you very much for your kind invitation to speak at your upcoming conference on the literature of place. I will be happy to oblige. I understand the conference will be held September 16 and 17 in the Sanders Auditorium.

I will address my remarks to the topic you suggested, "Writers of the Monadnock region." I understand you would like me to speak at 2:30 p.m. on September 16 for forty minutes, with twenty minutes of questions to follow. My talk will include a slide show. I presume you will have the necessary equipment—a slide projector and viewing screen—on hand.

My preference is to arrive in Manchester on the morning of September 16, and to depart that evening. It is easiest for me to use New York's LaGuardia Airport. I am grateful that your office will be taking care of my travel arrangements.

I look forward to meeting you in September.

Sincerely,

Jessica Grange

▼ INDEPENDENT CHALLENGE 2

Your company has recently installed Word 2003 on its company network. As the training manager, it's your responsibility to teach employees how to use the new software productively. Now that they have begun working with Word 2003, several employees have asked you about smart tags. In response to their queries, you decide to write a memo to all employees explaining how to use the smart tag feature. You know that smart tags are designed to help users perform tasks in Word that normally would require opening a different program, such as Microsoft Outlook (a desktop information-management program that includes e-mail, calendar, and address book features). Before writing your memo, you'll learn more about smart tags by searching the Word Help system.

a. Start Word and save a new blank document as **Smart Tags Memo** to the drive and folder where your Data Files are located.

b. Type **WORD TRAINING MEMORANDUM** at the top of the document, press [Enter] four times, then type the memo heading information shown in Figure A-17. Make sure to include your name in the From line and the current date in the Date line.

c. Press [Enter] twice to place the insertion point where you will begin typing the body of your memo.

d. Search the Word Help system for information on working with smart tags.

e. Type your memo after completing your research. In your memo, define smart tags, then explain what they look like, how to use smart tags, and how to remove smart tags from a document.

FIGURE A-17

> WORD TRAINING MEMORANDUM
>
>
> To: All employees
> From: Your Name, Training Manager
> Date: Today's date
> Re: Smart tags in Microsoft Word

Advanced Challenge Exercise

■ Search the Help system for information on how to check for new smart tags developed by Microsoft and third-party vendors.

■ Print the information you find.

■ Add a short paragraph to your memo explaining how to find new smart tags.

f. Save your changes, preview and print the memo, then close the document and exit Word.

▼ INDEPENDENT CHALLENGE 3

Yesterday you interviewed for a job as marketing director at Komata Web Designs. You spoke with several people at Komata, including Shige Murata, Director of Operations, whose business card is shown in Figure A-18. You need to write a follow-up letter to Mr. Murata, thanking him for the interview and expressing your interest in the company and the position. He also asked you to send him some samples of your marketing work, which you will enclose with the letter.

a. Start Word and save a new blank document as **Komata Letter** to the drive and folder where your Data Files are located.

b. Begin the letter by typing today's date.

c. Four lines below the date, type the inside address, referring to Figure A-18 for the address information. Be sure to include the recipient's title, company name, and full mailing address in the inside address. (*Hint*: When typing a foreign address, type the name of the country in capital letters by itself on the last line.)

d. Two lines below the inside address, type the salutation.

FIGURE A-18

> **Komata Web Designs**
>
> 5-8, Edobori 4-chome
> Minato-ku
> Tokyo 108-0034
> Japan
>
> **Shige Murata**   Phone: (03) 5555-3299
> *Director of Operations*   Fax: (03) 5555-7028
>   Email: smurata@komata.co.jp

▼ INDEPENDENT CHALLENGE 3 (CONTINUED)

e. Two lines below the salutation, type the body of the letter according to the following guidelines:

- In the first paragraph, thank him for the interview. Then restate your interest in the position and express your desire to work for the company. Add any specific details you think will enhance the power of your letter.
- In the second paragraph, note that you are enclosing three samples of your work and explain something about the samples you are enclosing.
- Type a short final paragraph.

f. Two lines below the last body paragraph, type a closing, then four lines below the closing, type the signature block. Be sure to include your name in the signature block.

g. Two lines below the signature block, type an enclosure notation. (*Hint*: An enclosure notation usually includes the word "Enclosures" or the abbreviation "Enc." followed by the number of enclosures in parentheses.)

h. Save your changes.

i. Preview and print the letter, then close the document and exit Word.

▼ INDEPENDENT CHALLENGE 4

Unlike personal letters or many e-mail messages, business letters are formal in tone and format. The World Wide Web is one source for information on writing styles, proper document formatting, and other business etiquette issues. In this independent challenge, you will research guidelines and tips for writing effective and professional business letters. Your online research should seek answers to the following questions: What is important to keep in mind when writing a business letter? What are the parts of a business letter? What are some examples of business letter types? What are some useful tips for writing business letters?

a. Use your favorite search engine to search the Web for information on writing and formatting business letters. Use the keywords **business letters** to conduct your search.

b. Review the Web sites you find. Print at least two Web pages that offer useful guidelines for writing business letters.

c. Start Word and save a new blank document as **Business Letters** to the drive and folder where your Data Files are located.

d. Type your name at the top of the document, then press [Enter] twice.

e. Type a brief report on the results of your research. Your report should answer the following questions:

- What are the URLs of the Web sites you visited to research guidelines for writing a business letter? (*Hint*: A URL is a Web page's address. An example of a URL is www.eHow.com.)
- What is important to keep in mind when writing a business letter?
- What are the parts of a business letter?
- In what situations do people write business letters? Provide at least five examples.

f. Save your changes to the document, preview and print it, then close the document and exit Word.

▼ VISUAL WORKSHOP

Create the cover letter shown in Figure A-19. Save the document with the name **Publishing Cover Letter** to the drive and folder where your Data Files are stored, print a copy of the letter, then close the document and exit Word.

FIGURE A-19

July 17, 2006

Ms. Charlotte Janoch
Managing Editor
Sunrise Press
6354 Baker Street
Townsend, MA 02181

Dear Ms. Janoch:

I read of the opening for an editorial assistant on the July 15 edition of Boston.com, and I would like to be considered for the position. A recent graduate of Merrimack College, I am interested in pursuing a career in publishing.

My desire for a publishing career springs from my interest in writing and editing. At Merrimack College, I was a frequent contributor to the student newspaper and was involved in creating a Web site for student poetry and short fiction.

I have a wealth of experience using Microsoft Word in professional settings. For the past several summers I worked as an office assistant for Packer Investment Consultants, where I used Word to create newsletters and financial reports for clients. During the school year, I also worked part-time in the Merrimack College admissions office. Here I used Word's mail merge feature to create form letters and mailing labels.

My enclosed resume details my talents and experience. I would welcome the opportunity to discuss the position and my qualifications with you. I can be reached at 617-555-3849.

Sincerely,

Your Name

Enc.

Editing Documents

OBJECTIVES

Open a document
Select text
Cut and paste text
Copy and paste text
Use the Office Clipboard
Find and replace text
Check spelling and grammar
Use the Thesaurus
Use wizards and templates

If you have a SAM user profile, you may have access to hands-on instruction, practice, and assessment of the skills covered in this unit. Log in to your SAM account and go to your assignments page to see what your instructor has assigned.

The sophisticated editing features in Word make it easy to revise and polish your documents. In this unit, you learn how to open an existing file, revise it by replacing, copying, and moving text, and then save the document as a new file. You also learn how to perfect your documents using proofing tools and how to quickly create attractive, professionally designed documents using wizards and templates. You have been asked to create a press release about a new MediaLoft lecture series in New York. The press release should provide information about the series so that newspapers, radio stations, and other media outlets can announce it to the public. MediaLoft press releases are disseminated by fax, so you also need to create a fax coversheet to use when you fax the press release to your list of press contacts.

Opening a Document

Sometimes the easiest way to create a document is to edit an existing document and save it with a new filename. To modify a document, you must first **open** it so that it displays in the document window. Word offers several methods for opening documents, described in Table B-1. Once you have opened a file, you can use the Save As command to create a new file that is a copy of the original. You can then edit the new file without making changes to the original. ▓▓▓▓ Rather than write your press release from scratch, you decide to modify a press release written for a similar event. You begin by opening the press release document and saving it with a new filename.

STEPS

TROUBLE
If the task pane is not open, click View on the menu bar, then click Task Pane.

1. **Start Word**

   Word opens and a blank document and the Getting Started task pane appear in the program window, as shown in Figure B-1. The Getting Started task pane contains links for opening existing documents and for creating new documents.

2. **Click the Open or More hyperlink at the bottom of the Getting Started task pane**

   The Open dialog box opens. You use the Open dialog box to locate and select the file you want to open. The Look in list box displays the current drive or folder. You also can use the Open button 📂 on the Standard toolbar or the Open command on the File menu to open the Open dialog box.

3. **Click the Look in list arrow, click the drive containing your Data Files, then double-click the folder containing your Data Files**

   A list of the Data Files for this unit appears in the Open dialog box, as shown in Figure B-2.

QUICK TIP
You also can double-click a filename in the Open dialog box to open the file.

4. **Click the filename WD B-1.doc in the Open dialog box to select it, then click Open**

   The document opens. Notice that the filename WD B-1.doc appears in the title bar. Once you have opened a file, you can edit it and use the Save or the Save As command to save your changes. You use the **Save** command when you want to save the changes you make to a file, overwriting the file that is stored on a disk. You use the **Save As** command when you want to create a new file with a different filename, leaving the original file intact.

5. **Click File on the menu bar, then click Save As**

   The Save As dialog box opens. By saving a file with a new filename, you create a document that is identical to the original document. The original filename is selected (highlighted) in the File name text box. Any text you type replaces the selected text.

6. **Type NY Press Release in the File name text box, then click Save**

   The original file closes and the NY Press Release file is displayed in the document window. Notice the new filename in the title bar. You can now make changes to the press release file without affecting the original file.

Clues to Use

Managing files and folders

The Open and Save As dialog boxes include powerful tools for navigating, creating, deleting, and renaming files and folders on your computer, a network, or the Web. By selecting a file or folder and clicking the Delete button ☒, you can delete the item and send it to the Recycle Bin. You can also create a new folder for storing files by clicking the Create New Folder button 📁 and typing a name for the folder. The new folder is created in the current folder. To rename a file or folder, simply right-click it in the dialog box, click Rename, type a new name, and then press [Enter].

Using the Save As dialog box, you can create new files that are based on existing files. To create a new file, you can save an existing file with a different filename or save it in a different location on your system. You also can save a file in a different file format so that it can be opened in a different software program. To save a file in a different format, click the Save as type list arrow, then click the type of file you want to create. For example, you can save a Word document (which has a .doc file extension) as a plain text file (.txt), as a Web page file (.htm), or in a variety of other file formats.

FIGURE B-1: Getting Started task pane

Open button

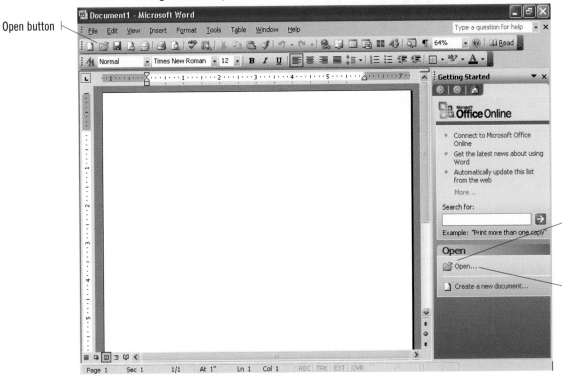

Your task pane might include hyperlinks to recently opened files here

Open hyperlink (yours might be the More hyperlink)

FIGURE B-2: Open dialog box

Current drive or folder

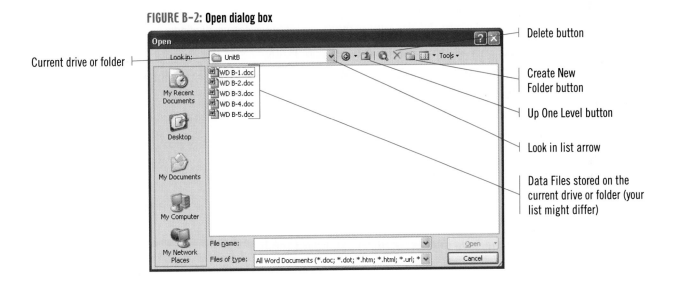

Delete button

Create New Folder button

Up One Level button

Look in list arrow

Data Files stored on the current drive or folder (your list might differ)

TABLE B-1: Methods for opening documents

use	to	if you want to
The Open button 📂 on the Standard toolbar, the Open command on the File menu, the Open or More hyperlink in the Getting Started task pane, or [Ctrl][O]	Open the Open dialog box	Open an existing file
A filename hyperlink in the Getting Started task pane	Open the file in the document window	Open the file; a fast way to open a file that was recently opened on your computer
The From existing document hyperlink in the New Document task pane	Open the New from Existing Document dialog box	Create a copy of an existing file; a fast way to open a document you intend to save with a new filename

Selecting Text

Before deleting, editing, or formatting text, you must **select** the text. Selecting text involves clicking and dragging the I-beam pointer across text to highlight it. You also can click with the ⬧ pointer in the blank area to the left of text to select lines or paragraphs. Table B-2 describes the many ways to select text. ▰▰▱▱
You revise the press release by selecting text and replacing it with new text.

TROUBLE

If you make a mistake, you can deselect the text by clicking anywhere in the document window.

1. **Click the** Zoom list arrow **on the Standard toolbar, click** Page Width, **click before** April 14, 2006, **then drag the** I **pointer over the text to select it**
   The date is selected, as shown in Figure B-3.

2. **Type** May 1, 2006
   The text you type replaces the selected text.

3. **Double-click** James, **type your first name, double-click** Callaghan, **then type your last name**
   Double-clicking a word selects the entire word.

4. **Place the pointer in the margin to the left of the phone number so that the pointer changes to** ⬧, **click to select the phone number, then type** (415) 555-8293
   Clicking to the left of a line of text with the ⬧ pointer selects the entire line.

5. **Click the** down scroll arrow **at the bottom of the vertical scroll bar until the headline Alex Fogg to Speak... is at the top of your document window**
   The scroll arrows or scroll bars allow you to scroll through a document. You scroll through a document when you want to display different parts of the document in the document window.

6. **Select** SAN FRANCISCO, **then type** NEW YORK

QUICK TIP

If you delete text by mistake, immediately click the Undo button ↩ on the Standard toolbar to restore the deleted text to the document.

7. **In the fourth body paragraph, select the sentence** All events will be held at the St. James Hotel., **then press** [Delete]
   Selecting text and pressing [Delete] removes the text from the document.

8. **Select and replace text in the second and last paragraphs using the following table:**

select	type
May 12	June 14
St. James Hotel in downtown San Francisco	Waldorf-Astoria Hotel
National Public Radio's Helen DeSaint	New York Times literary editor Janet Richard

   The edited press release is shown in Figure B-4.

9. **Click the** Save button 🖫 **on the Standard toolbar**
   Your changes to the press release are saved. Always save before and after editing text.

TABLE B-2: Methods for selecting text

to select	use the mouse pointer to
Any amount of text	Drag over the text
A word	Double-click the word
A line of text	Click with the ⬧ pointer to the left of the line
A sentence	Press and hold [Ctrl], then click the sentence
A paragraph	Triple-click the paragraph or double-click with the ⬧ pointer to the left of the paragraph
A large block of text	Click at the beginning of the selection, press and hold [Shift], then click at the end of the selection
Multiple nonconsecutive selections	Select the first selection, then press and hold [Ctrl] as you select each additional selection
An entire document	Triple-click with the ⬧ pointer to the left of any text, click Select All on the Edit menu, or press [Ctrl][A]

FIGURE B-3: Date selected in the press release

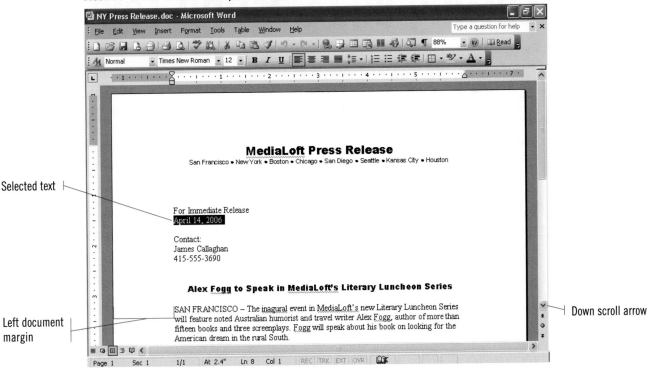

Selected text

Left document margin

Down scroll arrow

FIGURE B-4: Edited press release

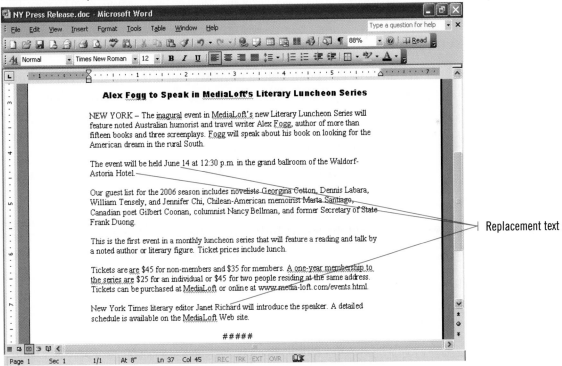

Replacement text

Clues to Use

Replacing text in Overtype mode

Normally you must select text before typing to replace the existing characters, but by turning on **Overtype mode** you can type over existing characters without selecting them first. To turn Overtype mode on and off on your computer, double-click OVR in the status bar. On some computers you also can turn Overtype mode on and off by pressing [Insert]. When Overtype mode is on, OVR appears in black in the status bar. When Overtype mode is off, OVR is dimmed.

Cutting and Pasting Text

The editing features in Word allow you to move text from one location to another in a document. The operation of moving text is often called **cut and paste**. When you cut text from a document, you remove it from the document and add it to the **Clipboard**, a temporary storage area for text and graphics that you cut or copy from a document. You cut text by selecting it and using the Cut command on the Edit menu or the Cut button. To insert the text from the Clipboard into the document, you place the insertion point where you want to insert the text, and then use the Paste command on the Edit menu or the Paste button to paste the text at that location. You also can move text by dragging it to a new location using the mouse. This operation is called **drag and drop**. ▒▒▒▒▒ You reorganize the information in the press release using the cut-and-paste and drag-and-drop methods.

STEPS

1. **Click the Show/Hide ¶ button ¶ on the Standard toolbar**

   Formatting marks appear in the document window. **Formatting marks** are special characters that appear on your screen and do not print. Common formatting marks include the paragraph symbol (¶), which shows the end of a paragraph—wherever you press [Enter]; the dot symbol (•), which represents a space—wherever you press [Spacebar]; and the arrow symbol (→), which shows the location of a tab stop—wherever you press [Tab]. Working with formatting marks turned on can help you to select, edit, and format text with precision.

   > **TROUBLE**
   > If the Clipboard task pane opens, close it.

2. **In the third paragraph, select Canadian poet Gilbert Coonan, (including the comma and the space after it), then click the Cut button ✂ on the Standard toolbar**

   The text is removed from the document and placed on the Clipboard. Word uses two different clipboards: the **system Clipboard** (the Clipboard), which holds just one item, and the **Office Clipboard**, which holds up to 24 items. The last item you cut or copy is always added to both clipboards. You'll learn more about the Office Clipboard in a later lesson.

3. **Place the insertion point before novelists (but after the space) in the first line of the third paragraph, then click the Paste button 📋 on the Standard toolbar**

   The text is pasted at the location of the insertion point, as shown in Figure B-5. The Paste Options button 📋 appears below text when you first paste it in a document. You'll learn more about the Paste Options button in the next lesson. For now, you can ignore it.

4. **Press and hold [Ctrl], click the sentence Ticket prices include lunch. in the fourth paragraph, then release [Ctrl]**

   The entire sentence is selected.

   > **TROUBLE**
   > If you make a mistake, click the Undo button ↶ on the Standard toolbar, then try again.

5. **Press and hold the mouse button over the selected text until the pointer changes to ▨, then drag the pointer's vertical line to the end of the fifth paragraph (between the period and the paragraph mark) as shown in Figure B-6**

   The pointer's vertical line indicates the location the text will be inserted when you release the mouse button.

6. **Release the mouse button**

   The selected text is moved to the location of the insertion point. It's convenient to move text using the drag-and-drop method when the locations of origin and destination are both visible on the screen. Text is not removed to the Clipboard when you move it using drag-and-drop.

7. **Deselect the text, then click the Save button 💾 on the Standard toolbar**

   Your changes to the press release are saved.

FIGURE B-5: Moved text with Paste Options button

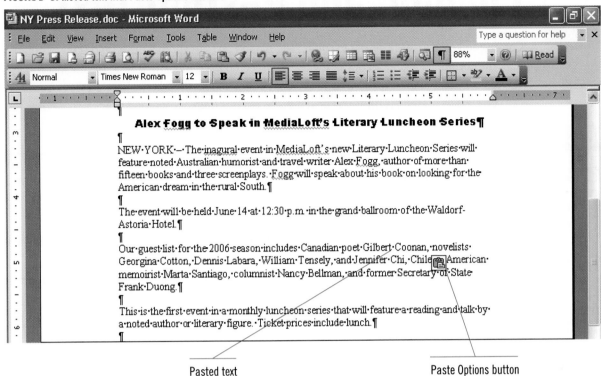

Pasted text   Paste Options button

FIGURE B-6: Text being dragged to a new location

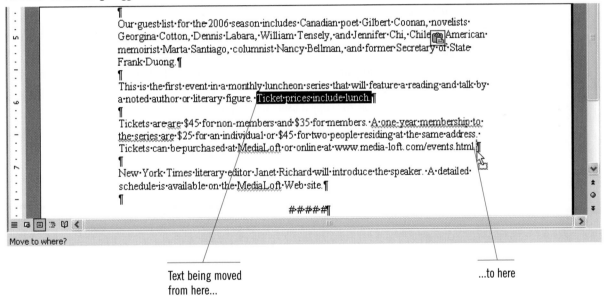

Text being moved from here...   ...to here

Clues to Use

Using keyboard shortcuts

Instead of using the Cut, Copy, and Paste commands to edit text in Word, you can use the **keyboard shortcuts** [Ctrl][X] to cut text, [Ctrl][C] to copy text, and [Ctrl][V] to paste text. A **shortcut key** is a function key, such as [F1], or a combination of keys, such as [Ctrl][S], that you press to perform a command. For example, pressing [Ctrl][S] saves changes to a document just as clicking the Save button or using the Save command on the File menu saves a document. Becoming skilled at using keyboard shortcuts can help you to quickly accomplish many of the tasks you perform frequently in Word. If a keyboard shortcut is available for a menu command, then it is listed next to the command on the menu.

Copying and Pasting Text

Copying and pasting text is similar to cutting and pasting text, except that the text you copy is not removed from the document. Rather, a copy of the text is placed on the Clipboard, leaving the original text in place. You can copy text to the Clipboard using the Copy command on the Edit menu or the Copy button, or you can copy text by pressing [Ctrl] as you drag the selected text from one location to another. You continue to edit the press release by copying text from one location to another.

STEPS

TROUBLE
If the Clipboard task pane opens, close it.

1. **In the headline, select** Literary Luncheon, **then click the** Copy button 🖺 **on the Standard toolbar**

   A copy of the text is placed on the Clipboard, leaving the text you copied in place.

2. **Place the insertion point before** season **in the third body paragraph, then click the** Paste button 🖺 **on the Standard toolbar**

   "Literary Luncheon" is inserted before "season," as shown in Figure B-7. Notice that the pasted text is formatted differently than the paragraph in which it was inserted.

QUICK TIP
If you don't like the result of a paste option, try another option or click the Undo button 🔄 and then paste the text again.

3. **Click the** Paste Options button 🖺, **then click** Match Destination Formatting

   The Paste Options button allows you to change the formatting of pasted text. The formatting of "Literary Luncheon" is changed to match the rest of the paragraph. The options available on the Paste Options menu depend on the format of the text you are pasting and the format of the surrounding text.

4. **Scroll down if necessary so that the last two paragraphs are visible on your screen**

5. **In the fifth paragraph, select** www.media-loft.com, **press and hold** [Ctrl], **then press the mouse button until the pointer changes to** 🖺

6. **Drag the pointer's vertical line to the end of the last paragraph, placing it between** site **and the period, release the mouse button, then release** [Ctrl]

   The text is copied to the last paragraph. Since the formatting of the text you copied is the same as the formatting of the paragraph in which you inserted it, you can ignore the Paste Options button. Text is not copied to the Clipboard when you copy it using the drag-and-drop method.

7. **Place the insertion point before** www.media-loft.com **in the last paragraph, type** at **followed by a space, then click the** Save button 🖺 **on the Standard toolbar**

   Compare your document with Figure B-8.

Clues to Use

Copying and moving items in a long document

If you want to copy or move items between parts of a long document, it can be useful to split the document window into two panes so that the item you want to copy or move is displayed in one pane and the destination for the item is displayed in the other pane. To split a window, click the Split command on the Window menu, drag the horizontal split bar that appears to the location you want to split the window, and then click. Once the document window is split into two panes, you can drag the split bar to resize the panes and use the scroll bars in each pane to display different parts of the document. To copy or move an item from one pane to another, you can use the Cut, Copy, and Paste commands, or you can drag the item between the panes. When you are finished editing the document, double-click the split bar to restore the window to a single pane.

FIGURE B-7: Text pasted in document

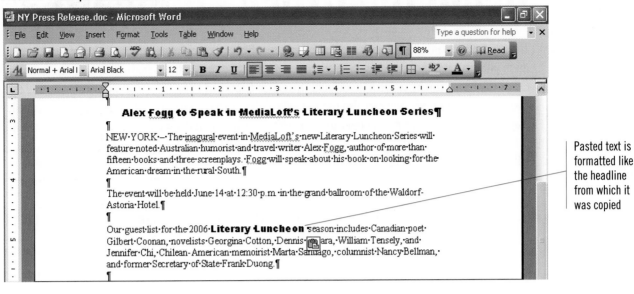

Pasted text is formatted like the headline from which it was copied

Word 2003

FIGURE B-8: Copied text in press release

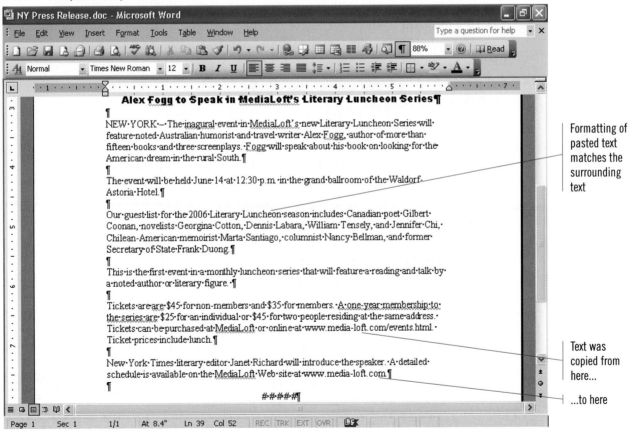

Formatting of pasted text matches the surrounding text

Text was copied from here...

...to here

Using the Office Clipboard

The Office Clipboard allows you to collect text and graphics from files created in any Office program and insert them into your Word documents. It holds up to 24 items and, unlike the system Clipboard, the items on the Office Clipboard can be viewed. By default, the Office Clipboard opens automatically when you cut or copy two items consecutively. You can also use the Office Clipboard command on the Edit menu to manually display the Office Clipboard if you prefer to work with it open. You add items to the Office Clipboard using the Cut and Copy commands. The last item you collect is always added to both the system Clipboard and the Office Clipboard. You use the Office Clipboard to move several sentences in your press release.

STEPS

TROUBLE
If the Office Clipboard does not open, click Office Clipboard on the Edit menu, click the Undo button on the Standard toolbar two times, click Clear All on the Clipboard task pane, then repeat Steps 1 and 2. To restore the default, click Options on the Clipboard task pane, click Show Office Clipboard Automatically to select it, then click outside the menu.

QUICK TIP
To delete an individual item from the Office Clipboard, click the list arrow next to the item, then click Delete.

QUICK TIP
Many Word users prefer to work with formatting marks turned on at all times. Experiment for yourself and see which method you prefer.

1. **In the last paragraph, select the sentence New York Times literary editor... (including the space after the period), then click the Cut button 🔀 on the Standard toolbar**
   The sentence is cut to the Clipboard.

2. **Select the sentence A detailed schedule is... (including the ¶ mark), then click 🔀**
   The Office Clipboard opens in the Clipboard task pane, as shown in Figure B-9. It displays the items you cut from the press release. The icon next to each item indicates the items are from a Word document.

3. **Place the insertion point at the end of the second paragraph (after Hotel. but before the ¶ mark), then click the New York Times literary editor... item on the Office Clipboard**
   Clicking an item on the Office Clipboard pastes the item in the document at the location of the insertion point. Notice that the item remains on the Office Clipboard even after you pasted it. Items remain on the Office Clipboard until you delete them or close all open Office programs. Also, if you add a 25th item to the Office Clipboard, the first item is deleted.

4. **Place the insertion point at the end of the third paragraph (after Duong.), then click the A detailed schedule is... item on the Office Clipboard**
   The sentence is pasted in the document.

5. **Select the fourth paragraph, which contains the sentence This is the first event... (including the ¶ mark), then click 🔀**
   The sentence is cut to the Office Clipboard. Notice that the last item collected displays at the top of the Clipboard task pane. The last item collected is also stored on the system Clipboard.

6. **Place the insertion point at the beginning of the third paragraph (before Our...), click the Paste button 📋 on the Standard toolbar, then press [Backspace]**
   The "This is the first..." sentence is pasted at the beginning of the "Our guest list..." paragraph. You can paste the last item collected using either the Paste command or the Office Clipboard.

7. **Place the insertion point at the end of the third paragraph (after www.media-loft.com and before the ¶ mark), then press [Delete] twice**
   The ¶ symbols and the blank line between the third and fourth paragraphs are deleted.

8. **Click the Show/Hide ¶ button ¶ on the Standard toolbar**
   Compare your press release with Figure B-10.

9. **Click the Clear All button on the Office Clipboard to remove the items from it, close the Clipboard task pane, press [Ctrl][Home], then click the Save button 💾**
   Pressing [Ctrl][Home] moves the insertion point to the top of the document.

FIGURE B-9: Office Clipboard in Clipboard task pane

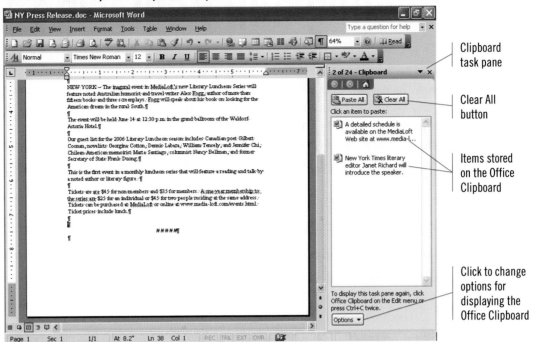

Clipboard task pane

Clear All button

Items stored on the Office Clipboard

Click to change options for displaying the Office Clipboard

FIGURE B-10: Revised press release

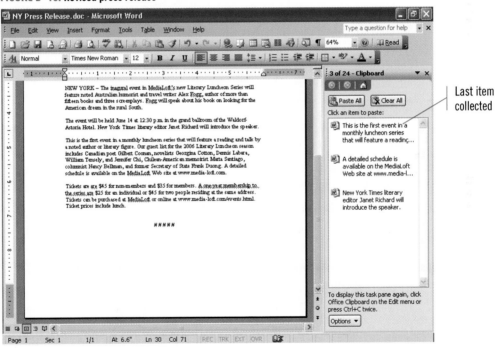

Last item collected

Clues to Use

Copying and moving items between documents

The system and Office Clipboards also can be used to copy and move items between Word documents. To copy or cut items from one Word document and paste them into another, first open both documents and the Clipboard task pane in the program window. With multiple documents open, you can copy and move items between documents by copying or cutting the item(s) from one document and then switching to another document and pasting the item(s). To switch between open documents, click the button on the taskbar for the document you want to appear in the document window. You can also display both documents at the same time by clicking the Arrange All command on the Window menu. The Office Clipboard stores all the items collected from all documents, regardless of which document is displayed in the document window. The system Clipboard stores the last item collected from any document.

Finding and Replacing Text

The Find and Replace feature in Word allows you to automatically search for and replace all instances of a word or phrase in a document. For example, you might need to substitute "bookstore" for "store," and it would be very time-consuming to manually locate and replace each instance of "store" in a long document. Using the Replace command you can automatically find and replace all occurrences of specific text at once, or you can choose to find and review each occurrence individually. You also can use the Find command to locate and highlight every occurrence of a specific word or phrase in a document. MediaLoft has decided to change the name of the New York series from "Literary Luncheon Series" to "Literary Limelight Series." You use the Replace command to search the document for all instances of "Luncheon" and replace them with "Limelight."

STEPS

1. **Click Edit on the menu bar, click Replace, then click More in the Find and Replace dialog box**
   The Find and Replace dialog box opens, as shown in Figure B-11.

2. **Click the Find what text box, then type Luncheon**
   "Luncheon" is the text that will be replaced.

3. **Press [Tab], then type Limelight in the Replace with text box**
   "Limelight" is the text that will replace "Luncheon."

4. **Click the Match case check box in the Search Options section to select it**
   Selecting the Match case check box tells Word to find only exact matches for the uppercase and lowercase characters you entered in the Find what text box. You want to replace all instances of "Luncheon" in the proper name "Literary Luncheon Series." You do not want to replace "luncheon" when it refers to a lunchtime event.

QUICK TIP
Click Find Next to find, review, and replace each occurrence individually.

5. **Click Replace All**
   Clicking Replace All changes all occurrences of "Luncheon" to "Limelight" in the press release. A message box reports three replacements were made.

6. **Click OK to close the message box, then click Close to close the Find and Replace dialog box**
   Word replaced "Luncheon" with "Limelight" in three locations, but did not replace "luncheon."

7. **Click Edit on the menu bar, then click Find**
   The Find and Replace dialog box opens with the Find tab displayed. The Find command allows you to quickly locate all instances of text in a document. You can use it to verify that Word did not replace "luncheon."

8. **Type luncheon in the Find what text box, click the Highlight all items found in check box to select it, click Find All, then click Close**
   The Find and Replace dialog box closes and "luncheon" is selected in the document, as shown in Figure B-12.

9. **Deselect the text, press [Ctrl][Home], then click the Save button on the Standard toolbar**

Clues to Use

Inserting text with AutoCorrect

As you type, AutoCorrect automatically corrects many commonly mis-spelled words. By creating your own AutoCorrect entries, you also can set Word to quickly insert text that you type often, such as your name or contact information, or to correct words you frequently misspell. For example, you could create an AutoCorrect entry so that the name "Alice Wegman" is automatically inserted whenever you type "aw" followed by a space. To create an AutoCorrect entry, click AutoCorrect Options on the Tools menu. On the AutoCorrect tab in the AutoCorrect dialog box, type the text you want to be automatically corrected in the Replace text box (such as "aw"), type the text you want to be automatically inserted in its place in the With text box (such as "Alice Wegman"), then click Add. The AutoCorrect entry is added to the list. Note that Word inserts an AutoCorrect entry in a document only when you press [Spacebar] after typing the text you want Word to correct. For example, Word will insert "Alice Wegman" when you type "aw" followed by a space, but not when you type "awful."

FIGURE B-11: Find and Replace dialog box

Replace only exact matches of uppercase and lowercase characters

Find only complete words

Use wildcards (*) in a search string

Find words that sound like the Find what text

Find and replace all forms of a word

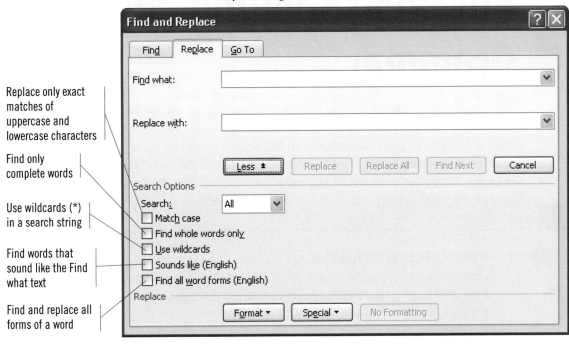

FIGURE B-12: Found text highlighted in document

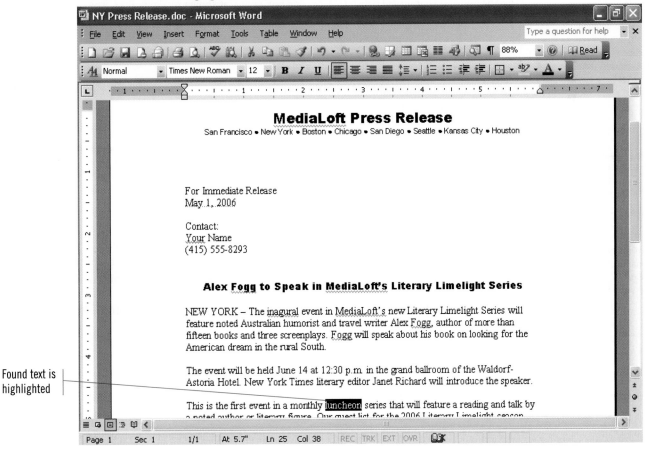

Found text is highlighted

Checking Spelling and Grammar

When you finish typing and revising a document, you can use the Spelling and Grammar command to search the document for misspelled words and grammar errors. The Spelling and Grammar checker flags possible mistakes, suggests correct spellings, and offers remedies for grammar errors such as subject-verb agreement, repeated words, and punctuation. ▰▰▰▰ You use the Spelling and Grammar checker to search your press release for errors. Before beginning the search, you set the Spelling and Grammar checker to ignore words, such as Fogg, that you know are spelled correctly.

STEPS

TROUBLE
If Word flags your name as misspelled, right-click it, then click Ignore All.

1. **Right-click Fogg in the headline**

   A shortcut menu that includes suggestions for correcting the spelling of "Fogg" opens. You can correct individual spelling and grammar errors by right-clicking text that is underlined with a red or green wavy line and selecting a correction. Although "Fogg" is not in the Word dictionary, it is spelled correctly in the document.

2. **Click Ignore All**

   Clicking Ignore All tells Word not to flag "Fogg" as misspelled.

TROUBLE
If "MediaLoft" and "MediaLoft's" are not flagged as misspelled, skip this step.

3. **Right-click MediaLoft at the top of the document, click Ignore All, right-click MediaLoft's in the headline, then click Ignore All**

   The red wavy underline is removed from all instances of "MediaLoft" and "MediaLoft's."

QUICK TIP
To change the language used by the Word proofing tools, click Tools on the menu bar, point to Language, then click Set Language.

4. **Press [Ctrl][Home], then click the Spelling and Grammar button ✓ on the Standard toolbar**

   The Spelling and Grammar: English (U.S.) dialog box opens, as shown in Figure B-13. The dialog box identifies "inagural" as misspelled and suggests possible corrections for the error. The word selected in the Suggestions box is the correct spelling.

5. **Click Change**

   Word replaces the misspelled word with the correctly spelled word. Next, the dialog box indicates "are" is repeated in a sentence.

TROUBLE
You might need to correct other spelling and grammar errors.

6. **Click Delete**

   Word deletes the second occurrence of the repeated word. Next, the dialog box flags a subject-verb agreement error and suggests using "is" instead of "are," as shown in Figure B-14. The phrase selected in the Suggestions box is correct.

QUICK TIP
If Word does not offer a valid correction, correct the error yourself.

7. **Click Change**

   The word "is" replaces the word "are" in the sentence and the Spelling and Grammar dialog box closes. Keep in mind that the Spelling and Grammar checker identifies many common errors, but you cannot rely on it to find and correct all spelling and grammar errors in your documents. Always proofread your documents carefully.

8. **Click OK to complete the spelling and grammar check, press [Ctrl][Home], then click the Save button 🖫 on the Standard toolbar**

FIGURE B-13: Spelling and Grammar: English (U.S.) dialog box

Word identified as misspelled

Suggested corrections

Adds the misspelled word and the correction to the AutoCorrect list

Ignores this occurrence of the word

Leaves all occurrences of the word unchanged

Adds the word to the Word dictionary

Changes the word to the selected suggestion

Changes all occurrences of the word to the selected suggestion

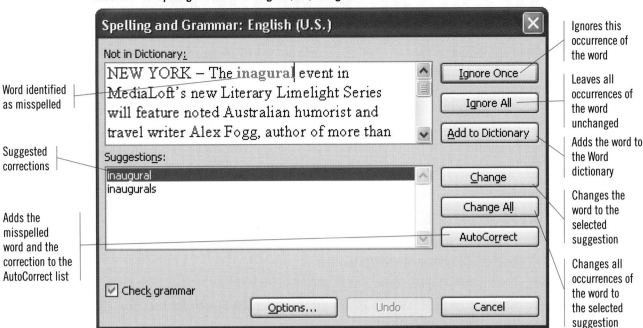

FIGURE B-14: Grammar error identified in Spelling and Grammar dialog box

Grammar error identified

Possible corrections

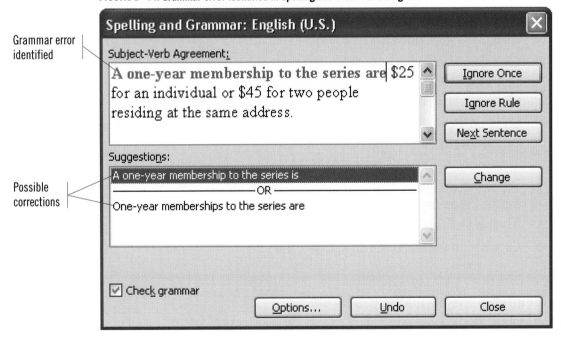

Clues to Use

Using the Undo, Redo, and Repeat commands

Word remembers the editing and formatting changes you make so that you can easily reverse or repeat them. You can reverse the last action you took by clicking the Undo button on the Standard toolbar, or you can undo a series of actions by clicking the Undo list arrow and selecting the action you want to reverse. When you undo an action using the Undo list arrow, you also undo all the actions above it in the list; that is, all actions that were performed after the action you selected. Similarly, you can keep the changes you just reversed by using the Redo button and the Redo list arrow.

If you want to repeat a change you just made, use the Repeat command on the Edit menu. The name of the Repeat command changes depending on the last action you took. For example, if you just typed "thank you," the name of the command is Repeat Typing. Clicking the Repeat Typing command inserts "thank you" at the location of the insertion point. You also can repeat the last action you took by pressing [F4].

Using the Thesaurus

Word also includes a Thesaurus, which you can use to look up synonyms for awkward or repetitive words. The Thesaurus is one of the reference sources available in the Research task pane. This task pane allows you to quickly search reference sources for information related to a word or phrase. When you are working with an active Internet connection, the Research task pane provides access to dictionary, encyclopedia, translation, and other reference sources and research services. ████ After proofreading your document for errors, you decide the press release would read better if several adjectives were more descriptive. You use the Thesaurus to find synonyms for "noted" and "new".

STEPS

1. **Scroll down until the headline is displayed at the top of your screen**

2. **In the first sentence of the third paragraph, select noted, then click the Research button 📖 on the Standard toolbar**
   The Research task pane opens. "Noted" appears in the Search for text box.

QUICK TIP
You can also select a word, click Tools on the menu bar, point to Language, and then click Thesaurus to open the Research task pane and display a list of synonyms for the word.

3. **Click the All Reference Books list arrow under the Search for text box, then click Thesaurus: English (U.S.)**
   Possible synonyms for "noted" are listed under the Thesaurus: English (U.S.) heading in the task pane, as shown in Figure B-15.

4. **Point to distinguished in the list of synonyms**
   A box containing an arrow appears around the word.

QUICK TIP
Right-click a word, then click Look up to open the Research task pane.

5. **Click the arrow in the box, click Insert on the menu that appears, then close the Research task pane**
   "Distinguished" replaces "noted" in the press release.

6. **Scroll up, right-click new in the first sentence of the first paragraph, point to Synonyms on the shortcut menu, then click innovative**
   "Innovative" replaces "new" in the press release.

7. **Press [Ctrl][Home], click the Save button 🖫 on the Standard toolbar, then click the Print button 🖨 on the Standard toolbar**
   A copy of the finished press release prints. Compare your document to Figure B-16.

8. **Click File on the menu bar, then click Close**

Clues to Use

Viewing and modifying the document properties

Document properties are details about a file that can help you to organize and search your files. The author name, the date the file was created, the title, and keywords that describe the contents of the file are examples of document property information. You can view and modify the properties of an open document by clicking Properties on the File menu to open the Properties dialog box. The General, Statistics, and Contents tabs of the Properties dialog box display information about the file that is automatically created and updated by Word. The General tab shows the file type, location, size, and date and time the file was created and last modified; the Statistics tab displays information about revisions to the document along with the number of pages, words, lines, paragraphs, and characters in the file; and the Contents tab shows the title of the document.

You can define other document properties using the Summary and Custom tabs of the Properties dialog box. The Summary tab includes identifying information about the document such as the title, subject, author, and keywords. Some of this information is entered by Word when the document is first saved, but you can modify or add to the summary details by typing new information in the text boxes on the Summary tab. The Custom tab allows you to create new document properties, such as client, project, or date completed. To create a custom property, select a property name in the Name list box on the Custom tab, use the Type list arrow to select the type of data you want for the property, and then type the identifying detail (such as a project name) in the Value text box. When you are finished viewing or modifying the document properties, click OK to close the Properties dialog box.

FIGURE B-15: Research task pane

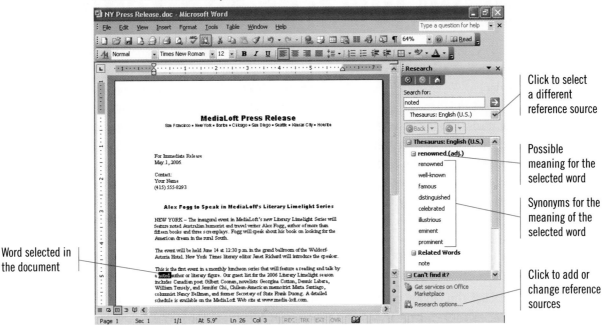

Word selected in the document

Click to select a different reference source

Possible meaning for the selected word

Synonyms for the meaning of the selected word

Click to add or change reference sources

FIGURE B-16: Completed press release

Using Wizards and Templates

Word includes many templates that you can use to quickly create memos, faxes, letters, reports, brochures, and other professionally designed documents. A **template** is a formatted document that contains place-holder text. To create a document that is based on a template, you replace the placeholder text with your own text and then save the document with a new filename. A **wizard** is an interactive set of dialog boxes that guides you through the process of creating a document. A wizard prompts you to provide information and select formatting options, and then it creates the document for you based on your specifications. You can create a document with a wizard or template using the New command on the File menu. ▰▰▰▰ You will fax the press release to your list of press contacts, beginning with the *New York Times*. You use a tem-plate to create a fax coversheet for the press release.

STEPS

1. **Click File on the menu bar, then click New**

   The New Document task pane opens.

2. **Click the On my computer hyperlink in the New Document task pane**

   The Templates dialog box opens. The tabs in the dialog box contain icons for the Word templates and wizards.

3. **Click the Letters & Faxes tab, then click the Professional Fax icon**

   A preview of the Professional Fax template appears in the Templates dialog box, as shown in Figure B-17.

   > **QUICK TIP**
   > Double-clicking an icon in the Templates dialog box also opens a new document based on the template.

4. **Click OK**

   The Professional Fax template opens as a new document in the document window. It contains placeholder text, which you can replace with your own information.

5. **Drag to select Company Name Here, then type MediaLoft**

6. **Click the Click here and type return address and phone and fax numbers placeholder**

   Clicking the placeholder selects it. When a placeholder says Click here... you do not need to drag to select it.

7. **Type MediaLoft San Francisco, press [Enter], then type Tel: (415) 555-8293**

   The text you type replaces the placeholder text.

   > **QUICK TIP**
   > Delete any placeholder text you do not want to replace.

8. **Replace the remaining placeholder text with the text shown in Figure B-18**

   Word automatically inserted the current date in the document. You do not need to replace the current date with the date shown in the figure.

9. **Click File on the menu bar, click Save As, use the Save in list arrow to navigate to the drive or folder where your Data Files are located, type NYT Fax in the File name text box, then click Save**

   The document is saved with the filename NYT Fax.

10. **Click the Print button ▤ on the Standard toolbar, click File on the menu bar, then click Exit**

    A copy of the fax coversheet prints and the document and Word close.

FIGURE B-17: Letters & Faxes tab in Templates dialog box

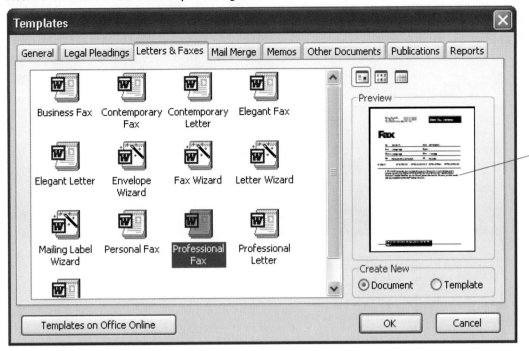

Preview of selected template

FIGURE B-18: Completed fax coversheet

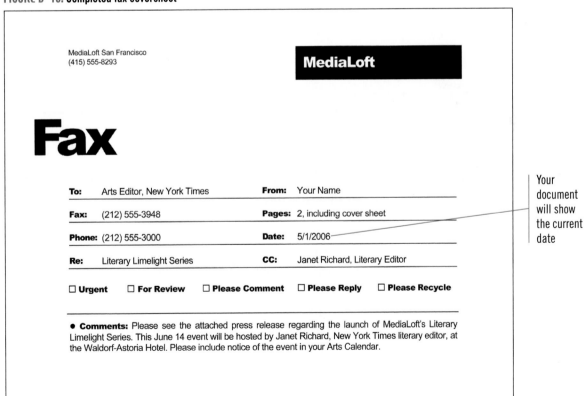

Your document will show the current date

Practice

▼ CONCEPTS REVIEW

Label the elements of the Open dialog box shown in Figure B-19.

FIGURE B-19

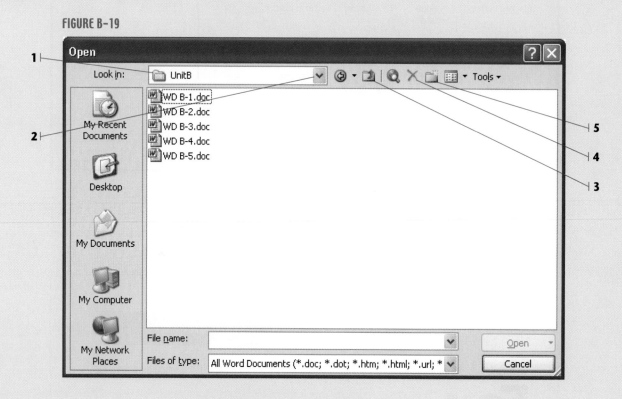

Match each term with the statement that best describes it.

6. **System Clipboard**	**a.** Command used to insert text stored on the Clipboard into a document
7. **Show/Hide**	**b.** Document that contains placeholder text
8. **Select**	**c.** Feature used to suggest synonyms for words
9. **Thesaurus**	**d.** Temporary storage area for only the last item cut or copied from a document
10. **Undo**	**e.** Command used to display formatting marks in a document
11. **Template**	**f.** Command used to locate and replace occurrences of specific text in a document
12. **Office Clipboard**	**g.** Command used to reverse the last action you took in a document
13. **Paste**	**h.** Temporary storage area for up to 24 items collected from any Office file
14. **Replace**	**i.** Action that must be taken before text can be cut, copied, or deleted

Select the best answer from the list of choices.

15. Which of the following is _not_ used to open an existing document?

    a. Blank document hyperlink in the New Document task pane

    b. Open button on the Standard toolbar

    c. Open or More hyperlink in the Getting Started task pane

    d. Open command on the File menu

16. To locate and change all instances of a word in a document, which menu command do you use?

   a. Find   **c.** Paste

   b. Search   **d.** Replace

17. Which of the following statements is *not* true?

   a. The last item cut or copied from a document is stored on the system Clipboard.

   b. You can view the contents of the Office Clipboard.

   c. When you move text by dragging it, a copy of the text you move is stored on the system Clipboard.

   d. The Office Clipboard can hold more than one item.

18. Which Word feature corrects errors as you type?

   a. Thesaurus   **c.** Spelling and Grammar

   b. AutoCorrect   **d.** Undo and Redo

19. Which command is used to display a document in two panes in the document window?

   a. Split   **c.** Arrange All

   b. New Window   **d.** Compare Side by Side with…

20. What does the symbol ¶ represent when it is displayed in the document window?

   a. Hidden text   **c.** A tab stop

   b. A space   **d.** The end of a paragraph

▼ SKILLS REVIEW

1. Open a document.

   a. Start Word, click the Open button, then open the file WD B-2.doc from the drive and folder where your Data Files are located.

   b. Save the document with the filename **CAOS Press Release**.

2. Select text.

   a. Select **Today's Date** and replace it with the current date.

   b. Select **Your Name** and **Your Phone Number** and replace them with the relevant information.

   c. Scroll down, then select and replace text in the body of the press release using the following table as a guide:

in paragraph	select	replace with
1	13 and 14	**16 and 17**
1	eighth	**eleventh**
4	open his renovated Pearl St studio for the first time this year	**offer a sneak-preview of his Peace sculpture commissioned by the city of Prague**

   d. In the fourth paragraph, delete the sentence **Exhibiting with him will be sculptor Francis Pilo**.

   e. Save your changes to the press release.

3. Cut and paste text.

   a. Display paragraph and other formatting marks in your document if they are not already displayed.

   b. Use the Cut and Paste buttons to switch the order of the two sentences in the fourth paragraph (which begins New group shows…).

   c. Use the drag-and-drop method to switch the order of the second and third paragraphs.

   d. Adjust the spacing if necessary so that there is one blank line between paragraphs, then save your changes.

4. Copy and paste text.

   a. Use the Copy and Paste buttons to copy **CAOS 2003** from the headline and paste it before the word **map** in the third paragraph.

   b. Change the formatting of the pasted text to match the formatting of the third paragraph, then insert a space between **2003** and **map** if necessary.

   c. Use the drag-and-drop method to copy **CAOS** from the third paragraph and paste it before the word **group** in the second sentence of the fourth paragraph, then save your changes.

5. Use the Office Clipboard.

   a. Use the Office Clipboard command on the Edit menu to open the Clipboard task pane.

   b. Scroll so that the first body paragraph is displayed at the top of the document window.

   c. Select the fifth paragraph (which begins Studio location maps...) and cut it to the Office Clipboard.

   d. Select the third paragraph (which begins Cambridgeport is easily accessible...) and cut it to the Office Clipboard.

   e. Use the Office Clipboard to paste the Studio location maps... item as the new fourth paragraph.

   f. Use the Office Clipboard to paste the Cambridgeport is easily accessible... item as the new fifth paragraph.

   g. Use any method to switch the order of the two sentences in the fourth paragraph (which begins Studio location maps...).

   h. Adjust the spacing if necessary so that there is one blank line between each of the six body paragraphs.

   i. Turn off the display of formatting marks, clear and close the Office Clipboard, then save your changes.

6. Find and replace text.

   a. Using the Replace command, replace all instances of **2003** with **2006**.

   b. Replace all instances of the abbreviation **st** with **street**, taking care to replace whole words only when you perform the replace. (*Hint*: Click More to expand the Find and Replace dialog box, and then deselect Match case if it is selected.)

   c. Use the Find command to find all instances of **st** in the document, and make sure no errors occurred when you replaced st with street. (*Hint*: Deselect the Find whole words only check box.)

   d. Save your changes to the press release.

7. Check Spelling and Grammar and use the Thesaurus.

   a. Set Word to ignore the spelling of Cambridgeport, if it is marked as misspelled. (*Hint*: Right-click Cambridgeport.)

   b. Move the insertion point to the top of the document, then use the Spelling and Grammar command to search for and correct any spelling and grammar errors in the press release.

   c. Use the Thesaurus to replace **thriving** in the second paragraph with a different suitable word.

   d. Proofread your press release, correct any errors, save your changes, print a copy, then close the document.

8. Use wizards and templates.

   a. Use the New command to open the New Document task pane.

   b. Use the On my computer hyperlink to open the Templates dialog box.

   c. Create a new document using the Business Fax template.

   d. Replace the placeholder text in the document using Figure B-20 as a guide. Delete any placeholders that do not apply to your fax. The date in your fax will be the current date.

   e. Save the document as **CAOS Fax**, print a copy, close the document, then exit Word.

FIGURE B-20

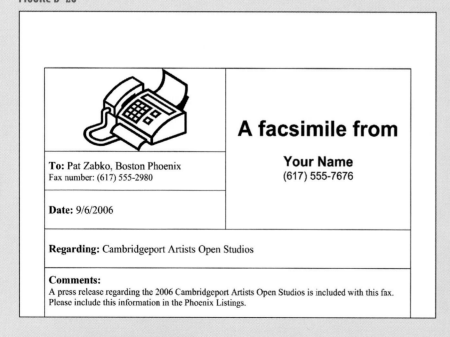

▼ INDEPENDENT CHALLENGE 1

Because of your success in revitalizing an historic theatre in Hobart, Tasmania, you were hired as the director of The Auckland Lyric Theatre in Auckland, New Zealand, to breathe life into its theatre revitalization efforts. After a year on the job, you are launching your first major fund-raising drive. You'll create a fund-raising letter for the Lyric Theatre by modifying a letter you wrote for the theatre in Hobart.

a. Start Word, open the file WD B-3.doc from the drive and folder where your Data Files are located, then save it as **Lyric Theatre Letter**.

b. Replace the theatre name and address, the date, the inside address, and the salutation with the text shown in Figure B-21.

c. Use the Replace command to replace all instances of **Hobart** with **Auckland**.

d. Use the Replace command to replace all instances of **Tasmanians** with **New Zealanders**.

e. Use the Find command to locate the word **considerable**, then use the Thesaurus to replace the word with a synonym.

f. Create an AutoCorrect entry that inserts **Auckland Lyric Theatre** whenever you type **alt**.

g. Select each XXXXX, then type **alt** followed by a space.

h. Move the fourth body paragraph so that it becomes the second body paragraph.

i. Replace Your Name with your name in the signature block.

j. Use the Spelling and Grammar command to check for and correct spelling and grammar errors.

FIGURE B-21

The Auckland Lyric Theatre
64-70 Queen Street, Auckland, New Zealand

September 24, 2006

Ms. Keri Marshall
718 Elliott Street
Auckland

Dear Ms. Marshall,

Advanced Challenge Exercise

- Open the Properties dialog box, then review the paragraph, line, word, and character count on the Statistics tab.
- On the Summary tab, change the title to **Auckland Lyric Theatre** and add the keyword **fund-raising**.
- On the Custom tab, add a property named Project with the value **Capital Campaign**, then close the dialog box.

k. Proofread the letter, correct any errors, save your changes, print a copy, close the document, then exit Word.

▼ INDEPENDENT CHALLENGE 2

An advertisement for job openings in London caught your eye and you have decided to apply. The ad, shown in Figure B-22, was printed in last weekend's edition of your local newspaper. You'll use the Letter Wizard to create a cover letter to send with your resume.

a. Read the ad shown in Figure B-22 and decide which position to apply for. Choose the position that most closely matches your qualifications.

b. Start Word and open the Templates dialog box.

c. Double-click Letter Wizard on the Letters & Faxes tab, then select Send one letter in the Letter Wizard dialog box.

d. In the Letter Wizard—Step 1 of 4 dialog box, choose to include a date on your letter, select Elegant Letter for the page design, select Modified block for the letter style, include a header and footer with the page design, then click Next.

e. In the Letter Wizard—Step 2 of 4 dialog box, enter the recipient's name (Ms. Katherine Winn) and the delivery address, referring to the ad for the address information. Also enter the salutation **Dear Ms. Winn** using the business style, then click Next.

f. In the Letter Wizard—Step 3 of 4 dialog box, include a reference line in the letter, enter the appropriate position code (see Figure B-22) in the Reference line text box, then click Next.

g. In the Letter Wizard—Step 4 of 4 dialog box, enter your name as the sender, enter your return address (including your country), and select an appropriate complimentary closing. Then, because you will be including your resume with the letter, include one enclosure. Click Finish when you are done.

h. Save the letter with the filename **Global Dynamics Letter** to the drive and folder where your Data Files are located.

i. Replace the placeholder text in the body of the letter with three paragraphs that address your qualifications for the job:

  • In the first paragraph, specify the job you are applying for, indicate where you saw the position advertised, and briefly state your qualifications and interest in the position.

  • In the second paragraph, describe your work experience and skills. Be sure to relate your experience and qualifications to the position requirements listed in the ad.

  • In the third paragraph, politely request an interview for the position and provide your phone number and e-mail address.

j. When you are finished typing the letter, check it for spelling and grammar errors and correct any mistakes.

k. Save your changes to the letter, print a copy, close the document, then exit Word.

FIGURE B-22

*Global*Dynamics

Career Opportunities in London

Global Dynamics, an established software development firm with offices in North America, Asia, and Europe, is seeking candidates for the following positions in its London facility:

Instructor
Responsible for delivering software training to our expanding European customer base. Duties include delivering hands-on training, keeping up-to-date with product development, and working with the Director of Training to ensure the high quality of course materials. Successful candidate will have excellent presentation skills and be proficient in Microsoft PowerPoint and Microsoft Word. **Position B12C6**

Administrative Assistant
Proficiency with Microsoft Word a must! Administrative office duties include making travel arrangements, scheduling meetings, taking notes and publishing meeting minutes, handling correspondence, and ordering office supplies. Must have superb multi-tasking abilities, excellent communication, organizational, and interpersonal skills, and be comfortable working with e-mail and the Internet. **Position B16F5**

Copywriter
The ideal candidate will have marketing or advertising writing experience in a high tech environment, including collateral, newsletters, and direct mail. Experience writing for the Web, broadcast, and multimedia is a plus. Fluency with Microsoft Word required. **Position C13D4**

Positions offer salary, excellent benefits, moving expenses, and career growth opportunities.

Send resume and cover letter referencing position code to:

Katherine Winn
Director of Recruiting
Global Dynamics
483 Briar Terrace
London LH3 9JH
United Kingdom

▼ INDEPENDENT CHALLENGE 3

As administrative director of continuing education, you drafted a memo to instructors asking them to help you finalize the course schedule for next semester. Today you'll examine the draft and make revisions before printing it.

a. Start Word and open the file WD B-4.doc from the drive and folder where your Data Files are located.

b. Open the Save As dialog box, navigate to the drive and folder where your Data Files are located, then use the Create New Folder button to create a new folder called **Memos**.

c. Click the Up One Level button in the dialog box, rename the Memos folder **Spring Memos**, then save the document as **Instructor Memo** in the Spring Memos folder.

d. Replace Your Name with your name in the From line, then scroll down until the first body paragraph is at the top of the screen.

Advanced Challenge Exercise

- Use the Split command on the Window menu to split the window under the first body paragraph, then scroll until the last paragraph of the memo is displayed in the bottom pane.
- Use the Cut and Paste buttons to move the sentence **If you are planning to teach...** from the first body paragraph to become the first sentence in the last paragraph of the memo.
- Double-click the split bar to restore the window to a single pane.

e. Use the [Delete] key to merge the first two paragraphs into one paragraph.

f. Use the Office Clipboard to reorganize the list of twelve-week courses so that the courses are listed in alphabetical order. (*Hint*: Use the Zoom list arrow to enlarge the document as needed.)

g. Use the drag-and-drop method to reorganize the list of one-day seminars so that the seminars are listed in alphabetical order.

h. Use the Spelling and Grammar command to check for and correct spelling and grammar errors.

i. Clear and close the Office Clipboard, save your changes, print a copy, close the document, then exit Word.

▼ INDEPENDENT CHALLENGE 4

Reference sources—dictionaries, thesauri, style and grammar guides, and guides to business etiquette and procedure—are essential for day-to-day use in the workplace. Much of this reference information is available on the World Wide Web. In this independent challenge, you will locate reference sources on the Web and use some of them to look up definitions, synonyms, and antonyms for words. Your goal is to familiarize yourself with online reference sources so you can use them later in your work.

a. Start Word, open the file WD B-5.doc from the drive and folder where your Data Files are located, and save it as **Web References**. This document contains the questions you will answer about the Web reference sources you find. You will type your answers to the questions in the document.

b. Replace the placeholder text at the top of the Web References document with your name and the date.

c. Use your favorite search engine to search the Web for grammar and style guides, dictionaries, and thesauri. Use the keywords **grammar**, **usage**, **dictionary**, **glossary**, and **thesaurus** to conduct your search.

d. Complete the Web References document, then proofread it and correct any mistakes.

e. Save the document, print a copy, close the document, then exit Word.

▼ VISUAL WORKSHOP

Using the Elegant Letter template, create the letter shown in Figure B-23. Save the document as **Visa Letter**. Check the letter for spelling and grammar errors, then print a copy.

FIGURE B-23

YOUR NAME

March 17, 2006

Embassy of Australia
Suite 710
50 O'Connor Street
Ottawa, Ontario K1P 6L2

Dear Sir or Madam:

I am applying for a long-stay (six-month) tourist visa to Australia, valid for four years. I am scheduled to depart for Sydney on July 1, 2006, returning to Vancouver on December 23, 2006.

While in Australia, I plan to conduct research for a book I am writing on coral reefs. I am interested in a multiple entry visa valid for four years so that I can return to Australia after this trip to follow-up on my initial research. I will be based in Cairns, but will be traveling frequently to other parts of Australia to meet with scientists, policy-makers, and environmentalists.

Enclosed please find my completed visa application form, my passport, a passport photo, a copy of my return air ticket, and the visa fee. Please let me know if I can provide further information.

Sincerely,

Your Name

35 HARDY STREET • VANCOUVER, BC • V6C 3K4
PHONE: (604) 555-8989 • FAX: (604) 555-8981

UNIT C
Word 2003

Formatting Text and Paragraphs

OBJECTIVES

Format with fonts
Change font styles and effects
Change line and paragraph spacing
Align paragraphs
Work with tabs
Work with indents
Add bullets and numbering
Add borders and shading

If you have a SAM user profile, you may have access to hands-on instruction, practice, and assessment of the skills covered in this unit. Log in to your SAM account and go to your assignments page to see what your instructor has assigned.

Formatting can enhance the appearance of a document, create visual impact, and help illustrate a document's structure. The formatting of a document can also add personality to it and lend it a degree of professionalism. In this unit you learn how to format text using different fonts and font-formatting options. You also learn how to change the alignment, indentation, and spacing of paragraphs, and how to spruce up documents with borders, shading, bullets, and other paragraph-formatting effects. You have finished drafting the quarterly marketing report for the MediaLoft Chicago store. You now need to format the report so it is attractive and highlights the significant information.

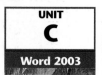

Formatting with Fonts

Formatting text with different fonts is a quick and powerful way to enhance the appearance of a document. A **font** is a complete set of characters with the same typeface or design. Arial, Times New Roman, Comic Sans, Courier, and Tahoma are some of the more common fonts, but there are hundreds of others, each with a specific design and feel. Another way to alter the impact of text is to increase or decrease its **font size**, which is measured in points. A **point** is ½ of an inch. When formatting a document with fonts, it's important to pick fonts and font sizes that augment the document's purpose. You apply fonts and font sizes to text using the Font and Font Size list arrows on the Formatting toolbar. You change the font and font size of the title and headings in the report, selecting a font that enhances the business tone of the document. By formatting the title and headings in a font different from the body text, you help to visually structure the report for readers.

STEPS

1. **Start Word, open the file** WD C-1.doc **from the drive and folder where your Data Files are located, then save it as** Chicago Marketing Report

   The file opens in Print Layout view.

2. **Click the** Normal View button **≡** **on the horizontal scroll bar, click the** Zoom list arrow **on the Standard toolbar, then click** 100% **if necessary**

   The document switches to Normal view, a view useful for simple text formatting. The name of the font used in the document, Times New Roman, is displayed in the Font list box on the Formatting toolbar. The font size, 12, appears next to it in the Font Size list box.

> **QUICK TIP**
> There are two types of fonts: serif fonts have a small stroke, called a serif, at the ends of characters; sans serif fonts do not have a serif. Times New Roman is a serif font. Arial is a sans serif font.

3. **Select the title** MediaLoft Chicago Quarterly Marketing Report, **then click the** Font list arrow **on the Formatting toolbar**

   The Font list, which shows the fonts available on your computer, opens as shown in Figure C-1. Fonts you have used recently appear above the double line. All the fonts on your computer are listed in alphabetical order below the double line. You can click the font name in either location on the Font list to apply the font to the selected text.

4. **Click** Arial

   The font of the report title changes to Arial.

5. **Click the** Font Size list arrow **on the Formatting toolbar, then click** 20

   The font size of the title increases to 20 points.

6. **Click the** Font Color list arrow **A·** **on the Formatting toolbar**

   A palette of colors opens.

7. **Click** Plum **on the Font Color palette as shown in Figure C-2, then deselect the text**

   The color of the report title text changes to plum. The active color on the Font Color button also changes to plum.

8. **Scroll down until the heading Advertising is at the top of your screen, select** Advertising, **press and hold** [Ctrl], **select the heading** Events, **then release** [Ctrl]

   The Advertising and Events headings are selected. Selecting multiple items allows you to format several items at once.

> **QUICK TIP**
> For a clean look, limit the number of fonts you use in a document to two or three.

9. **Click the** Font list arrow, **click** Arial, **click the** Font Size list arrow, **click** 14, **click the** Font Color button **A**, **then deselect the text**

   The headings are formatted in 14-point Arial with a plum color.

10. **Press** [Ctrl][Home], **then click the** Save button **🖫** **on the Standard toolbar**

    Pressing [Ctrl][Home] moves the insertion point to the beginning of the document. Compare your document to Figure C-3.

FIGURE C-1: Font list

Font list arrow

Font Size list arrow

Font names are formatted in the font (your list of fonts might differ)

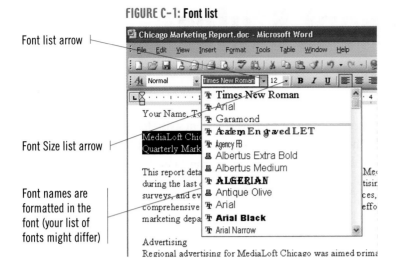

FIGURE C-2: Font Color palette

Font Color list arrow

Name of color appears as a ScreenTip

Click to create a custom color

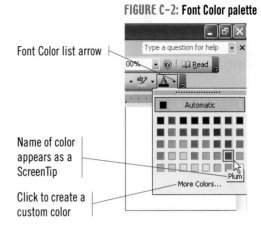

FIGURE C-3: Document formatted with fonts

Title formatted in 20-point Arial, plum

Headings formatted in 14-point Arial, plum

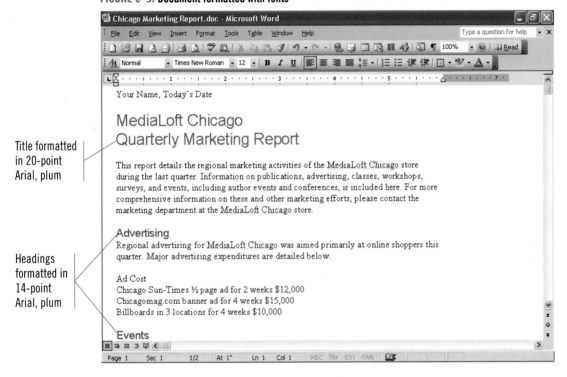

Clues to Use

Adding a drop cap

A fun way to illustrate a document with fonts is to add a drop cap to a paragraph. A **drop cap** is a large initial capital letter, often used to set off the first paragraph of an article. To create a drop cap, place the insertion point in the paragraph you want to format, and then click Drop Cap on the Format menu to open the Drop Cap dialog box. In the Drop Cap dialog box, shown in Figure C-4, select the position, font, number of lines to drop, and the distance you want the drop cap to be from the paragraph text, and then click OK to create the drop cap. The drop cap is added to the paragraph as a graphic object.

Once a drop cap is inserted in a paragraph, you can modify it by selecting it and then changing the settings in the Drop Cap dialog box. For even more interesting effects, try enhancing a drop cap with font color, font styles, or font effects, or try filling the graphic object with shading or adding a border around it. To enhance a drop cap, first select it, and then experiment with the formatting options available in the Font dialog box and in the Borders and Shading dialog box.

FIGURE C-4: Drop Cap dialog box

Changing Font Styles and Effects

You can dramatically change the appearance of text by applying different font styles, font effects, and character-spacing effects. For example, you can use the buttons on the Formatting toolbar to make text darker by applying **bold**, or to slant text by applying **italic**. You can also use the Font command on the Format menu to apply font effects and character-spacing effects to text.  You spice up the appearance of the text in the document by applying different font styles and effects.

STEPS

QUICK TIP

Click the Underline button U on the Formatting toolbar to underline text.

1. **Select** MediaLoft Chicago Quarterly Marketing Report, **then click the** Bold button B **on the Formatting toolbar**

   Applying bold makes the characters in the title darker and thicker.

2. **Select** Advertising, **click** B, **select** Events, **then press** [F4]

   Pressing [F4] repeats the last action you took, in this case applying bold. The Advertising and Events headings are both formatted in bold.

3. **Select the** paragraph **under the title, then click the** Italic button I **on the Formatting toolbar**

   The paragraph is formatted in italic.

4. **Scroll down until the subheading Author Events is at the top of your screen, select** Author Events, **click** Format **on the menu bar, then click** Font

   The Font dialog box opens, as shown in Figure C-5. You can use options on the Font tab to change the font, font style, size, and color of text, and to add an underline and apply font effects to text.

QUICK TIP

To hide the selected text, click the Hidden check box on the Font tab. Hidden text is displayed when formatting marks are turned on.

5. **Scroll up the Font list, click** Arial, **click** Bold Italic **in the Font style list box, select the** Small caps check box, **then click** OK

   The subheading is formatted in Arial, bold, italic, and small caps. When you change text to small caps, the lowercase letters are changed to uppercase letters in a smaller font size.

6. **Select the subheading** Travel Writers & Photographers Conference, **then press** [F4]

   Because you formatted the previous subheading in one action (using the Font dialog box), the Travel Writers subheading is formatted in Arial, bold, italic, and small caps. If you apply formats one by one, then pressing [F4] repeats only the last format you applied.

7. **Under Author Events, select the book title** Just H2O Please: Tales of True Adventure on the Environmental Frontline, **click** I, **select** 2 **in the book title, click** Format **on the menu bar, click** Font, **click the** Subscript check box, **click** OK, **then deselect the text**

   The book title is formatted in italic and the character 2 is subscript, as shown in Figure C-6.

QUICK TIP

To animate the selected text, click the Text Effects tab in the Font dialog box, then select an animation style. The animation appears only when a document is viewed in Word; animation effects do not print.

8. **Press** [Ctrl][Home], **select the** report title, **click** Format **on the menu bar, click** Font, **then click the** Character Spacing tab **in the Font dialog box**

   You use the Character Spacing tab to change the scale, or width, of the selected characters, to alter the spacing between characters, or to raise or lower the position of the characters.

9. **Click the** Scale list arrow, **click** 150%, **click** OK, **deselect the text, then click the** Save button 🖫 **on the Standard toolbar**

   Increasing the scale of the characters makes them wider and gives the text a short, squat appearance, as shown in Figure C-7.

FIGURE C-5: Font tab in Font dialog box

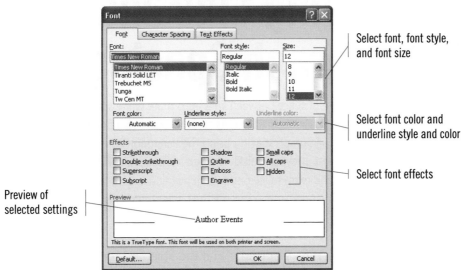

Select font, font style, and font size

Select font color and underline style and color

Select font effects

Preview of selected settings

Word 2003

FIGURE C-6: Font effects applied to text

Subhead formatted in 12-point Arial, bold, italic, and small caps

Book title formatted in italic

Subscript text

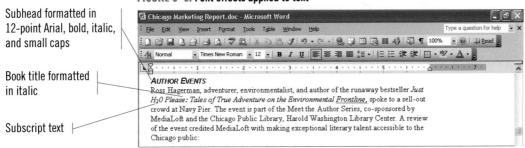

FIGURE C-7: Character spacing effects applied to text

Report title formatted in bold with a character scale of 150%

Paragraph formatted in italic

Headings formatted in bold

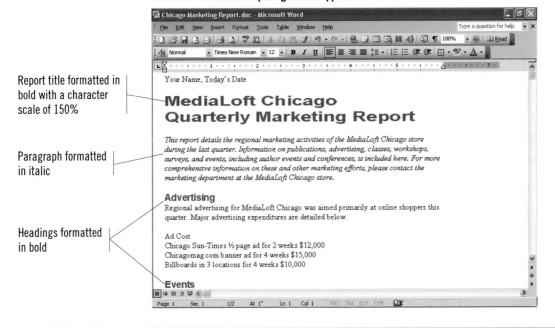

Clues to Use

Changing the case of letters

The Change Case command on the Format menu allows you to quickly change letters from uppercase to lowercase—and vice versa—saving you the time it takes to retype text you want to change. To change the case of selected text, use the Change Case command to open the Change Case dialog box, then select the case style you want to use. Sentence case capitalizes the first letter of a sentence, title case capitalizes the first letter of each word, and toggle case switches all letters to the opposite case.

Changing Line and Paragraph Spacing

Increasing the amount of space between lines adds more white space to a document and can make it easier to read. Adding space between paragraphs can also open up a document and improve its appearance. You can change line and paragraph spacing using the Paragraph command on the Format menu. You can also use the Line Spacing list arrow to quickly change line spacing. You increase the line spacing of several paragraphs and add extra space under each heading to give the report a more open feel. You work with formatting marks turned on, so you can see the paragraph marks (¶).

STEPS

QUICK TIP

The check mark on the Line Spacing list indicates the current line spacing.

1. **Click the** Show/Hide ¶ button **on the Standard toolbar, place the insertion point in the italicized paragraph under the report title, then click the** Line Spacing list arrow **on the Formatting toolbar**

   The Line Spacing list opens. This list includes options for increasing the space between lines.

2. **Click** 1.5

   The space between the lines in the paragraph increases to 1.5 lines. Notice that you do not need to select an entire paragraph to change its paragraph formatting; simply place the insertion point in the paragraph you want to format.

QUICK TIP

Word recognizes any string of text that ends with a paragraph mark as a paragraph, including titles, headings, and single lines in a list.

3. **Scroll down until the heading** Advertising **is at the top of your screen, select the** four-line list **that begins with Ad Cost, click** , **then click** 1.5

   The line spacing between the selected paragraphs changes to 1.5. To change the paragraph-formatting features of more than one paragraph, you must select the paragraphs.

4. **Place the insertion point in the heading** Advertising, **click** Format **on the menu bar, then click** Paragraph

   The Paragraph dialog box opens, as shown in Figure C-8. You can use the Indents and Spacing tab to change line spacing and the spacing above and below paragraphs. Spacing between paragraphs is measured in points.

QUICK TIP

Adjusting the space between paragraphs is a more precise way to add white space to a document than inserting blank lines.

5. **Click the** After up arrow **in the Spacing section so that 6 pt appears, then click** OK

   Six points of space are added below the Advertising heading paragraph.

6. **Select** Advertising, **then click the** Format Painter button **on the Standard toolbar**

   The pointer changes to . The **Format Painter** is a powerful Word feature that allows you to copy all the format settings applied to the selected text to other text that you want to format the same way. The Format Painter is especially useful when you want to copy multiple format settings, but you can also use it to copy individual formats.

QUICK TIP

Using the Format Painter is not the same as using [F4]. Pressing [F4] repeats only the last action you took. You can use the Format Painter at any time to copy multiple format settings.

7. **Select** Events **with the** pointer, **then deselect the text**

   Six points of space are added below the Events heading paragraph and the pointer changes back to the I-beam pointer. Compare your document with Figure C-9.

8. **Select** Events, **then double-click**

   Double-clicking the Format Painter button allows the Format Painter to remain active until you turn it off. By keeping the Format Painter turned on you can apply formatting to multiple items.

9. **Scroll down, select the headings** Classes & Workshops, Publications, **and** Surveys **with the** pointer, **then click** **to turn off the Format Painter**

   The headings are formatted in 14-point Arial, bold, plum, with six points of space added below each heading paragraph.

10. **Press** [Ctrl][Home], **click** , **then click the** Save button **on the Standard toolbar**

FIGURE C-8: Indents and Spacing tab in Paragraph dialog box

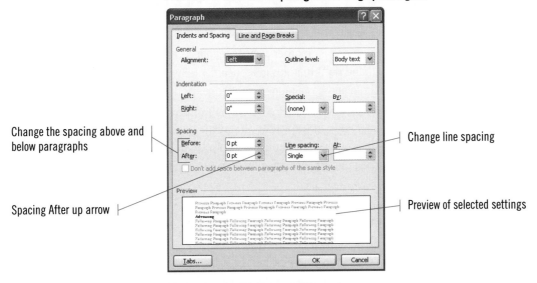

Change the spacing above and below paragraphs

Change line spacing

Spacing After up arrow

Preview of selected settings

FIGURE C-9: Line and paragraph spacing applied to document

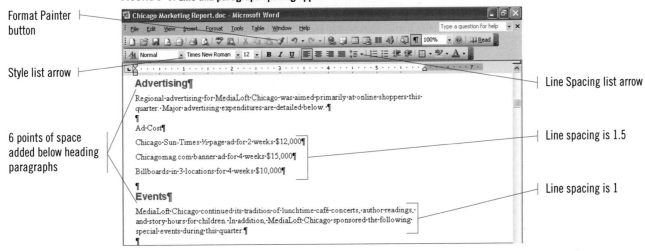

Format Painter button

Style list arrow

6 points of space added below heading paragraphs

Line Spacing list arrow

Line spacing is 1.5

Line spacing is 1

Word 2003

Clues to Use

Formatting with styles

You can also apply multiple format settings to text in one step by applying a style. A **style** is a set of formats, such as font, font size, and paragraph alignment, that are named and stored together. Styles can be applied to text, paragraphs, lists, and tables. To work with styles, click the Styles and Formatting button 🔠 on the Formatting toolbar to open the Styles and Formatting task pane, shown in Figure C-10. The task pane displays the list of available styles and the formats you have created for the current document. To view all the styles available in Word, click the Show list arrow at the bottom of the task pane, then click All Styles.

A **character style**, indicated by **a** in the list of styles, includes character format settings, such as font and font size. A **paragraph style**, indicated by ¶ in the list, is a combination of character and paragraph formats, such as font, font size, paragraph alignment, paragraph spacing, indents, and bullets and numbering. A **table style** indicated by ⊞ in the list, includes format settings for text in tables, as well as for table borders, shading, and alignment. Finally, a **list style**, indicated by ⬛ in the list, includes indent and numbering format settings for an outline numbered list.

To apply a style, select the text, paragraph, or table you want to format, then click the style name in the Pick formatting to apply list box. To remove styles from text, select the text, then click Clear Formatting in the Pick formatting to apply list box. You can also apply and remove styles using the Style list arrow on the Formatting toolbar.

FIGURE C-10: Styles and Formatting task pane

Aligning Paragraphs

Changing paragraph alignment is another way to enhance a document's appearance. Paragraphs are aligned relative to the left and right margins in a document. By default, text is **left-aligned**, which means it is flush with the left margin and has a ragged right edge. Using the alignment buttons on the Formatting toolbar, you can **right-align** a paragraph—make it flush with the right margin—or **center** a paragraph so that it is positioned evenly between the left and right margins. You can also **justify** a paragraph so that both the left and right edges of the paragraph are flush with the left and right margins. You change the alignment of several paragraphs at the beginning of the report to make it more visually interesting.

STEPS

1. **Replace** Your Name, Today's Date **with your name, a comma, and the date**

2. **Select your name, the comma, and the date, then click the** Align Right button ☰ **on the Formatting toolbar**

   The text is aligned with the right margin. In Normal view, the junction of the white and shaded sections of the horizontal ruler indicates the location of the right margin. The left end of the ruler indicates the left margin.

3. **Place the insertion point between your name and the comma, press** [Delete] **to delete the comma, then press** [Enter]

   The new paragraph containing the date is also right-aligned. Pressing [Enter] in the middle of a paragraph creates a new paragraph with the same text and paragraph formatting as the original paragraph.

4. **Select the** report title, **then click the** Center button ☰ **on the Formatting toolbar**

   The two paragraphs that make up the title are centered between the left and right margins.

QUICK TIP
Click the Align Left button ☰ on the Formatting toolbar to left-align a paragraph.

5. **Place the insertion point in the** Advertising **heading, then click** ☰

   The Advertising heading is centered.

6. **Place the insertion point in the italicized paragraph under the report title, then click the** Justify button ☰

   The paragraph is aligned with both the left and right margins, as shown in Figure C-11. When you justify a paragraph, Word adjusts the spacing between words so that each line in the paragraph is flush with the left and the right margins.

7. **Place the insertion point in** MediaLoft **in the report title, click** Format **on the menu bar, then click** Reveal Formatting

   The Reveal Formatting task pane opens in the Word program window, as shown in Figure C-12. The Reveal Formatting task pane shows the formatting applied to the text and paragraph where the insertion point is located. You can use the Reveal Formatting task pane to check or change the formatting of any character, word, paragraph, or other aspect of a document.

8. **Select** Advertising, **then click the** Alignment **hyperlink in the Reveal Formatting task pane**

   The Paragraph dialog box opens with the Indents and Spacing tab displayed. It shows the settings for the selected text.

9. **Click the** Alignment list arrow, **click** Left, **click** OK, **then deselect the text**

   The Advertising heading is left-aligned.

10. **Close the Reveal Formatting task pane, then click the** Save button 🖫 **on the Standard toolbar**

FIGURE C-11: Modified paragraph alignment

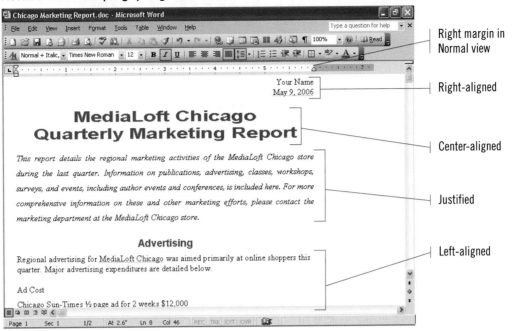

Right margin in Normal view

Right-aligned

Center-aligned

Justified

Left-aligned

FIGURE C-12: Reveal Formatting task pane

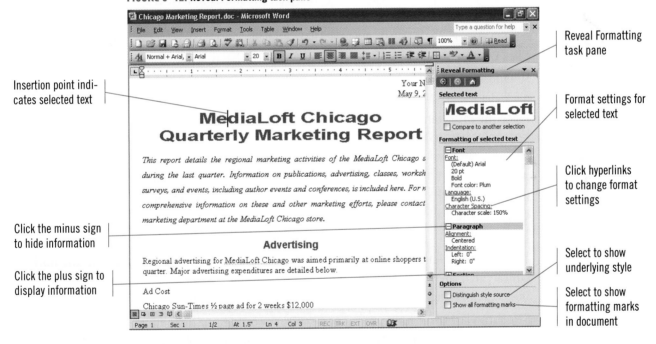

Insertion point indicates selected text

Click the minus sign to hide information

Click the plus sign to display information

Reveal Formatting task pane

Format settings for selected text

Click hyperlinks to change format settings

Select to show underlying style

Select to show formatting marks in document

Word 2003

Clues to Use

Comparing formatting

When two words or paragraphs in a document do not look exactly the same but you are not sure how they are formatted differently, you can use the Reveal Formatting task pane to compare the two selections to determine the differences. To compare the formatting of two text selections, select the first instance, select the Compare to another selection check box in the Reveal Formatting task pane, and then select the second instance. Differences in formatting between the two selections are listed in the Formatting differences section in the Reveal Formatting task pane. You can then use the hyperlinks in the Formatting differences section to make changes to the formatting of the second selection. If you want to format the second selection so that it matches the first, you can click the list arrow next to the second selection in the Selected text section, and then click Apply Formatting of Original Selection on the menu that appears. On the same menu, you can also click Select All Text with Similar Formatting to select all the text in the document that is formatted the same, or Clear Formatting to return the formatting of the selected text to the default.

Working with Tabs

Tabs allow you to align text vertically at a specific location in a document. A **tab stop** is a point on the horizontal ruler that indicates the location at which to align text. By default, tab stops are located every ½" from the left margin, but you can also set custom tab stops. Using tabs, you can align text to the left, right, or center of a tab stop, or you can align text at a decimal point or bar character. You set tabs using the horizontal ruler or the Tabs command on the Format menu.  You use tabs to format the information on advertising expenditures so it is easy to read.

STEPS

1. **Scroll down until the heading Advertising is at the top of your screen, then select the four-line list beginning with Ad Cost**

   Before you set tab stops for existing text, you must select the paragraphs for which you want to set tabs.

   TROUBLE
   If the horizontal ruler is not visible, click Ruler on the View menu.

2. **Point to the tab indicator ⌊L⌋ at the left end of the horizontal ruler**

   The icon that appears in the tab indicator indicates the active type of tab; pointing to the tab indicator displays a ScreenTip with the name of the active tab type. By default, left tab is the active tab type. Clicking the tab indicator scrolls through the types of tabs and indents.

3. **Click the tab indicator to see each of the available tab and indent types, make left tab ⌊L⌋ the active tab type, then click the 1" mark on the horizontal ruler**

   A left tab stop is inserted at the 1" mark on the horizontal ruler. Clicking the horizontal ruler inserts a tab stop of the active type for the selected paragraph or paragraphs.

4. **Click the tab indicator twice so the Right Tab icon ⌐ is active, then click the 4½" mark on the horizontal ruler**

   A right tab stop is inserted at the 4½" mark on the horizontal ruler, as shown in Figure C-13.

   QUICK TIP
   Never use the Spacebar to vertically align text; always use tabs or a table.

5. **Place the insertion point before Ad in the first line in the list, press [Tab], place the insertion point before Cost, then press [Tab]**

   Inserting a tab before Ad left-aligns the text at the 1" mark. Inserting a tab before Cost right-aligns Cost at the 4½" mark.

6. **Insert a tab at the beginning of each remaining line in the list, then insert a tab before each $ in the list**

   The paragraphs left-align at the 1" mark. The prices right-align at the 4½" mark.

7. **Select the four lines of tabbed text, drag the right tab stop to the 5" mark on the horizontal ruler, then deselect the text**

   Dragging the tab stop moves it to a new location. The prices right-align at the 5" mark.

   QUICK TIP
   Place the insertion point in a paragraph to see the tab stops for that paragraph on the horizontal ruler.

8. **Select the last three lines of tabbed text, click Format on the menu bar, then click Tabs**

   The Tabs dialog box opens, as shown in Figure C-14. You can use the Tabs dialog box to set tab stops, change the position or alignment of existing tab stops, clear tab stops, and apply tab leaders to tabs. **Tab leaders** are lines that appear in front of tabbed text.

9. **Click 5" in the Tab stop position list box, click the 2 option button in the Leader section, click OK, deselect the text, then click the Save button ⊟ on the Standard toolbar**

   A dotted tab leader is added before each 5" tab stop, as shown in Figure C-15.

FIGURE C-13: Left and right tab stops on the horizontal ruler

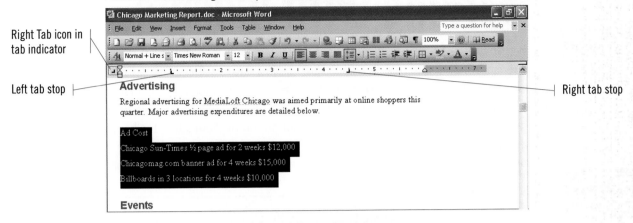

Right Tab icon in tab indicator

Left tab stop

Right tab stop

FIGURE C-14: Tabs dialog box

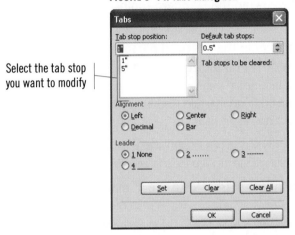

Select the tab stop you want to modify

FIGURE C-15: Tab leaders

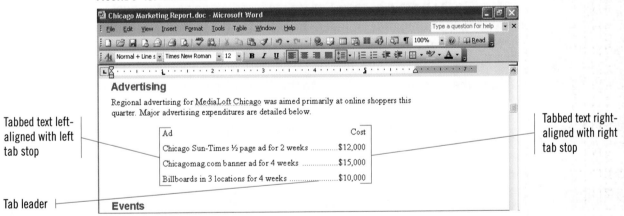

Tabbed text left-aligned with left tab stop

Tabbed text right-aligned with right tab stop

Tab leader

Clues to Use

Working with Click and Type

The **Click and Type** feature in Word allows you to automatically apply the paragraph formatting (alignment and indentation) necessary to insert text, graphics, or tables in a blank area of a document in Print Layout or Web Layout view. As you move the pointer around in a blank area of a document, the pointer changes depending on its location. Double-clicking with a click and type pointer in a blank area of a document automatically applies the appropriate alignment and indentation for that location, so that when you begin typing, the text is already formatted. The pointer shape indicates which formatting is applied at each location when you double-click. For example, if you click with the ‡ pointer, the text you type is center-aligned. Clicking with I ‡ creates a left tab stop at the location of the insertion point so that the text you type is left-aligned at the tab stop. Clicking with ‡ I right-aligns the text you type. The I‡ pointer creates left-aligned text with a first line indent. The best way to learn how to use Click and Type is to experiment in a blank document.

Working with Indents

When you **indent** a paragraph, you move its edge in from the left or right margin. You can indent the entire left or right edge of a paragraph, just the first line, or all lines except the first line. The **indent markers** on the horizontal ruler indicate the indent settings for the paragraph in which the insertion point is located. Dragging the indent markers to a new location on the ruler is one way to change the indentation of a paragraph; using the indent buttons on the Formatting toolbar is another. You can also use the Paragraph command on the Format menu to indent paragraphs. Table C-1 describes different types of indents and the methods for creating each. ▟▟▟ You indent several paragraphs in the report.

STEPS

1. **Press [Ctrl][Home], click the** Print Layout View button 🔲 **on the horizontal scroll bar, click the** Zoom list arrow **on the Standard toolbar, then click** Page Width

   The document is displayed in Print Layout view, making it easier to see the document margins.

QUICK TIP

Press [Tab] at the beginning of a paragraph to indent the first line ½". You can also set a custom indent using the Indents and Spacing tab in the Paragraph dialog box.

2. **Place the insertion point in the italicized paragraph under the title, then click the** Increase Indent button ▤ **on the Formatting toolbar**

   The entire paragraph is indented ½" from the left margin, as shown in Figure C-16. The indent marker ▤ also moves to the ½" mark on the horizontal ruler. Each time you click the Increase Indent button, the left edge of a paragraph moves another ½" to the right.

3. **Click the** Decrease Indent button ▤ **on the Formatting toolbar**

   The left edge of the paragraph moves ½" to the left, and the indent marker moves back to the left margin.

TROUBLE

Take care to drag only the First Line Indent marker. If you make a mistake, click the Undo button ↶ , then try again.

4. **Drag the** First Line Indent marker ▽ **to the ¼" mark on the horizontal ruler as shown in Figure C-17**

   The first line of the paragraph is indented ¼". Dragging the first line indent marker indents only the first line of a paragraph.

5. **Scroll to the bottom of page 1, place the insertion point in the** quotation (the last paragraph), **then drag the** Left Indent marker ☐ **to the ½" mark on the horizontal ruler**

   When you drag the Left Indent marker, the First Line and Hanging Indent markers move as well. The left edge of the paragraph is indented ½" from the left margin.

6. **Drag the** Right Indent marker △ **to the 5½" mark on the horizontal ruler**

   The right edge of the paragraph is indented ½" from the right margin, as shown in Figure C-18.

7. **Click the** Save button 🖫 **on the Standard toolbar**

TABLE C-1: **Types of indents**

indent type	description	to create
Left indent	The left edge of a paragraph is moved in from the left margin	Drag the Left Indent marker ☐ right to the position where you want the left edge of the paragraph to align, or click the Increase Indent button ▤ to indent the paragraph in ½" increments
Right indent	The right edge of a paragraph is moved in from the right margin	Drag the Right Indent marker △ left to the position where you want the right edge of the paragraph to end
First-line indent	The first line of a paragraph is indented more than the subsequent lines	Drag the First Line Indent marker ▽ right to the position where you want the first line of the paragraph to start
Hanging indent	The subsequent lines of a paragraph are indented more than the first line	Drag the Hanging Indent marker ⌂ right to the position where you want the hanging indent to start
Negative indent (or Outdent)	The left edge of a paragraph is moved to the left of the left margin	Drag the Left Indent marker ☐ left to the position where you want the negative indent to start

FIGURE C-16: Indented paragraph

First Line Indent marker

Hanging Indent marker

Left Indent marker

Indented paragraph

Right Indent marker

Increase Indent button

Decrease Indent button

FIGURE C-17: Dragging the First Line Indent marker

First Line Indent marker being dragged to the ¼" mark

Dotted line shows positon of First Line Indent marker

FIGURE C-18: Paragraph indented from the left and right

Paragraph indented ½" from left margin

Paragraph indented ½" from right margin

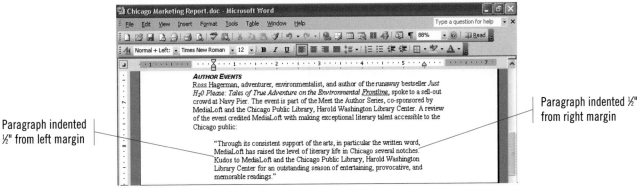

Clues to Use

Clearing formatting

If you are unhappy with the way text is formatted, you can use the Clear Formats command to return the text to the default format settings. By default, text is formatted in 12-point Times New Roman and paragraphs are left-aligned and single-spaced with no indents.

To clear formatting from text, select the text you want to clear, point to Clear on the Edit menu, then click Formats. Alternately, click the Styles list arrow on the Formatting toolbar, then click Clear Formatting.

Adding Bullets and Numbering

Formatting a list with bullets or numbering can help to organize the ideas in a document. A **bullet** is a character, often a small circle, that appears before the items in a list to add emphasis. Formatting a list as a numbered list helps illustrate sequences and priorities. You can quickly format a list with bullets or numbering by using the Bullets and Numbering buttons on the Formatting toolbar. You can also use the Bullets and Numbering command on the Format menu to change or customize bullet and numbering styles. You format the lists in your report with numbers and bullets.

STEPS

1. **Scroll down until the first paragraph on the second page (Authors on our...) is at the top of your screen**

2. **Select the three-line list of names under the paragraph, then click the Numbering button on the Formatting toolbar**
   The paragraphs are formatted as a numbered list.

3. **Place the insertion point after Jack Seneschal, press [Enter], then type Polly Flanagan**
   Pressing [Enter] in the middle of the numbered list creates a new numbered paragraph and automatically renumbers the remainder of the list. Similarly, if you delete a paragraph from a numbered list, Word automatically renumbers the remaining paragraphs.

> **QUICK TIP**
> To change the numbers to letters, Roman numerals, or another numbering style, right-click the list, click Bullets and Numbering, then select a new numbering style on the Numbered tab.

4. **Click 1 in the list**
   Clicking a number in a list selects all the numbers, as shown in Figure C-19.

5. **Click the Bold button B on the Formatting toolbar**
   The numbers are all formatted in bold. Notice that the formatting of the items in the list does not change when you change the formatting of the numbers. You can also use this technique to change the formatting of bullets in a bulleted list.

> **QUICK TIP**
> To remove a bullet or number, select the paragraph(s), then click 📃 or 📃.

6. **Select the list of classes and workshops under the Classes & Workshops heading, scrolling down if necessary, then click the Bullets button 📃 on the Formatting toolbar**
   The five paragraphs are formatted as a bulleted list.

7. **With the list still selected, click Format on the menu bar, then click Bullets and Numbering**
   The Bullets and Numbering dialog box opens with the Bulleted tab displayed, as shown in Figure C-20. You use this dialog box to apply bullets and numbering to paragraphs, or to change the style of bullets or numbers.

8. **Click the Square bullets box or select another style if square bullets are not available to you, click OK, then deselect the text**
   The bullet character changes to a small square, as shown in Figure C-21.

9. **Click the Save button 🖫 on the Standard toolbar**

Clues to Use

Creating outlines

You can create lists with hierarchical structures by applying an outline numbering style to a list. To create an outline, begin by applying an outline numbering style from the Outline Numbered tab in the Bullets and Numbering dialog box, then type your outline, pressing [Enter] after each item. To demote items to a lower level of importance in the outline, place the insertion point in the item, then click the Increase Indent button 📄 on the Formatting toolbar. Each time you indent a paragraph, the item is demoted to a lower lever in the outline. Similarly, you can use the Decrease Indent button 📄 to promote an item to a higher level in the outline. You can also create a hierarchical structure in any bulleted or numbered list by using 📄 and 📄 to demote and promote items in the list. To change the outline numbering style applied to a list, select a new style from the Outline Numbered tab in the Bullets and Numbering dialog box.

FIGURE C-19: Numbered list

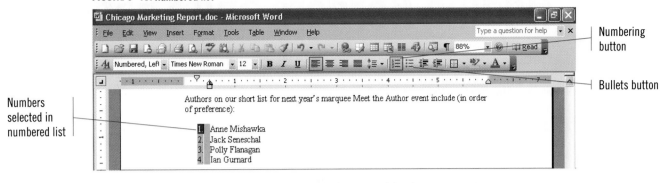

Numbering button

Bullets button

Numbers selected in numbered list

FIGURE C-20: Bulleted tab in the Bullets and Numbering dialog box

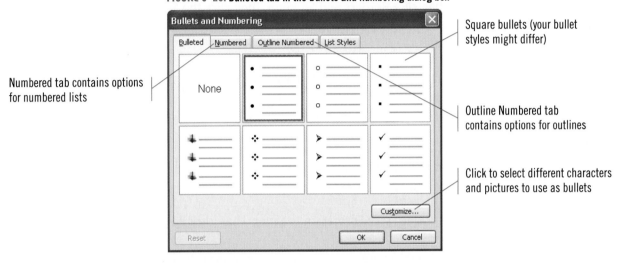

Square bullets (your bullet styles might differ)

Numbered tab contains options for numbered lists

Outline Numbered tab contains options for outlines

Click to select different characters and pictures to use as bullets

Word 2003

FIGURE C-21: Square bullets applied to list

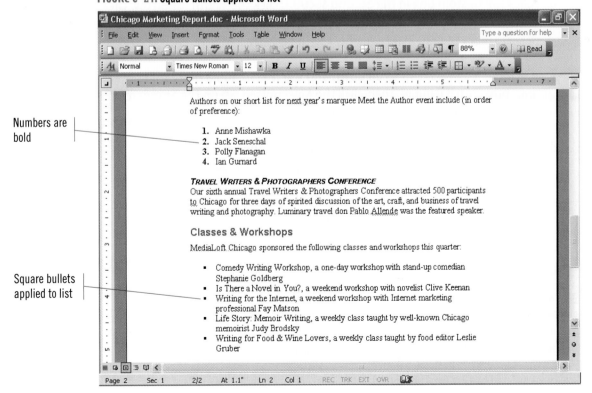

Numbers are bold

Square bullets applied to list

Adding Borders and Shading

Borders and shading can add color and splash to a document. **Borders** are lines you add above, below, to the side, or around words or a paragraph. You can format borders using different line styles, colors, and widths. **Shading** is a color or pattern you apply behind words or paragraphs to make them stand out on a page. You apply borders and shading using the Borders and Shading command on the Format menu. You enhance the advertising expenses table by adding shading to it. You also apply a border under every heading to visually punctuate the sections of the report.

STEPS

1. **Scroll up until the heading Advertising is at the top of your screen**

2. **Select the four paragraphs of tabbed text under the Advertising heading, click Format on the menu bar, click Borders and Shading, then click the Shading tab**
   The Shading tab in the Borders and Shading dialog box is shown in Figure C-22. You use this tab to apply shading to words and paragraphs.

3. **Click the Lavender box in the bottom row of the Fill section, click OK, then deselect the text**
   Lavender shading is applied to the four paragraphs. Notice that the shading is applied to the entire width of the paragraphs, despite the tab settings.

4. **Select the four paragraphs, drag the Left Indent marker ▢ to the ¾" mark on the horizontal ruler, drag the Right Indent marker △ to the 5¼" mark, then deselect the text**
   The shading for the paragraphs is indented from the left and right, making it look more attractive.

5. **Select Advertising, click Format on the menu bar, click Borders and Shading, then click the Borders tab**
   The Borders tab is shown in Figure C-23. You use this tab to add boxes and lines to words or paragraphs.

QUICK TIP

When creating custom borders, it's important to select the style, color, and width settings before applying the borders in the Preview section.

6. **Click the Custom box in the Setting section, click the Width list arrow, click ¾ pt, click the Bottom Border button ▦ in the Preview section, click OK, then deselect the text**
   A ¾-point black border is added below the Advertising paragraph.

7. **Click Events, press [F4], scroll down and use [F4] to add a border under each plum heading, press [Ctrl][Home], then click the Save button 🖫 on the Standard toolbar**
   The completed document is shown in Figure C-24.

8. **Click the Print button 🖨, close the document, then exit Word**
   A copy of the report prints. Depending on your printer, colors might appear differently when you print. If you are using a black-and-white printer, colors will print in shades of gray.

Clues to Use

Highlighting text in a document
The Highlight tool allows you to mark and find important text in a document. **Highlighting** is transparent color that is applied to text using the Highlight pointer 🖊. To highlight text, click the Highlight list arrow 🔲 on the Formatting toolbar, select a color, then use the I-beam part of the 🖊 pointer to select the text. Click 🔲 to turn off the Highlight pointer. To remove highlighting, select the highlighted text, click 🔲, then click None. Highlighting prints, but it is used most effectively when a document is viewed on screen.

FIGURE C-22: Shading tab in Borders and Shading dialog box

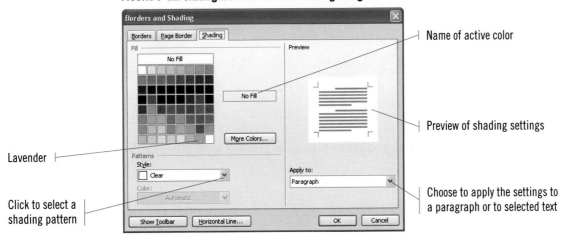

Name of active color

Preview of shading settings

Lavender

Click to select a shading pattern

Choose to apply the settings to a paragraph or to selected text

FIGURE C-23: Borders tab in Borders and Shading dialog box

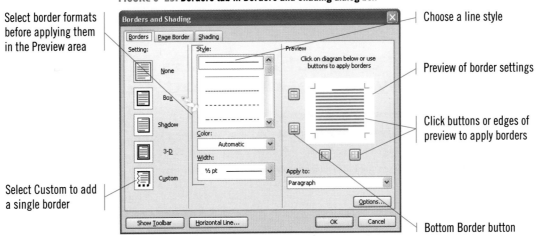

Select border formats before applying them in the Preview area

Choose a line style

Preview of border settings

Click buttons or edges of preview to apply borders

Select Custom to add a single border

Bottom Border button

FIGURE C-24: Borders and shading applied to the document

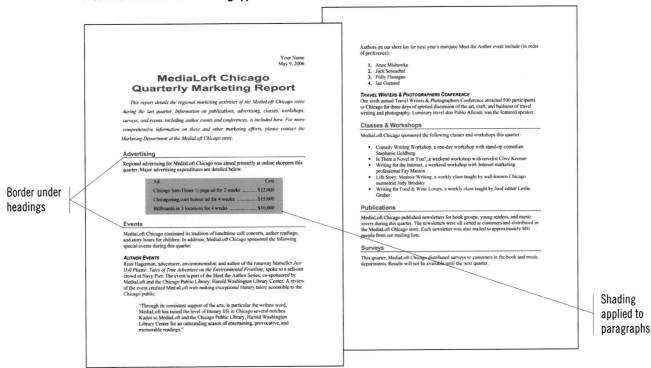

Border under headings

Shading applied to paragraphs

Practice

▼ CONCEPTS REVIEW

Label each element of the Word program window shown in Figure C-25.

FIGURE C-25

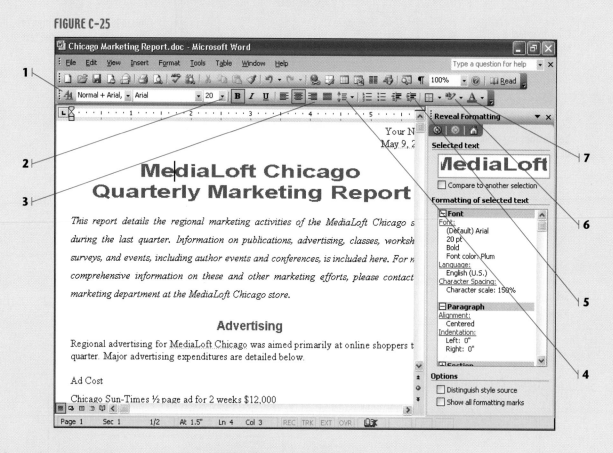

Match each term with the statement that best describes it.

8. Bold
9. Shading
10. Point
11. Style
12. Italic
13. Highlight
14. Bullet
15. Border

a. A character that appears at the beginning of a paragraph to add emphasis

b. Transparent color that is applied to text to mark it in a document

c. A text style in which characters are slanted

d. Color or a pattern that is applied behind text to make it look attractive

e. A set of format settings

f. A unit of measurement equal to ½ of an inch

g. A line that can be applied above, below, or to the sides of a paragraph

h. A text style in which characters are darker and thicker

Select the best answer from the list of choices.

16. Which button is used to align a paragraph with both the left and right margins?

a.

c.

b.

d.

17. What is Arial?

a. A style

c. A text effect

b. A character format

d. A font

18. What is the most precise way to increase the amount of white space between two paragraphs?

a. Insert an extra blank line between the paragraphs.

b. Change the line spacing of the paragraphs.

c. Indent the paragraphs.

d. Use the Paragraph command to change the spacing below the first paragraph.

19. What element of the Word program window can be used to check the tab settings applied to text?

a. Formatting toolbar

c. Reveal Formatting task pane

b. Standard toolbar

d. Styles and Formatting task pane

20. Which command would you use to apply color behind a paragraph?

a. Background

c. Borders and Shading

b. Styles and Formatting

d. Paragraph

▼ SKILLS REVIEW

1. Format with fonts.

a. Start Word, open the file WD C-2.doc from the drive and folder where your Data Files are located, save it as **EDA Report**, then scroll through the document to get a feel for its contents.

b. Press [Ctrl][Home], format the report title **Richmond Springs Economic Development Report Executive Summary** in 26-point Tahoma. Choose a different font if Tahoma is not available to you.

c. Change the font color of the report title to Teal, then press [Enter] after Springs in the title.

d. Place the insertion point in the first body paragraph under the title, then add a two-line drop cap to the paragraph using the Dropped position.

e. Format each of the following headings in 14-point Tahoma with the Teal font color: **Mission Statement**, **Guiding Principles**, **Issues**, **Proposed Actions**.

f. Press [Ctrl][Home], then save your changes to the report.

2. Change font styles and effects.

a. Apply bold to the report title and to each heading in the report.

b. Show formatting marks, then format the paragraph under the Mission Statement heading in italic.

c. Format **Years Population Growth**, the first line in the four-line list under the Issues heading, in bold, small caps, with a Teal font color.

d. Change the font color of the next two lines under Years Population Growth to Teal.

e. Format the line **Source: Office of State Planning** in italic.

f. Scroll to the top of the report, change the character scale of **Richmond Springs Economic Development Report** to 80%, then save your changes.

3. Change line and paragraph spacing.

   a. Change the line spacing of the three-line list under the first body paragraph to 1.5 lines.

   b. Add 12 points of space before the Executive Summary line in the title.

   c. Add 12 points of space after each heading in the report (but not the title).

   d. Add 6 points of space after each paragraph in the list under the Guiding Principles heading.

   e. Add 6 points of space after each paragraph under the Proposed Actions heading.

   f. Press [Ctrl][Home], then save your changes to the report.

4. Align paragraphs.

   a. Press [Ctrl][A] to select the entire document, then justify all the paragraphs.

   b. Center the three-line report title.

   c. Press [Ctrl][End], type your name, press [Enter], type the current date, then right-align your name and the date.

   d. Save your changes to the report.

5. Work with tabs.

   a. Scroll up and select the four-line list of population information under the Issues heading.

   b. Set left tab stops at the 1¾" mark and the 3" mark.

   c. Insert a tab at the beginning of each line in the list.

   d. In the first line, insert a tab before Population. In the second line, insert a tab before 4.5%. In the third line, insert a tab before 53%.

   e. Select the first three lines, then drag the second tab stop to the 2¾" mark on the horizontal ruler.

   f. Press [Ctrl][Home], then save your changes to the report.

6. Work with indents.

   a. Indent the paragraph under the Mission Statement heading ½" from the left and ½" from the right.

   b. Indent the first line of the paragraph under the Guiding Principles heading ½".

   c. Indent the first line of the three body paragraphs under the Issues heading ½".

   d. Press [Ctrl][Home], then save your changes to the report.

7. Add bullets and numbering.

   a. Apply bullets to the three-line list under the first body paragraph.

   b. Change the bullet style to small black circles (or choose another bullet style if small black circles are not available to you).

   c. Change the font color of the bullets to Teal.

   d. Scroll down until the Guiding Principles heading is at the top of your screen.

   e. Format the six-paragraph list under Guiding Principles as a numbered list.

   f. Format the numbers in 12-point Tahoma bold, then change the font color to Teal.

   g. Scroll down until the Proposed Actions heading is at the top of your screen, then format the paragraphs under the heading as a bulleted list using check marks as the bullet style. If checkmarks are not available, click Reset or choose another bullet style.

   h. Change the font color of the bullets to Teal, press [Ctrl][Home], then save your changes to the report.

8. Add borders and shading.

   a. Change the font color of the report title to Light Yellow, then apply Teal shading.

   b. Add a 1-point Teal border below the Mission Statement heading.

   c. Use the Format Painter to copy the formatting of the Mission Statement heading to the other headings in the report.

   d. Under the Issues heading, select the first three lines of tabbed text, which are formatted in Teal.

e. Apply Light Yellow shading to the paragraphs, then add a 1-point Teal box border around the paragraphs.

f. Indent the shading and border around the paragraphs 1½" from the left and 1½" from the right.

g. Press [Ctrl][Home], save your changes to the report, view the report in Print Preview, then print a copy. The formatted report is shown in Figure C-26.

h. Close the file and exit Word.

FIGURE C-26

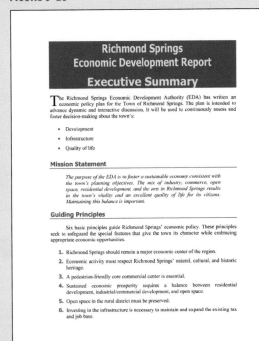
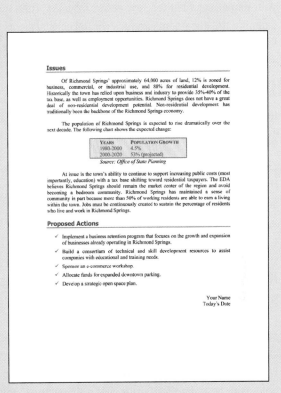

▼ INDEPENDENT CHALLENGE 1

You are an estimator for Zephir Construction in the Australian city of Wollongong. You have drafted an estimate for a home renovation job, and need to format it. It's important that your estimate have a clean, striking design, and reflect your company's professionalism.

a. Start Word, open the file WD C-3.doc from the drive and folder where your Data Files are located, save it as **Zephir Construction**, then read the document to get a feel for its contents. Figure C-27 shows how you will format the letterhead.

FIGURE C-27

ZEPHIRConstruction
73 Corrimal Street, Wollongong, NSW 2500
Tel: 02-4225-3202; www.zephir.com.au

b. In the first paragraph, format **ZEPHIR** in 24-point Arial Black, then apply bold. (*Hint*: Select a similar font if Arial Black is not available to you.)

c. Format **Construction** in 24-point Arial, then change the character scale to 90%.

d. Format the next two lines in 9-point Arial bold, center the three-line letterhead, then add a 1-point black border below the last line.

e. Format the title **Proposal of Renovation** in 16-point Arial Black, then center the title.

f. Format the following headings (including the colons) in 12-point Arial Black: **Date**, **Work to be performed for and at**, **Scope of work**, **Payment schedule**, and **Agreement**.

g. Format the 14-line list under **Scope of work** that begins with **Demo of all ...** as a numbered list, then apply bold to the numbers.

▼ INDEPENDENT CHALLENGE 1 (CONTINUED)

h. Change the paragraph spacing to add 4 points of space after each paragraph in the list. (*Hint*: Select 0 pt in the After text box, then type 4.)

i. With the list selected, set a right tab stop at the 5¾" mark, then insert tabs before every price in the list.

j. Apply bold to the two lines, **Total estimated job cost...** and **Approximate job time**... below the list.

k. Replace Your Name with your name in the signature block, select the signature block (Respectfully submitted through your name), set a left tab stop at the 3½" mark, then indent the signature block.

l. Examine the document carefully for formatting errors and make any necessary adjustments.

m. Save and print the document, then close the file and exit Word.

▼ INDEPENDENT CHALLENGE 2

Your employer, The Lange Center for Contemporary Arts in Halifax, Nova Scotia, is launching a membership drive. Your boss has written the text for a flyer advertising Lange membership, and asks you to format it so that it is eye catching and attractive.

a. Open the file WD C-4.doc from the drive and folder where your Data Files are located, save it as **Membership Flyer**, then read the document. Figure C-28 shows how you will format the first several paragraphs of the flyer.

b. Select the entire document and format it in 10-point Arial Narrow.

FIGURE C-28

c. Center the first line, **Membership Drive**, and apply indigo shading to the paragraph. Format the text in 26-point Arial Narrow, bold, with a white font color. Expand the character spacing by 7 points.

d. Format the second line, **2006**, in 36-point Arial Black. Expand the character spacing by 25 points and change the character scale to 200%. Center the line.

e. Format each **What we do for...** heading in 12-point Arial, bold, with an indigo font color. Add a single line ½-point border under each heading.

f. Format each subheading (**Gallery**, **Lectures**, **Library**, **All members...**, and **Membership Levels**) in 10-point Arial, bold. Add 3 points of spacing before each paragraph.

g. Indent each body paragraph ¼", except for the lines under the **What we do for YOU** heading.

h. Format the four lines under the All members... subheading as a bulleted list. Use a bullet symbol of your choice and format the bullets in the indigo color.

i. Indent the five lines under the Membership Levels heading ¼". For these five lines, set left tab stops at the 1¼" mark and the 2" mark on the horizontal ruler. Insert tabs before the price and before the word **All** in each of the five lines.

j. Format the name of each membership level (**Artistic**, **Conceptual**, etc.) in 10-point Arial, bold, italic, with an indigo font color.

k. Format the **For more information** heading in 14-point Arial, bold, with an indigo font color, then center the heading.

l. Format the last two lines in 11-point Arial Narrow, and center the lines. In the contact information, replace Your Name with your name, then apply bold to your name.

Advanced Challenge Exercise

- Change the font color of **2006** to 80% gray and add a shadow effect.
- Add an emboss effect to each subheading.
- Add a 3-point dotted black border above the **For more information** heading.

m. Examine the document carefully for formatting errors and make any necessary adjustments.

n. Save and print the flyer, then close the file and exit Word.

▼ INDEPENDENT CHALLENGE 3

FIGURE C-29

One of your responsibilities as program coordinator at Solstice Mountain Sports is to develop a program of winter outdoor learning and adventure workshops. You have drafted a memo to your boss to update her on your progress. You need to format the memo so it is professional looking and easy to read.

a. Start Word, open the file WD C-5.doc from the drive and folder where your Data Files are located, then save it as **Solstice Memo**.

b. Select the heading **Solstice Mountain Sports Memorandum**, then apply the paragraph style Heading 1 to it. (*Hint:* Open the Styles and Formatting task pane, click the Show list arrow, click Available Styles if necessary, then click Heading 1.)

c. In the memo header, replace Today's Date and Your Name with the current date and your name.

d. Select the four-line memo header, set a left tab stop at the ¾" mark, then insert tabs before the date, the recipient's name, your name, and the subject of the memo.

e. Double-space the four lines in the memo header, then apply the character style Strong to **Date:**, **To:**, **From:**, and **Re:**.

f. Apply a 1½-point double line border below the blank line under the memo header. (*Hint*: Turn on formatting marks, select the paragraph symbol below the memo header, then apply a border below it.)

g. Apply the paragraph style Heading 3 to the headings **Overview**, **Workshops**, **Accommodation**, **Fees**, and **Proposed winter programming**.

h. Under the Fees heading, format the words **Workshop fees** and **Accommodation fees** in bold italic.

i. Add 6 points of space after the Workshop fees paragraph.

Advanced Challenge Exercise

- Format **Fees** as animated text using the Las Vegas Lights animation style.
- After Fees, type **Verify prices with the Moose Lodge**, then format the text as hidden text.
- In the Fees section, apply yellow highlighting to the prices.

j. On the second page of the document, format the list under the **Proposed winter programming** heading as an outline. Figure C-29 shows the hierarchical structure of the outline. (*Hint:* Format the list as an outline numbered list, then use the Increase Indent and Decrease Indent buttons to change the level of importance of each item.)

k. Change the outline numbering style to the bullet numbering style shown in Figure C-29, if necessary.

l. Save and print the document, then close the file and exit Word.

▼ INDEPENDENT CHALLENGE 4

The fonts you choose for a document can have a major effect on the document's tone. Not all fonts are appropriate for use in a business document, and some fonts, especially those with a definite theme, are appropriate only for specific purposes. The World Wide Web includes hundreds of Web sites devoted to fonts and text design. Some Web sites sell fonts, others allow you to download fonts for free and install them on your computer. In this Independent Challenge, you will research Web sites related to fonts and find examples of fonts you can use in your work.

a. Start Word, open the file WD C-6.doc from the drive and folder where your Data Files are located, and save it as **Fonts**. This document contains the questions you will answer about the fonts you find.

b. Use your favorite search engine to search the Web for Web sites related to fonts. Use the keyword **font** to conduct your search.

c. Explore the fonts available for downloading. As you examine the fonts, notice that fonts fall into two general categories: serif fonts, which have a small stroke, called a serif, at the ends of each character, and sans serif fonts, which do not have a serif. Times New Roman is an example of a serif font and Arial is an example of a sans serif font.

d. Replace Your Name and Today's Date with the current date and your name, type your answers in the Fonts document, save it, print a copy, then close the file and exit Word.

Figure C-29

Proposed winter programming

- ❖ Skiing, Snowboarding, and Snowshoeing
  - ➢ Skiing and Snowboarding
    - Cross-country skiing
      - Cross-country skiing for beginners
      - Intermediate cross-country skiing
      - Inn-to-inn ski touring
      - Moonlight cross-country skiing
    - Telemarking
      - Basic telemark skiing
      - Introduction to backcountry skiing
      - Exploring on skis
    - Snowboarding
      - Backcountry snowboarding
  - ➢ Snowshoeing
    - Beginner
      - Snowshoeing for beginners
      - Snowshoeing and winter ecology
    - Intermediate and Advanced
      - Intermediate snowshoeing
      - Guided snowshoe trek
      - Above tree line snowshoeing
- ❖ Winter Hiking, Camping, and Survival
  - ➢ Hiking
    - Beginner
      - Long-distance hiking
      - Winter summits
      - Hiking for women
  - ➢ Winter camping and survival
    - Beginner
      - Introduction to winter camping
      - Basic winter mountain skills
      - Building snow shelters
    - Intermediate
      - Basic winter mountain skills II
      - Ice climbing
      - Avalanche awareness and rescue

Word 2003

Using the file WD C-7.doc found in the drive and folder where your Data Files are located, create the menu shown in Figure C-30. (*Hints*: Use Centaur or a similar font. Change the font size of the heading to 56 points, scale the font to 90%, and expand the spacing by 1 point. For the rest of the text, change the font size of the daily specials to 18 points and the descriptions to 14 points. Format the prices using tabs. Use paragraph spacing to adjust the spacing between paragraphs so that all the text fits on one page.) Save the menu as **Melting Pot Specials**, then print a copy.

FIGURE C-30

The Melting Pot Café

····· ·· ····· ····· ····· ····· ····· ····· ····· ····· ·····

Daily Specials

Monday: Veggie Chili
Hearty veggie chili with melted cheddar in our peasant French bread bowl. Topped with sour cream & scallions...$5.95

Tuesday: Greek Salad
Our large garden salad with kalamata olives, feta cheese, and garlic vinaigrette. Served with an assortment of rolls. $5.95

Wednesday: French Dip
Lean roast beef topped with melted cheddar on our roasted garlic roll. Served with a side of au jus and red bliss mashed potatoes. $6.95

Thursday: Chicken Cajun Bleu
Cajun chicken, chunky blue cheese, cucumbers, leaf lettuce, and tomato on our roasted garlic roll. $6.50

Friday: Clam Chowder
Classic New England thick, rich, clam chowder in our peasant French bread bowl. Served with a garden salad...$5.95

Saturday: Hot Chicken and Gravy
Delicious chicken and savory gravy served on a thick slice of toasted honest white. Served with red bliss mashed potatoes...$6.95

Sunday: Turkey-Bacon Club
Double-decker roasted turkey, crisp bacon, leaf lettuce, tomato, and sun-dried tomato mayo on toasted triple seed...$6.50

■■■■ ■■ ■■■■■ ■■■■■ ■■■■■ ■■■■■ ■■■■■ ■■■■■ ■■■■■ ■■■■■

Chef: Your Name

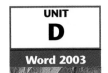

Formatting Documents

OBJECTIVES

Set document margins
Divide a document into sections
Insert page breaks
Insert page numbers
Add headers and footers
Edit headers and footers
Format columns
Insert a table
Insert WordArt
Insert clip art

If you have a SAM user profile, you may have access to hands-on instruction, practice, and assessment of the skills covered in this unit. Log in to your SAM account and go to your assignments page to see what your instructor has assigned.

The page-formatting features of Word allow you to creatively lay out and design the pages of your documents. In this unit, you learn how to change the document margins, determine page orientation, add page numbers, and insert headers and footers. You also learn how to format text in columns and how to illustrate your documents with tables, clip art, and WordArt. ▨▨▨ You have written and formatted the text for the quarterly newsletter for the marketing staff. You are now ready to lay out and design the newsletter pages. You plan to organize the articles in columns and to illustrate the newsletter with a table, clip art, and WordArt.

Setting Document Margins

Changing a document's margins is one way to change the appearance of a document and control the amount of text that fits on a page. The **margins** of a document are the blank areas between the edge of the text and the edge of the page. When you create a document in Word, the default margins are 1" at the top and bottom of the page, and 1.25" on the left and right sides of the page. You can adjust the size of a document's margins using the Page Setup command on the File menu, or using the rulers. ░░░░ The newsletter should be a four-page document when finished. You begin formatting the pages by reducing the size of the document margins so that more text fits on each page.

STEPS

1. **Start Word, open the file** WD D-1.doc **from the drive and folder where your Data Files are located, then save it as** MediaLoft Buzz

   The newsletter opens in Print Layout view.

2. **Scroll through the newsletter to get a feel for its contents, then press** [Ctrl][Home]

   The newsletter is currently five pages long. Notice the status bar indicates the page where the insertion point is located and the total number of pages in the document.

3. **Click** File **on the menu bar, click** Page Setup, **then click the** Margins tab **in the Page Setup dialog box if it is not already selected**

   The Margins tab in the Page Setup dialog box is shown in Figure D-1. You can use the Margins tab to change the top, bottom, left, or right document margins, to change the orientation of the pages from portrait to landscape, and to alter other page layout settings. **Portrait orientation** means a page is taller than it is wide; **landscape orientation** means a page is wider than it is tall. This newsletter uses portrait orientation.

QUICK TIP
The minimum allowable margin settings depend on your printer and the size of the paper you are using. Word displays a warning message if you set margins that are too narrow for your printer.

4. **Click the** Top down arrow **three times until 0.7" appears, then click the** Bottom down arrow **until 0.7" appears**

   The top and bottom margins of the newsletter will be .7". Notice that the margins in the Preview section of the dialog box change as you adjust the margin settings.

5. **Press** [Tab], **type** .7 **in the Left text box, press** [Tab], **then type** .7 **in the Right text box**

   The left and right margins of the newsletter will also be .7". You can change the margin settings by using the arrows or by typing a value in the appropriate text box.

6. **Click** OK

   The document margins change to .7", as shown in Figure D-2. The bar at the intersection of the white and shaded areas on the horizontal and vertical rulers indicates the location of the margin. You can also change a document's margins by dragging the bar to a new location.

QUICK TIP
Use the Reveal Formatting task pane to quickly check the margin, orientation, paper size, and other page layout settings for a document.

7. **Click the** Zoom list arrow **on the Standard toolbar, then click** Two Pages

   The first two pages of the document appear in the document window.

8. **Scroll down to view all five pages of the newsletter, press** [Ctrl][Home], **click the** Zoom list arrow, **click** Page Width, **then click the** Save button 🖫 **on the Standard toolbar to save the document**

FIGURE D-1: Margins tab in Page Setup dialog box

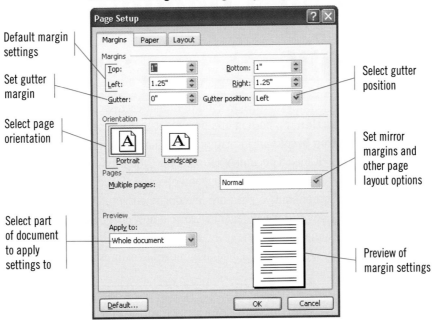

Default margin settings

Set gutter margin

Select page orientation

Select part of document to apply settings to

Select gutter position

Set mirror margins and other page layout options

Preview of margin settings

FIGURE D-2: Newsletter with smaller margins

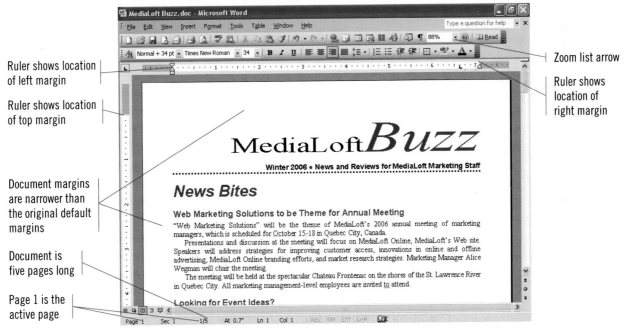

Ruler shows location of left margin

Ruler shows location of top margin

Document margins are narrower than the original default margins

Document is five pages long

Page 1 is the active page

Zoom list arrow

Ruler shows location of right margin

Clues to Use

Changing orientation, margin settings, and paper size

By default, the documents you create in Word use an 8½" × 11" paper size in portrait orientation with the default margin settings. You can adjust these settings in the Page Setup dialog box to create documents that are a different size, shape, or layout. On the Margins tab, change the orientation of the pages by selecting Portrait or Landscape. To change the layout of multiple pages, use the Multiple pages list arrow to create pages that use mirror margins, that include two pages per sheet of paper, or that are formatted like a folded booklet. **Mirror margins** are used in documents with facing pages, such as a maga-zine, where the margins on the left page of the document are a mirror image of the margins on the right page. Documents with mirror margins have inside and outside margins, rather than right and left margins. Another type of margin is a gutter margin, which is used in documents that are bound, such as books. A **gutter** adds extra space to the left, top, or inside margin to allow for the binding. Add a gutter to a document by adjusting the setting in the Gutter text box on the Margins tab. If you want to change the size of the paper used in a document, use the Paper tab in the Page Setup dialog box. Use the Paper size list arrow to select a standard paper size, or enter custom measure-ments in the Width and Height text boxes.

Word 2003

Dividing a Document into Sections

Dividing a document into sections allows you to format each section of the document with different page layout settings. A **section** is a portion of a document that is separated from the rest of the document by section breaks. **Section breaks** are formatting marks that you insert in a document to show the end of a section. Once you have divided a document into sections, you can format each section with different column, margin, page orientation, header and footer, and other page layout settings. By default, a document is formatted as a single section, but you can divide a document into as many sections as you like. You want to format the body of the newsletter in two columns, but leave the masthead and the headline "News Bites" as a single column. You insert a section break before the body of the newsletter to divide the document into two sections, and then change the number of columns in the second section to two.

STEPS

1. **Click the Show/Hide ¶ button ¶ on the Standard toolbar to display formatting marks if they are not visible**

   Turning on formatting marks allows you to see the section breaks you insert in a document.

QUICK TIP
When you insert a section break at the beginning of a paragraph, Word inserts the break at the end of the previous paragraph. A section break stores the formatting information for the preceding section.

2. **Place the insertion point before the headline** Web Marketing Solutions to be..., **click** Insert **on the menu bar, then click** Break

   The Break dialog box opens, as shown in Figure D-3. You use this dialog box to insert different types of section breaks. Table D-1 describes the different types of section breaks.

3. **Click the** Continuous option button, **then click** OK

   Word inserts a continuous section break, shown as a dotted double line, above the headline. A continuous section break begins a new section of the document on the same page. The document now has two sections. Notice that the status bar indicates that the insertion point is in section 2.

4. **With the insertion point in section 2, click the** Columns button ▦ **on the Standard toolbar**

   A grid showing four columns opens. You use the grid to select the number of columns you want to create.

5. **Point to the** second column **on the grid, then click**

   Section 2 is formatted in two columns, as shown in Figure D-4. The text in section 1 remains formatted in a single column. Notice the status bar now indicates the document is four pages long. Formatting text in columns is another way to increase the amount of text that fits on a page.

6. **Click the** Zoom list arrow **on the Standard toolbar, click** Two Pages, **then scroll down to examine all four pages of the document**

   The text in section 2—all the text below the continuous section break—is formatted in two columns. Text in columns flows automatically from the bottom of one column to the top of the next column.

7. **Press** [Ctrl][Home], **click the** Zoom list arrow, **click** Page Width, **then save the document**

TABLE D-1: Types of section breaks

section	function
Next page	Begins a new section and moves the text following the break to the top of the next page
Continuous	Begins a new section on the same page
Even page	Begins a new section and moves the text following the break to the top of the next even-numbered page
Odd page	Begins a new section and moves the text following the break to the top of the next odd-numbered page

FIGURE D-3: Break dialog box

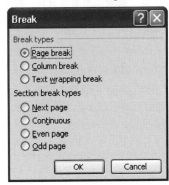

FIGURE D-4: Continuous section break and columns

Text in section 1 is formatted in one column

Insertion point in section 2

Text in section 2 is formatted in two columns

Section 2 is the active section

Continuous section break

Columns of text

Document is now four pages long

Clues to Use

Changing page layout settings for a section

Dividing a document into sections allows you to vary the layout of a document. In addition to applying different column settings to sections, you can apply different margins, page orientation, paper size, vertical alignment, header and footer, page numbering, and other page layout settings. For example, if you are formatting a report that includes a table with many columns, you might want to change the table's page orientation to landscape so that it is easier to read. To do this, you would insert a section break before and after the table to create a section that contains only the table. Then you would use the Margins tab in the Page Setup dialog box to change the page orientation of the section that contains the table to landscape.

To change the page layout settings for an individual section, place the insertion point in the section, open the Page Setup (or Columns) dialog box, select the options you want to change, click the Apply to list arrow, click This section, then click OK. When you select This section in the Apply to list box, the settings are applied to the current section only. If you select Whole document in the Apply to list box, the settings are applied to all the sections in the document.

Inserting Page Breaks

As you type text in a document, Word automatically inserts an **automatic page break** (also called a soft page break) when you reach the bottom of a page, allowing you to continue typing on the next page. You can also force text onto the next page of a document by using the Break command to insert a **manual page break** (also called a hard page break). You insert manual page breaks where you know you want to begin each new page of the newsletter.

STEPS

1. **Scroll down to the bottom of page 1, place the insertion point before the headline** Career Corner, **click** Insert **on the menu bar, then click** Break

   The Break dialog box opens. You also use this dialog box to insert page, column, and text-wrapping breaks. Table D-2 describes these types of breaks.

QUICK TIP

To delete a break, double-click the break to select it, then press [Delete].

2. **Make sure the** Page break option button **is selected, then click** OK

   Word inserts a manual page break before "Career Corner" and moves all the text following the page break to the beginning of the next page, as shown in Figure D-5. The page break appears as a dotted line in Print Layout view when formatting marks are displayed. Page break marks are visible on the screen but do not print. Manual and automatic page breaks are always visible in Normal view.

3. **Scroll down to the bottom of page 2, place the insertion point before the headline** Webcasts Slated for Spring, **press and hold** [Ctrl], **then press** [Enter]

   Pressing [Ctrl][Enter] is a fast way to insert a manual page break. The headline is forced to the top of the third page.

QUICK TIP

To fit more text on the screen in Print Layout view, you can hide the white space on the top and bottom of each page and the gray space between pages. To toggle between hiding and showing white space, move the pointer to the top of a page until the pointer changes to ⬇, then click.

4. **Scroll down page 3, place the insertion point before the headline** Staff News, **then press** [Ctrl][Enter]

   The headline is forced to the top of the fourth page.

5. **Press** [Ctrl][Home], **click the** Zoom list arrow **on the Standard toolbar, then click** Two Pages

   The first two pages of the document are displayed, as shown in Figure D-6.

6. **Scroll down to view pages 3 and 4, click the** Zoom list arrow, **click** Page Width, **then save the document**

Clues to Use

Vertically aligning text on a page

By default, text is vertically aligned with the top margin of a page, but you can change the vertical alignment of text so that it is centered between the top and bottom margins, justified between the top and bottom margins, or aligned with the bottom margin of the page. You vertically align text on a page only when the text does not fill the page; for example, if you are creating a flyer or a title page for a report. To change the vertical alignment of text in a section (or a document), place the insertion point in the section you want to align, open the Page Setup dialog box, use the Vertical alignment list arrow on the Layout tab to select the alignment you want—top, center, justified, or bottom—use the Apply to list arrow to select the part of the document you want to align, and then click OK.

FIGURE D-5: **Manual page break in document**

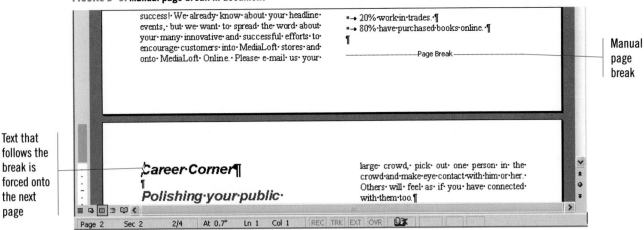

Text that follows the break is forced onto the next page

Manual page break

FIGURE D-6: **Pages 1 and 2**

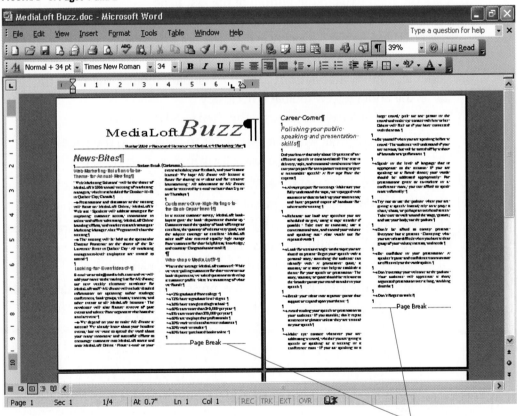

Manual page breaks

TABLE D-2: **Types of breaks**

break	function
Page break	Forces the text following the break to begin at the top of the next page
Column break	Forces the text following the break to begin at the top of the next column
Text wrapping break	Forces the text following the break to begin at the beginning of the next line

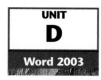
Inserting Page Numbers

If you want to number the pages of a multiple-page document, you can insert a page number field at the top or bottom of each page. A **field** is a code that serves as a placeholder for data that changes in a document, such as a page number or the current date. When you use the Page Numbers command on the Insert menu to add page numbers to a document, Word automatically numbers the pages for you. ▰▰▰▰ You insert a page number field so that page numbers will appear at the bottom of each page in the document.

STEPS

1. **Click** Insert **on the menu bar, then click** Page Numbers
   The Page Numbers dialog box opens, as shown in Figure D-7. You use this dialog box to specify the position—top or bottom of the page—and the alignment for the page numbers. Bottom of page (Footer) is the default position.

QUICK TIP
You can also align page numbers with the left, right, inside, or outside margins of a document.

2. **Click the** Alignment list arrow, **then click** Center
   The page numbers will be centered between the left and right margins at the bottom of each page.

3. **Click** OK, **then scroll to the bottom of the first page**
   The page number 1 appears in gray at the bottom of the first page, as shown in Figure D-8. The number is gray, or dimmed, because it is located in the Footer area. When the document is printed, the page numbers appear as normal text. You will learn more about headers and footers in the next lesson.

4. **Click the** Print Preview button 🔍 **on the Standard toolbar, then click the** One Page button 🔳 **on the Print Preview toolbar if necessary**
   The first page of the newsletter appears in Print Preview. Notice the page number.

5. **Click the** page number **with the** 🔍 **pointer to zoom in on the page**
   The page number is centered at the bottom of the page, as shown in Figure D-9.

6. **Scroll down the document to see the page number at the bottom of each page**
   Word automatically numbered each page of the newsletter.

QUICK TIP
To display more than six pages of a document in Print Preview, drag to expand the Multiple Pages grid.

7. **Click the** Multiple Pages button 🔳 **on the Print Preview toolbar, point to the** second box **in the bottom row on the grid to select** 2 × 2 pages, **then click**
   All four pages of the newsletter appear in the Print Preview window.

8. **Click** Close **on the Print Preview toolbar, press** [Ctrl][Home], **then save the document**

Clues to Use

Inserting the date and time

Using the Date and Time command on the Insert menu, you can insert the current date or the current time into a document, either as a field or as static text. Word uses the clock on your computer to compute the current date and time. To insert the current date or time at the location of the insertion point, click Date and Time on the Insert menu, then select the date or time format you want to use

from the list of available formats in the Date and Time dialog box. If you want to insert the date or time as a field that is updated automatically each time you open or print the document, select the Update automatically check box, and then click OK. If you want the current date or time to remain in the document as static text, deselect the Update automatically check box, and then click OK.

FIGURE D-7: Page Numbers dialog box

Set location for page number (header or footer)

Set alignment of page number

Clear to hide the page number on the first page

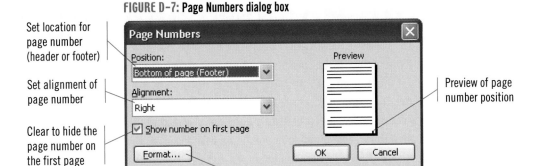

Preview of page number position

Click to change numbering format

FIGURE D-8: Page number in document

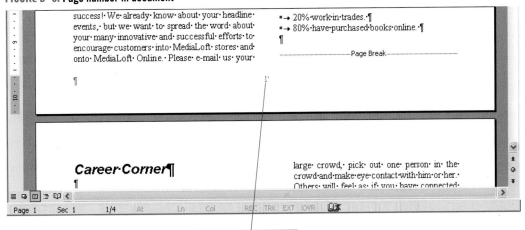

Page number is dimmed

FIGURE D-9: Page number in Print Preview

One Page button

Multiple Pages button

Page number in Print Preview

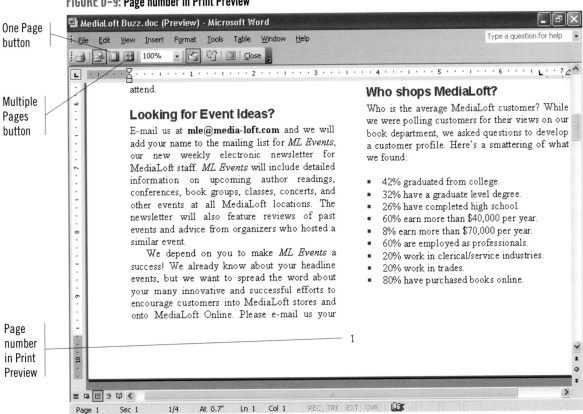

Word 2003

Adding Headers and Footers

A **header** is text or graphics that appears at the top of every page of a document. A **footer** is text or graphics that appears at the bottom of every page. In longer documents, headers and footers often contain information such as the title of the publication, the title of the chapter, the name of the author, the date, or a page number. You can add headers and footers to a document by using the Header and Footer command on the View menu to open the Header and Footer areas, and then inserting text and graphics in them. ⬛⬛⬛ You create a header that includes the name of the newsletter and the current date.

STEPS

1. **Click View on the menu bar, then click Header and Footer**

   The Header and Footer areas open and the document text is dimmed, as shown in Figure D-10. When the document text is dimmed, it cannot be edited. The Header and Footer toolbar also opens. It includes buttons for inserting standard text into headers and footers and for navigating between headers and footers. See Table D-3. The Header and Footer areas of a document are independent of the document itself and must be formatted separately. For example, if you select all the text in a document and then change the font, the header and footer font does not change.

   QUICK TIP

   You can change the date format by right-clicking the field, clicking Edit Field on the shortcut menu, and then selecting a new date format in the Field properties list in the Field dialog box.

2. **Type Buzz in the Header area, press [Spacebar] twice, then click the Insert Date button 🗓️ on the Header and Footer toolbar**

   Clicking the Insert Date button inserts a date field into the header. The date is inserted using the default date format (usually month/date/year, although your default date format might be different). The word "Buzz" and the current date will appear at the top of every page in the document.

3. **Select Buzz and the date, then click the Center button ☰ on the Formatting toolbar**

   The text is centered in the Header area. In addition to the alignment buttons on the Formatting toolbar, you can use tabs to align text in the Header and Footer areas. Notice the tab stops shown on the ruler. The tab stops are the default tab stops for the Header and Footer areas and are based on the default margin settings. If you change the margins in a document, you can adjust the tab stops in the Header or Footer area to align with the new margin settings.

   QUICK TIP

   Unless you set different headers and footers for different sections, the information you insert in any Header or Footer area appears on every page in the document.

4. **With the text still selected, click the Font list arrow on the Formatting toolbar, click Arial, click the Bold button B, then click in the Header area to deselect the text**

   The header text is formatted in 12-point Arial bold.

5. **Click the Switch Between Header and Footer button 🖹 on the Header and Footer toolbar**

   The insertion point moves to the Footer area, where a page number field is centered in the Footer area.

6. **Double-click the page number to select the field, click the Font list arrow, click Arial, click B, then click in the Footer area to deselect the field**

   The page number is formatted in 12-point Arial bold.

   QUICK TIP

   To change the distance between the header and footer and the edge of the page, change the From edge settings on the Layout tab in the Page Setup dialog box.

7. **Click Close on the Header and Footer toolbar, save the document, then scroll down until the bottom of page 1 and the top of page 2 appear in the document window**

   The Header and Footer areas close and the header and footer text is dimmed, as shown in Figure D-11. The header text—"Buzz" and the current date—appear at the top of every page in the document, and a page number appears at the bottom of every page.

FIGURE D-10: Header area

Header area is open

Header and Footer toolbar (yours may open in a different location)

Tab stops for the header are set for the default document margins

Document text is dimmed

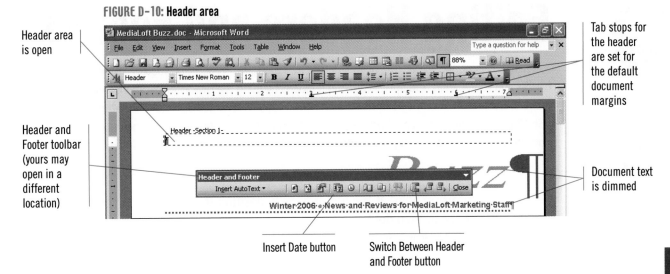

Insert Date button

Switch Between Header and Footer button

FIGURE D-11: Header and footer in document

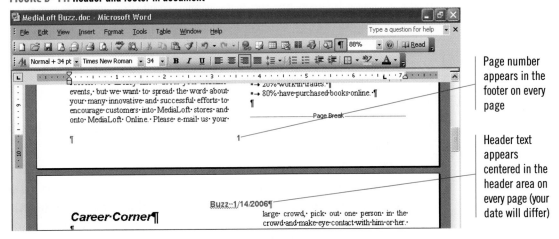

Page number appears in the footer on every page

Header text appears centered in the header area on every page (your date will differ)

Word 2003

TABLE D-3: Buttons on the Header and Footer toolbar

button	function
Insert AutoText ▾	Inserts an AutoText entry, such as a field for the filename, or the author's name
Insert Page Number	Inserts a field for the page number so that the pages are numbered automatically
Insert Number of Pages	Inserts a field for the total number of pages in the document
Format Page Number	Opens the Page Number Format dialog box; use to change the numbering format or to begin automatic page numbering with a specific number
Insert Date	Inserts a field for the current date
Insert Time	Inserts a field for the current time
Page Setup	Opens the Page Setup dialog box
Show/Hide Document Text	Hides and displays the document text
Link to Previous	Switches the link between headers and footers in adjoining sections on and off; use to make headers and footers in adjoining sections the same or different
Switch Between Header and Footer	Moves the insertion point between the Header and Footer areas
Show Previous	Moves the insertion point to the header or footer in the next section
Show Next	Moves the insertion point to the header or footer in the previous section

Editing Headers and Footers

To change header and footer text or to alter the formatting of headers and footers, you must first open the Header and Footer areas. You open headers and footers by using the Header and Footer command on the View menu or by double-clicking a header or footer in Print Layout view. ▓▓▓▓ You modify the header by adding a small circle symbol between "Buzz" and the date. You also add a border under the header text to set it off from the rest of the page. Finally, you remove the header and footer text from the first page of the document.

STEPS

1. **Place the insertion point at the top of page 2, position the pointer over the header text at the top of page 2, then double-click**
   The Header and Footer areas open.

QUICK TIP
To insert a character such as an em dash (—) or an ellipsis (...), select the character on the Special Characters tab in the Symbol dialog box, then click Insert.

2. **Place the insertion point between the two spaces after Buzz, click Insert on the menu bar, then click Symbol**
   The Symbol dialog box opens and is similar to Figure D-12. **Symbols** are special characters, such as graphics, shapes, and foreign language characters, that you can insert into a document. The symbols shown in Figure D-12 are the symbols included with the (normal text) font. You can use the Font list arrow on the Symbols tab to view the symbols included with each font on your computer.

TROUBLE
If you cannot locate the symbol, type 25CF in the Character code text box.

3. **Scroll the list of symbols if necessary to locate the black circle symbol shown in Figure D-12, select the black circle symbol, click Insert, then click Close**
   A circle symbol is added at the location of the insertion point.

4. **With the insertion point in the header text, click Format on the menu bar, then click Borders and Shading**
   The Borders and Shading dialog box opens.

5. **Click the Borders tab if it is not already selected, click Custom in the Setting section, click the dotted line in the Style scroll box (the second line style), click the Width list arrow, click 2¼ pt, click the Bottom border button in the Preview section, make sure Paragraph is selected in the Apply to list box, click OK, click Close on the Header and Footer toolbar, then scroll as needed to see the top of page 2**
   A dotted line border is added below the header text, as shown in Figure D-13.

6. **Press [Ctrl][Home] to move the insertion point to the beginning of the document**
   The newsletter already includes the name of the document at the top of the first page, making the header information redundant. You can modify headers and footers so that the header and footer text does not appear on the first page of a document or a section.

7. **Click File on the menu bar, click Page Setup, then click the Layout tab**
   The Layout tab of the Page Setup dialog box includes options for creating a different header and footer for the first page of a document or a section, and for creating different headers and footers for odd- and even-numbered pages. For example, in a document with facing pages, such as a magazine, you might want the publication title to appear in the left-page header and the publication date to appear in the right-page header.

QUICK TIP
You can enter different text in the First Page Header and First Page Footer areas when the Different first page check box is selected.

8. **Click the Different first page check box to select it, click the Apply to list arrow, click Whole document, then click OK**
   The header and footer text is removed from the Header and Footer areas on the first page.

9. **Scroll to see the header and footer on pages 2, 3, and 4, then save the document**

FIGURE D-12: Symbol dialog box

Special Characters tab

The subset changes as you scroll the list of symbols

Black circle symbol (yours might be located in a different position)

Available symbols (yours might differ)

Name of selected symbol

Character code for selected symbol

Inserts selected symbol at location of insertion point

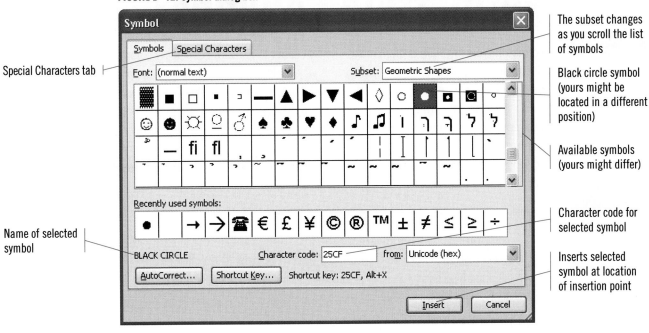

FIGURE D-13: Symbol and border added to header

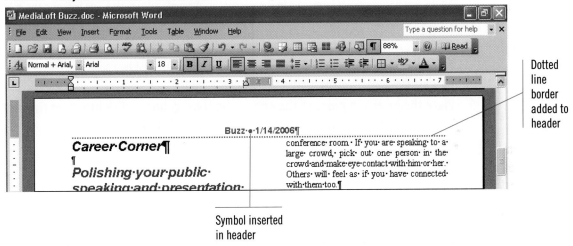

Dotted line border added to header

Symbol inserted in header

Clues to Use

Inserting and creating AutoText entries

Word includes a number of built-in AutoText entries, including salutations and closings for letters, as well as information for headers and footers. To insert a built-in AutoText entry at the location of the insertion point, point to AutoText on the Insert menu, point to a category on the AutoText menu, then click the AutoText entry you want to insert. You can also use the Insert AutoText button on the Header and Footer toolbar to insert an AutoText entry from the Header/Footer category into a header or footer.

The Word AutoText feature also allows you to store text and graphics that you use frequently so that you can easily insert them in

a document. To create a custom AutoText entry, enter the text or graphic you want to store—such as a company name or logo—in a document, select it, point to AutoText on the Insert menu, and then click New. In the Create AutoText dialog box, type a name for your AutoText entry, then click OK. The text or graphic is saved as a custom AutoText entry. To insert a custom AutoText entry in a document, point to AutoText on the Insert menu, click AutoText, select the entry name on the AutoText tab in the AutoCorrect dialog box, click Insert, then click OK.

Formatting Columns

Formatting text in columns often makes the text easier to read. You can apply column formatting to a whole document, to a section, or to selected text. The Columns button on the Standard toolbar allows you to quickly create columns of equal width. In addition, you can use the Columns command on the Format menu to create columns and to customize the width and spacing of columns. To control the way text flows between columns, you can insert a **column break**, which forces the text following the break to move to the top of the next column. You can also balance columns of unequal length on a page by inserting a continuous section break at the end of the last column on the page. You format the Staff News page in three columns, and then adjust the flow of text.

STEPS

1. **Scroll to the top of page 4, place the insertion point before Boston, click Insert on the menu bar, click Break, click the Continuous option button, then click OK**

   A continuous section break is inserted before Boston. The newsletter now contains three sections.

> **QUICK TIP**
> To change the width and spacing of existing columns, you can use the Columns dialog box or drag the column markers on the horizontal ruler.

2. **Refer to the status bar to confirm that the insertion point is in section 3, click Format on the menu bar, then click Columns**

   The Columns dialog box opens, as shown in Figure D-14.

3. **Select Three in the Presets section, click the Spacing down arrow twice until 0.3" appears, select the Line between check box, then click OK**

   All the text in section 3 is formatted in three columns of equal width with a line between the columns, as shown in Figure D-15.

> **QUICK TIP**
> To create a banner headline that spans the width of a page, select the headline text, click the Columns button, then click 1 Column.

4. **Click the Zoom list arrow on the Standard toolbar, then click Whole Page**

   Notice that the third column of text is much shorter than the first two columns. Page 4 would look better if the three columns were balanced—each the same length.

5. **Place the insertion point at the end of the third column, click Insert on the menu bar, click Break, click the Continuous option button, then click OK**

   The columns in section 3 adjust to become roughly the same length.

6. **Scroll up to page 3**

   The two columns on page 3 are also uneven. You want the information about Jack Niven to appear at the top of the second column.

> **QUICK TIP**
> If a section contains a column break, you cannot balance the columns by inserting a continuous section break.

7. **Click the Zoom list arrow, click Page Width, scroll down page 3, place the insertion point before the heading Jack Niven, click Insert on the menu bar, click Break, click the Column break option button, then click OK**

   The text following the column break is forced to the top of the next column.

8. **Click the Zoom list arrow, click Two Pages, then save the document**

   The columns on pages 3 and 4 are formatted as shown in Figure D-16.

Clues to Use

Hyphenating text in a document

Hyphenating a document is another way to control the flow of text in columns. Hyphens are small dashes that break words that fall at the end of a line. Hyphenation diminishes the gaps between words in justified text and reduces ragged right edges in left-aligned text. If a document includes narrow columns, hyphenating the text can help give the pages a cleaner look. To hyphenate a document automatically, point to Language on the Tools menu, click Hyphenation, select the Automatically hyphenate document check box in the Hyphenation dialog box, and then click OK. You can also use the Hyphenation dialog box to change the hyphenation zone—the distance between the margin and the end of the last word in the line. A smaller hyphenation zone results in a greater number of hyphenated words and a cleaner look to columns of text.

FIGURE D-14: Columns dialog box

Select a preset format for columns

Change the number of columns

Select to add a line between columns

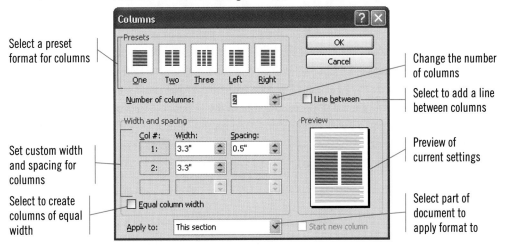

Set custom width and spacing for columns

Preview of current settings

Select to create columns of equal width

Select part of document to apply format to

FIGURE D-15: Text formatted in three columns

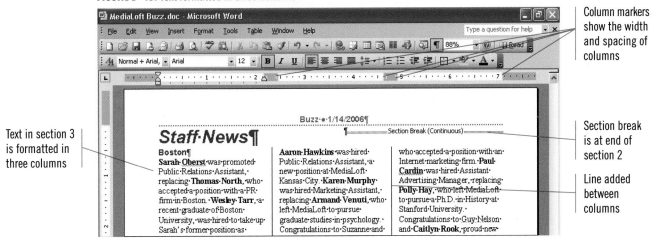

Column markers show the width and spacing of columns

Text in section 3 is formatted in three columns

Section break is at end of section 2

Line added between columns

FIGURE D-16: Columns on pages 3 and 4 of the newsletter

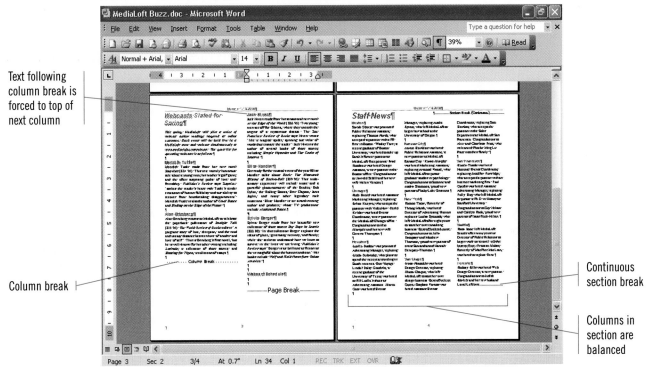

Text following column break is forced to top of next column

Column break

Continuous section break

Columns in section are balanced

Inserting a Table

Adding a table to a document is a useful way to illustrate information that is intended for quick reference and analysis. A **table** is a grid of columns and rows of cells that you can fill with text and graphics. A **cell** is the box formed by the intersection of a column and a row. The lines that divide the columns and rows of a table and help you see the grid-like structure of the table are called **borders**. A simple way to insert a table into a document is to use the Insert command on the Table menu. This command allows you to determine the dimensions and format of a table before it is inserted. ▰▰▰▰▰ You add a table showing the schedule for Webcasts to the bottom of page 3.

STEPS

1. **Click the** Zoom list arrow **on the Standard toolbar, click** Page Width, **then scroll down page 3 until the heading** Webcast Schedule **is at the top of your screen**

   The bottom of page three is displayed.

2. **Place the insertion point before the heading** Webcast Schedule, **click** Insert **on the menu bar, click** Break, **click the** Continuous option button, **then click** OK

   A continuous section break is inserted before the heading Webcast Schedule. The document now includes four sections, with the heading Webcast Schedule in the third section.

3. **Click the** Columns button ▦ **on the Standard toolbar, point to the** first column **on the grid, then click**

   Section 3 is formatted as a single column.

4. **Place the insertion point before the second paragraph mark below the heading Webcast Schedule, click** Table **on the menu bar, point to** Insert, **then click** Table

   The Insert Table dialog box opens, as shown in Figure D-17. You use this dialog box to create a blank table with a set number of columns and rows, and to choose an option for sizing the width of the columns in the table.

QUICK TIP
To apply a different table style to a table once it is created, place the insertion point in the table, click Table Auto-Format on the Table menu, and then modify the selections in the Table Auto-Format dialog box.

5. **Type** 4 **in the Number of columns text box, press** [Tab], **type** 6 **in the Number of rows text box, make sure the** Fixed column width option button **is selected, then click** AutoFormat

   The Table AutoFormat dialog box opens. You use this dialog box to apply a table style to the table. Table styles include format settings for the text, borders, and shading in a table. A preview of the selected style appears in the Preview section of the dialog box.

6. **Scroll down the list of table styles, click** Table Grid 8, **clear the** First column, Last row, **and** Last column check boxes **in the Apply special formats to section, then click** OK **twice**

   A blank table with four columns and six rows is inserted in the document at the location of the insertion point. The table is formatted in the Table Grid 8 style, with blue shading in the header row and blue borders that define the table cells. The insertion point is in the upper-left cell of the table, the first cell in the header row.

7. **Type** Date **in the first cell in the first row, press** [Tab], **type** Time, **press** [Tab], **type** Guest, **press** [Tab], **type** Store, **then press** [Tab]

   Pressing [Tab] moves the insertion point to the next cell in the row. At the end of a row, pressing [Tab] moves the insertion point to the first cell in the next row. You can also click in a cell to move the insertion point to it.

TROUBLE
If you pressed [Tab] after the last row, click the Undo button ⟲ on the Standard toolbar to remove the blank row.

8. **Type the text shown in Figure D-18 in the table cells, pressing** [Tab] **to move from cell to cell**

   You can edit the text in a table by placing the insertion point in a cell and then typing. You can also select the text in a table and then format it using the buttons on the Formatting toolbar. If you want to modify the structure of a table, you can use the Insert and Delete commands on the Table menu to add and remove rows and columns. You can also use the AutoFit command on the Table menu to change the width of table columns and the height of table rows. To select a column, row, or table before performing an action, place the insertion point in the row, column, or table you want to select, and then use the Select command on the Table menu.

9. **Save the document**

FIGURE D-17: Insert Table dialog box

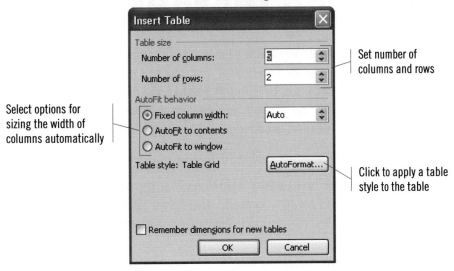

Set number of columns and rows

Select options for sizing the width of columns automatically

Click to apply a table style to the table

FIGURE D-18: Completed table

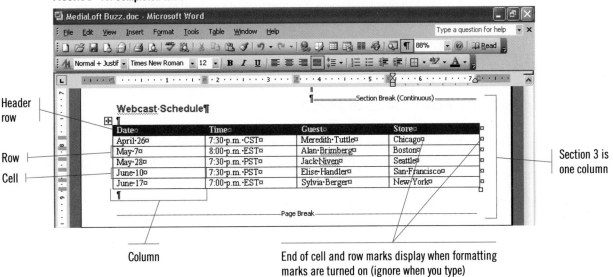

Header row

Row

Cell

Section 3 is one column

Column

End of cell and row marks display when formatting marks are turned on (ignore when you type)

Word 2003

Clues to Use

Moving around in a long document

Rather than scrolling to move to a different place in a long document, you can use the Browse by Object feature, the Go To command, or the Document Map to quickly move the insertion point to a specific location. Browse by Object allows you to browse to the next or previous page, section, line, table, graphic, or other item of the same type in a document. To do this, first click the Select Browse Object button below the vertical scroll bar to open a palette of object types. On this palette, click the button for the type of item by which you want to browse, and then click the Next or Previous buttons to scroll through the items of that type in the document.

To move a specific page, section, or other item in a document,

you can click the Go To command on the Edit menu. On the Go To tab in the Find and Replace dialog box, select the type of item in the Go to what list box, type the item number in the text box, and then click Go To to move the insertion point to the item.

If your document is formatted with heading styles, you can also use the Document Map to navigate a document. The Document Map is a separate pane in the document window that displays a list of headings in the document. You click a heading in the Document Map to move the insertion point to that heading in the document. To open and close the Document Map, click Document Map on the View menu or click the Document Map button on the Standard toolbar.

OFFICE–183

FORMATTING DOCUMENTS WORD D-17

Inserting WordArt

Illustrating a document with WordArt is a fun way to spice up the layout of a page. **WordArt** is an object that contains specially formatted, decorative text. The text in a WordArt object can be skewed, rotated, stretched, shadowed, patterned, or fit into shapes to create interesting effects. To insert a WordArt object into a document, you use the WordArt command on the Insert menu. You decide to format the Staff News headline as WordArt to add some zest to the final page of the newsletter.

STEPS

1. **Scroll down until the heading** Staff News **is at the top of your screen, select** Staff News **(not including the paragraph mark), then press** [Delete]

   The insertion point is at the top of page 4 in the third section of the document. The third section is formatted as a single column.

2. **Click** Insert **on the menu bar, point to** Picture, **then click** WordArt

   The WordArt Gallery dialog box opens, as shown in Figure D-19. You use the WordArt Gallery to select a style for the WordArt object.

3. **Click the** fourth style in the third row, **then click** OK

   The Edit WordArt Text dialog box opens. You type the text you want to format as WordArt in this dialog box. You can also use the Edit WordArt Text dialog box to change the font and font size of the WordArt text.

   > **QUICK TIP**
   > Use the Text Wrapping button on the WordArt toolbar to convert the object to a floating graphic.

4. **Type** Staff News, **then click** OK

   The WordArt object appears at the location of the insertion point. The object is an **inline graphic**, or part of the line of text in which it was inserted.

5. **Click the** WordArt object **to select it**

   The black squares that appear on the corners and sides of the object are the **sizing handles**. Sizing handles appear when a graphic object is selected. You can drag a sizing handle to change the size of the object. The WordArt toolbar also appears when a WordArt object is selected. You use the buttons on the WordArt toolbar to edit and modify the format of WordArt objects.

6. **Position the pointer over the** lower-right sizing handle, **when the pointer changes to** ↖ **drag down and to the right to make the object about 1½" tall and 5½" wide**

   Refer to the vertical and horizontal rulers for guidance as you drag the sizing handle to resize the object. When you release the mouse button, the WordArt object is enlarged, as shown in Figure D-20.

7. **Click the** Center button ▤ **on the Formatting toolbar**

   The WordArt object is centered between the margins.

8. **Click the** WordArt Shape button ▨ **on the WordArt toolbar, then click the** Wave 1 shape **(the fifth shape in the third row)**

   The shape of the WordArt text changes.

   > **TROUBLE**
   > If the newsletter is five pages instead of four, reduce the height of the WordArt object.

9. **Click outside the WordArt object to deselect it, click the** Zoom list arrow **on the Standard toolbar, click** Two Pages, **then save the document**

   The completed pages 3 and 4 are displayed, as shown in Figure D-21.

FIGURE D-19: **WordArt Gallery dialog box**

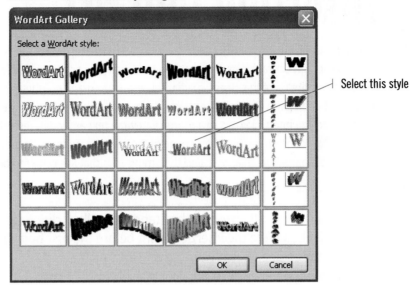

Select this style

FIGURE D-20: **Resized WordArt object**

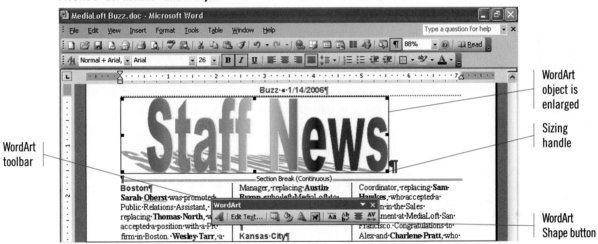

WordArt object is enlarged

Sizing handle

WordArt toolbar

WordArt Shape button

FIGURE D-21: **Completed pages 3 and 4**

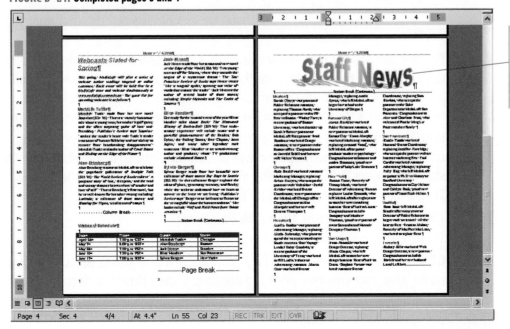

WordArt centered with the Wave 1 shape applied

Inserting Clip Art

Illustrating a document with clip art images can give it visual appeal and help to communicate your ideas. **Clip art** is a collection of graphic images that you can insert into a document. Clip art images are stored in the **Clip Organizer**, a library of the **clips**—media files, including graphics, photographs, sounds, movies, and animations—that come with Word. You can add a clip to a document using the Clip Art command on the Insert menu. Once you insert a clip art image, you can wrap text around it, resize it, and move it to a different location. ▓▓▓▓ You illustrate the second page of the newsletter with a clip art image. After you insert the image, you wrap text around it, enlarge it, and then move it so that it is centered between the two columns of text.

STEPS

1. **Click the** Zoom list arrow **on the Standard toolbar, click** Page Width, **scroll to the top of page 2, then place the insertion point before the first body paragraph, which begins** Did you know...
   You insert the clip art graphic at the location of the insertion point.

2. **Click** Insert **on the menu bar, point to** Picture, **then click** Clip Art
   The Clip Art task pane opens. You can use this task pane to search for clips related to a keyword. If you are working with an active Internet connection, your search results will include clip art from the Microsoft Office Online Web site.

TROUBLE

Make sure the All media types check box in the Results should be in list box has a check mark. Select a different clip if the clip shown in Figure D-22 is not available to you.

3. **Select the text in the Search for text box if necessary, type** communication, **then click** Go
   Clips that include the keyword "communication" appear in the Clip Art task pane, as shown in Figure D-22. When you point to a clip, a ScreenTip showing the first few keywords applied to the clip (listed alphabetically), the width and height of the clip in pixels, and the file size and file type for the clip appears.

4. **Point to the** clip **called out in Figure D-22, click the** list arrow **that appears next to the clip, click** Insert **on the menu, then close the Clip Art task pane**
   The clip is inserted at the location of the insertion point. You want to center the graphic on the page. Until you apply text wrapping to a graphic, it is part of the line of text in which it was inserted (an **inline graphic**). To move a graphic independently of text, you must wrap the text around it to make it a **floating graphic**, which can be moved anywhere on a page.

5. **Double-click the** clip art image, **click the** Layout tab **in the Format Picture dialog box, click** Tight, **then click** OK
   The text in the first body paragraph wraps around the irregular shape of the clip art image. The white circles that appear on the square edges of the graphic are the sizing handles. The white sizing handles indicate the graphic is a floating graphic.

QUICK TIP

To verify the size of a graphic or to set precise measurements, double-click the graphic to open the Format Picture dialog box, then adjust the Height and Width settings on the Size tab.

6. **Position the pointer over the** lower-right sizing handle, **when the pointer changes to** ↖ **drag down and to the right until the graphic is about 2½" wide and 2½" tall**
   As you drag a sizing handle, the dotted lines show the outline of the graphic. Refer to the dotted lines and the rulers as you resize the graphic. When you release the mouse button, the image is enlarged.

7. **With the graphic still selected, position the pointer over the graphic, when the pointer changes to** ⊹ **drag the graphic down and to the right so it is centered on the page as shown in Figure D-23, release the mouse button, then deselect the graphic**
   The graphic is now centered between the two columns of text.

TROUBLE

If page 3 is a blank page or contains text continued from page 2, reduce the size of the graphic on page 2.

8. **Click the** Zoom list arrow, **then click** Two Pages
   The completed pages 1 and 2 are displayed, as shown in Figure D-24.

9. **Click the** Zoom list arrow, **click** Page Width, **press** [Ctrl][End], **press** [Enter] **twice, type your name, save your changes, print the document, then close the document and exit Word**

FIGURE D-22: Clip Art task pane

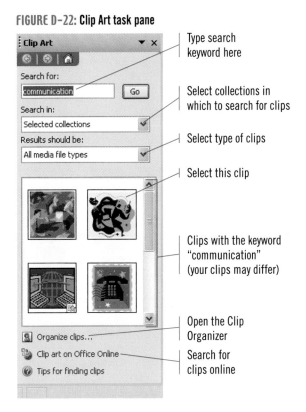

Type search keyword here

Select collections in which to search for clips

Select type of clips

Select this clip

Clips with the keyword "communication" (your clips may differ)

Open the Clip Organizer

Search for clips online

FIGURE D-23: Graphic being moved to a new location

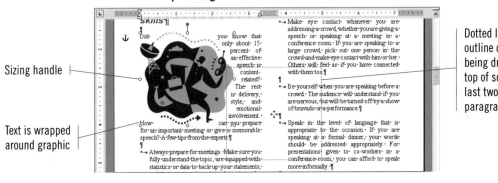

Sizing handle

Text is wrapped around graphic

Dotted line shows square outline of graphic as it is being dragged; position top of square between the last two lines of the first paragraph in column 2

FIGURE D-24: Completed pages 1 and 2 of newsletter

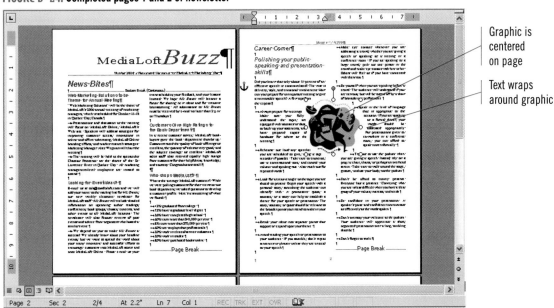

Graphic is centered on page

Text wraps around graphic

Practice

▼ CONCEPTS REVIEW

Label each element shown in Figure D-25.

FIGURE D-25

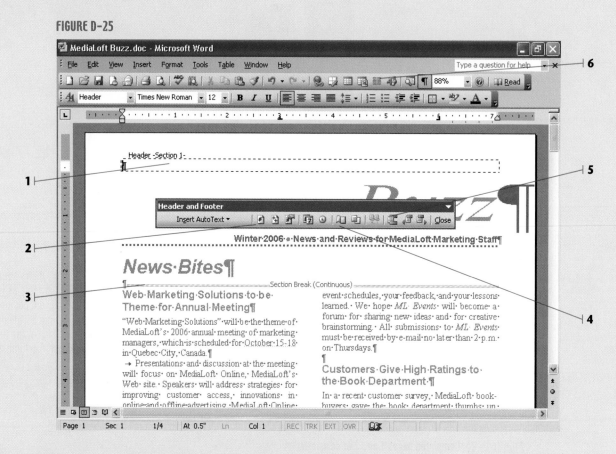

Match each term with the statement that best describes it.

7. **Section break**

8. **Header**

9. **Footer**

10. **Field**

11. **Manual page break**

12. **Margin**

13. **Inline graphic**

14. **Floating graphic**

a. A placeholder for information that changes

b. A formatting mark that divides a document into parts that can be formatted differently

c. The blank area between the edge of the text and the edge of the page

d. A formatting mark that forces the text following the mark to begin at the top of the next page

e. An image that is inserted as part of a line of text

f. An image to which text wrapping has been applied

g. Text or graphics that appear at the bottom of every page in a document

h. Text or graphics that appear at the top of every page in a document

Select the best answer from the list of choices.

15. Which of the following do documents with mirror margins always have?

a. Inside and outside margins

b. Different first page headers and footers

c. Gutters

d. Landscape orientation

16. Which button is used to insert a field into a header or footer?

a. [icon]   **c.** [icon]

b. [icon]   **d.** [icon]

17. Which type of break do you insert if you want to force text to begin on the next page?

a. Text wrapping break   **c.** Automatic page break

b. Manual page break   **d.** Continuous section break

18. Which type of break do you insert if you want to balance the columns in a section?

a. Text wrapping break   **c.** Continuous section break

b. Column break   **d.** Automatic page break

19. What must you do to change an inline graphic to a floating graphic?

a. Move the graphic   **c.** Anchor the graphic

b. Resize the graphic   **d.** Apply text wrapping to the graphic

20. Pressing [Ctrl][Enter] does which of the following?

a. Inserts a manual page break

b. Moves the insertion point to the beginning of the document

c. Inserts a continuous section break

d. Inserts an automatic page break

▼ SKILLS REVIEW

1. Set document margins.

a. Start Word, open the file WD D-2.doc from the drive and folder where your Data Files are located, then save it as **Happy Valley Fitness**.

b. Change the top and bottom margins to 1.2" and the left and right margins to 1".

c. Save your changes to the document.

2. Divide a document into sections.

a. Hide the white space in the document by moving the pointer to the top of a page, then clicking the Hide White Space pointer that appears.

b. Scroll down, then insert a continuous section break before the **Facilities** heading.

c. Format the text in section 2 in two columns, then save your changes to the document.

3. Insert page breaks.

a. Insert a manual page break before the heading **Welcome to the Happy Valley Fitness Center!**.

b. Scroll down and insert a manual page break before the heading **Services**.

c. Scroll down and insert a manual page break before the heading **Membership**.

d. Show the white space in the document by moving the pointer over the thick black line that separates the pages, then clicking the Show White Space pointer that appears.

e. Press [Ctrl][Home], then save your changes to the document.

4. Insert page numbers.

a. Insert page numbers in the document. Center the page numbers at the bottom of the page.

b. View the page numbers on each page in Print Preview, close Print Preview, then save your changes to the document.

5. Add headers and footers.

   a. Change the view to Page Width, then open the Header and Footer areas.

   b. Type your name in the Header area, press [Tab] twice, then use the Insert Date button on the Header and Footer toolbar to insert the current date.

   c. On the horizontal ruler, drag the right tab stop from the 6" mark to the 6½" mark so that the date aligns with the right margin of the document.

   d. Move the insertion point to the Footer area.

   e. Double-click the page number to select it, then format the page number in bold italic.

   f. Close headers and footers, preview the header and footer on each page in Print Preview, close Print Preview, then save your changes to the document.

6. Edit headers and footers.

   a. Open headers and footers, then apply italic to the text in the header.

   b. Move the insertion point to the Footer area, double-click the page number to select it, then press [Delete].

   c. Click the Align Right button on the Formatting toolbar.

   d. Use the Symbol command on the Insert menu to open the Symbol dialog box.

   e. Insert a black right-pointing triangle symbol (character code: 25BA), then close the Symbol dialog box.

   f. Use the Insert Page Number button on the Header and Footer toolbar to insert a page number.

   g. Use the Page Setup button on the Header and Footer toolbar to open the Page Setup dialog box.

   h. Use the Layout tab to create a different header and footer for the first page of the document.

   i. Scroll to the beginning of the document, type your name in the First Page Header area, then apply italic to your name.

   j. Close headers and footers, preview the header and footer on each page in Print Preview, close Print Preview, then save your changes to the document.

7. Format columns.

   a. On page 2, select **Facilities** and the paragraph mark below it, use the Columns button to format the selected text as one column, then center **Facilities** on the page.

   b. Balance the columns on page 2 by inserting a continuous section break at the bottom of the second column.

   c. On page 3, select **Services** and the paragraph mark below it, format the selected text as one column, then center the text.

   d. Balance the columns on page 3.

   e. On page 4, select **Membership** and the paragraph mark below it, format the selected text as one column, then center the text.

   f. Insert a column break before the **Membership Cards** heading, press [Ctrl][Home], then save your changes to the document.

8. Insert a table.

   a. Click the Document Map button on the Standard toolbar to open the Document Map.

   b. In the Document Map, click the heading Membership Rates, then close the Document Map. (*Hint*: The Document Map button is a toggle button.)

   c. Select the word Table at the end of the Membership Rates section, press [Delete], then open the Insert Table dialog box.

   d. Create a table with two columns and five rows, open the AutoFormat dialog box, and then apply the Table Classic 3 style to the table, clearing the Last row check box. Close the dialog box.

   e. Press [Tab] to leave the first cell in the header row blank, then type **Rate**.

   f. Press [Tab], then type the following text in the table, pressing [Tab] to move from cell to cell.

Enrollment/Individual	$100
Enrollment/Couple	$150
Monthly membership/Individual	$35
Monthly membership/Couple	$60

g. With the insertion point in the table, right-click the table, point to AutoFit on the shortcut menu, then click AutoFit to Contents.

h. With the insertion point in the table, right-click again, point to AutoFit, then click AutoFit to Window.

i. Save your changes to the document.

9. Insert WordArt.

a. Scroll to page 3, place the insertion point before the **Personal Training** heading, then insert a WordArt object.

b. Select any horizontal WordArt style, type **Get Fit!**, then click OK.

c. Click the WordArt object to select it, click the Text Wrapping button on the WordArt toolbar, then apply the Tight text-wrapping style to the object so that it is a floating object.

d. Move the object so that it is centered below the text at the bottom of the page (below the page break mark).

e. Adjust the size and position of the object so that the page looks attractive. (*Hint*: The sizing handles on floating objects are white circles.)

f. Apply a different WordArt shape to the object, preview the page, adjust the size and position if necessary, then save your changes to the document.

10. Insert clip art.

a. On page 1, place the insertion point in the second blank paragraph below **A Rehabilitation and Exercise Facility**. (*Hint*: Place the insertion point to the left of the paragraph mark.)

b. Open the Clip Art task pane. Search for clips related to the keyword **fitness**.

c. Insert the clip shown in Figure D-26. (*Note*: An active Internet connection is needed to select the clip shown in the figure. Select a different clip if this one is not available to you. If you are working offline, you might need to search using a keyword such as sports.)

d. Select the graphic, then drag the lower-right sizing handle down and to the right so that the graphic is about 2.5" wide and 3" tall. Size the graphic so that all the text and the manual page break fit on page 1. (*Hint*: The sizing handles on inline graphics are black squares.)

e. Save your changes to the document. Preview the document, print a copy, then close the document and exit Word.

FIGURE D-26

The Happy Valley Fitness Center

A Rehabilitation and Exercise Facility

Member Services

▼ INDEPENDENT CHALLENGE 1

You are the owner of a small business in Latona, Ontario, called Small World Catering. You have begun work on the text for a brochure advertising your business and are now ready to lay out the pages and prepare the final copy. The brochure will be printed on both sides of an 8½" × 11" sheet of paper, and folded in thirds.

a. Start Word, open the file WD D-3.doc from the drive and folder where your Data Files are located, then save it as **Small World**. Read the document to get a feel for its contents.

b. Change the page orientation to landscape, and change all four margins to .6".

c. Format the document in three columns of equal width.

d. Insert a manual page break before the heading **Catering Services**.

e. On page 1, insert column breaks before the headings **Sample Indian Banquet Menu** and **Sample Tuscan Banquet Menu**.

f. On page 1, insert a continuous section break at the end of the third column to create separate sections on pages one and two.

g. Add lines between the columns on the first page, then center the text in the columns.

h. Create a different header and footer for the first page. Type **Call for custom menus designed to your taste and budget** in the First Page Footer area.

i. Center the text in the footer area, format it in 20-point Comic Sans MS, all caps, with a violet font color, then close headers and footers.

j. On page 2, insert a column break before Your Name. Press [Enter] as many times as necessary to move the contact information to the bottom of the second column. Be sure all five lines of the contact information are in column 2 and do not flow to the next column.

k. Replace Your Name with your name, then center the contact information in the column.

l. Insert a column break at the bottom of the second column. Then, type the text shown in Figure D-27 in the third column. Refer to the figure as you follow the instructions for formatting the text in the third column.

m. Use the Font dialog box to format Small World Catering in 32-point Comic Sans MS, bold, with a violet font color.

n. Format the remaining text in 12-point Comic Sans MS, with a violet font color. Center the text in the third column.

o. Insert the clip art graphic shown in Figure D-27 or another appropriate clip art graphic. Do not wrap text around the graphic.

p. Resize the graphic and add and remove blank paragraphs in the third column of your brochure so that the spacing between elements roughly matches the spacing shown in Figure D-27.

Advanced Challenge Exercise

- Format Small World as a WordArt object using a WordArt style and shape of your choice.
- Format Catering as a WordArt object using a WordArt style and shape of your choice.
- Adjust the size, position, and spacing of the WordArt objects, clip art graphic, and text in the third column so that the brochure is attractive and eye-catching.

q. Save your changes, preview the brochure in Print Preview, then print a copy. If possible, print the two pages of the brochure back to back so that the brochure can be folded in thirds.

r. Close the document and exit Word.

FIGURE D-27

Small World

Catering

Complete catering services available for all types of events. Menus and estimates provided upon request.

▼ INDEPENDENT CHALLENGE 2

You work in the Campus Safety Department at Hudson State College. You have written the text for an informational flyer about parking regulations on campus and now you need to format the flyer so it is attractive and readable.

a. Start Word, open the file WD D-4.doc from the drive and folder where your Data Files are located, then save it as **Hudson Parking FAQ**. Read the document to get a feel for its contents.

b. Change all four margins to .7".

c. Insert a continuous section break before **1. May I bring a car to school?** (*Hint*: Place the insertion point before May.)

d. Scroll down and insert a next page section break before **Sample Parking Permit**.

e. Format the section 2 text in three columns of equal width with .3" of space between the columns.

f. Hyphenate the document using the automatic hyphenation feature. (*Hint*: If the Hyphenation feature is not installed on your computer, skip this step.)

g. Add a 3-point dotted-line bottom border to the blank paragraph under Hudson State College. (*Hint*: Place the insertion point before the paragraph mark under Hudson State College, then apply a bottom border to the paragraph.)

h. Add your name to the header. Right-align your name and format it in 10-point Arial.

i. Add the following text to the footer, inserting symbols between words as indicated: **Parking and Shuttle Service Office • 54 Buckley Street • Hudson State College • 942-555-2227.**

j. Format the footer text in 9-point Arial Black and center it in the footer. Use a different font if Arial Black is not available to you. If necessary, adjust the font and font size so that the entire address fits on one line.

k. Apply a 3-point dotted-line border above the footer text. Make sure to apply the border to the paragraph.

l. Balance the columns in section 2.

m. Add the clip art graphic shown in Figure D-28 or another appropriate clip art graphic to the upper-right corner of the document, above the border. Make sure the graphic does not obscure the border. (*Hint*: Apply text wrapping to the graphic before positioning it.)

FIGURE D-28

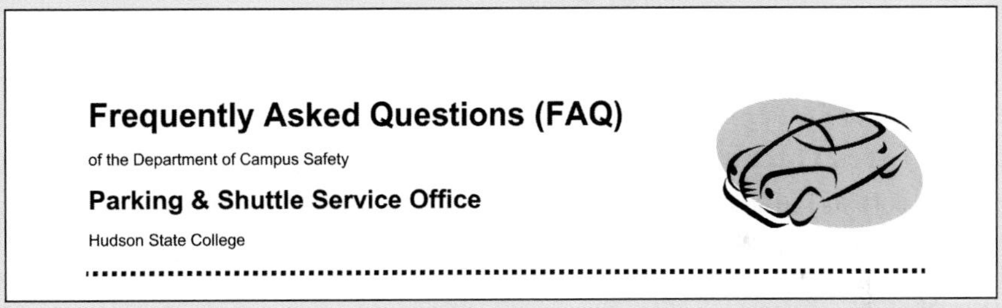

> **Frequently Asked Questions (FAQ)**
> of the Department of Campus Safety
> **Parking & Shuttle Service Office**
> Hudson State College

n. Place the insertion point on page 2 (which is section 4). Change the left and right margins in section 4 to 1". Also change the page orientation of section 4 to landscape.

o. Change the vertical alignment of section 4 to Center.

p. Save your changes, preview the flyer in Print Preview, then print a copy. If possible, print the two pages of the flyer back to back.

q. Close the document and exit Word.

FORMATTING DOCUMENTS WORD D-27

▼ INDEPENDENT CHALLENGE 3

A book publisher would like to publish an article you wrote on stormwater pollution in Australia as a chapter in a forthcoming book called *Environmental Issues for the New Millennium*. The publisher has requested that you format your article like a book chapter before submitting it for publication, and has provided you with a style sheet.

a. Start Word, open the file WD D-5.doc from the drive and folder where your Data Files are located, then save it as **Stormwater**.

b. Change the font of the entire document to 11-point Book Antiqua. If this font is not available to you, select a different font suitable for the pages of a book. Change the alignment to justified.

c. Change the paper size to 6" × 9".

d. Create mirror margins. (*Hint*: Use the Multiple Pages list arrow.) Change the top and bottom margins to .8", change the inside margin to .4", change the outside margin to .6", and create a .3" gutter to allow room for the book's binding.

e. Change the Zoom level to Two Pages, then apply the setting to create different headers and footers for odd- and even-numbered pages.

f. Change the Zoom level to Page Width. In the odd-page header, type **Chapter 5**, insert a symbol of your choice, then type **Stormwater Pollution in the Fairy Creek Catchment**.

g. Format the header text in 9-point Book Antiqua italic, then right-align the text.

h. In the even-page header, type your name, insert a symbol of your choice, then insert the current date. (*Hint*: Scroll down or use the Show Next button to move the insertion point to the even-page header.)

i. Change the format of the date to include just the month and the year. (*Hint*: Right-click the date field, then click Edit Field.)

j. Format the header text in 9-point Book Antiqua italic. The even-page header should be left-aligned.

k. Insert page numbers that are centered in the footer. Format the page number in 10-point Book Antiqua. Make sure to insert a page number field in both the odd- and even-page footer areas.

l. Format the page numbers so that the first page of your chapter, which is Chapter 5 in the book, begins on page 53. (*Hint*: Select a page number field, then use the Format Page Number button.)

m. Go to the beginning of the document, press [Enter] 10 times, type **Chapter 5: Stormwater Pollution in the Fairy Creek Catchment**, press [Enter] twice, type your name, then press [Enter] twice.

n. Format the chapter title in 16-point Book Antiqua bold, format your name in 14-point Book Antiqua using small caps, then left-align the title text and your name.

Advanced Challenge Exercise

- Use the Browse by Object feature to move the insertion point to page 4 in the document, scroll down, place the insertion point at the end of the paragraph above the Potential health effects... heading, press [Enter] twice, type **Table 1: Total annual pollutant loads per year in the Fairy Creek Catchment**, format the text as bold, then press [Enter] twice.

- Insert a table with four columns and four rows that is formatted in the Table Professional style.

- Type the text shown in Figure D-29 in the table. Do not be concerned when the text wraps to the next line in a cell.

- Format the text as bold in the header row, then remove the bold formatting from the text in the remaining rows.

- Place the insertion point in the table, point to AutoFit on the Table menu, click Distribute Rows Evenly, point to AutoFit on the Table menu a second time, then click AutoFit to Contents.

o. Save your changes, preview the chapter in Print Preview, print the first four pages of the chapter, then close the document and exit Word.

FIGURE D-29

Area	Nitrogen	Phosphorus	Suspended solids
Fairy Creek	9.3 tonnes	1.2 tonnes	756.4 tonnes
Durras Arm	6.2 tonnes	.9 tonnes	348.2 tonnes
Cabbage Tree Creek	9.8 tonnes	2.3 tonnes	485.7 tonnes

▼ INDEPENDENT CHALLENGE 4

One of the most common opportunities to use the page layout features of Word is when formatting a research paper. The format recommended by the *MLA Handbook for Writers of Research Papers*, a style guide that includes information on preparing, writing, and formatting research papers, is the standard format used by many schools, colleges, and universities. In this independent challenge, you will research the MLA (Modern Language Association) guidelines for formatting a research paper and use the guidelines you find to prepare a sample first page of a research report.

a. Start Word, open the file WD D-6.doc from the drive and folder where your Data Files are located, then save it as **MLA Style**. This document contains the questions you will answer about MLA style guidelines.

b. Use your favorite search engine to search the Web for information on the MLA guidelines for formatting a research report. Use the keywords **MLA Style** and **research paper format** to conduct your search.

c. Look for information on the proper formatting for the following aspects of a research paper: paper size, margins, title page or first page of the report, line spacing, paragraph indentation, page numbers, and works cited.

d. Type your answers to the questions in the MLA Style document, save it, print a copy, then close the document.

e. Using the information you learned, start a new document and create a sample first page of a research report. Use **MLA Format for Research Papers** as the title for your sample report, and make up information about the course and instructor, if necessary. For the body of the report, type several sentences about MLA style. Make sure to format the page exactly as the MLA style dictates.

f. Save the document as **MLA Sample Format** to the drive and folder where your Data Files are located, print a copy, close the document, then exit Word.

▼ VISUAL WORKSHOP

Use the file WD D-7.doc, found on the drive and folder where your Data Files are located, to create the article shown in Figure D-30. (*Hint*: Change all four margins to .6". To locate the flower clip art image, search using the keyword **flower**, and be sure only the Photographs check box in the Results should be in list box in the Clip Art task pane has a check mark. Select a different clip if the clip shown in the figure is not available to you.) Save the document with the filename **Gardener's Corner**, then print a copy.

FIGURE D-30

GARDENER'S CORNER

Putting a Perennial Garden to Bed

By Your Name

A certain sense of peace descends when a perennial garden is put to bed for the season. The plants are safely tucked in against the elements, and the garden is ready to welcome the first signs of life. When the work is done, you can sit back and anticipate the bright blooms of spring. Many gardeners are uncertain of how to close a perennial garden. This week's column demystifies the process.

Clean up

Garden clean up can be a gradual process—plants will deteriorate at different rates, allowing you to do a little bit each week.

1. Edge beds and borders and remove stakes and other plant supports.
2. Dig and divide irises, daylilies, and other early bloomers.
3. Cut back plants when foliage starts to deteriorate.
4. Rake all debris out of the garden and pull any weeds that remain.

Plant perennials

Fall is the perfect time to plant perennials! The warm, sunny days and cool nights provide optimal conditions for new root growth.

1. Dig deeply and enhance soil with organic matter.
2. Use a good starter fertilizer to speed up new root growth.
3. Untangle the roots of new plants before planting them.
4. Water deeply after planting as the weather dictates.

Add compost

Organic matter is the key ingredient to healthy soil. If you take care of the soil, your plants will become strong and disease resistant.

1. Use an iron rake to loosen the top few inches of soil.
2. Spread a one to two inch layer of compost over the entire garden.
3. Refrain from stepping on the area and compacting the soil.

To mulch or not to mulch?

Winter protection for perennial beds can only help plants survive the winter. Here's what works and what doesn't:

1. Always apply mulch after the ground is frozen.
2. Never apply generic hay because is contains billions of weed seeds. Also, whole leaves and bark mulch hold too much moisture.
3. Straw and salt marsh hay are excellent choices for mulch.

For copies of earlier Gardener's Corner columns, call 1-800-555-3827.

Creating and Formatting Tables

OBJECTIVES

Insert a table

Insert and delete rows and columns

Modify table rows and columns

Sort table data

Split and merge cells

Perform calculations in tables

Use Table AutoFormat

Create a custom format for a table

If you have a SAM user profile, you may have access to hands-on instruction, practice, and assessment of the skills covered in this unit. Log in to your SAM account and go to your assignments page to see what your instructor has assigned.

Tables are commonly used to display information for quick reference and analysis. In this unit, you learn how to create and modify a table in Word, how to sort table data and perform calculations, and how to format a table with borders and shading. You also learn how to use a table to structure the layout of a page. You are preparing a summary budget for an advertising campaign aimed at the Boston market. The goal of the ad campaign is to promote MediaLoft Online, the MediaLoft Web site. You decide to format the budget information as a table so that it is easy to read and analyze.

Inserting a Table

A **table** is a grid made up of rows and columns of cells that you can fill with text and graphics. A **cell** is the box formed by the intersection of a column and a row. The lines that divide the columns and rows and help you see the grid-like structure of a table are called **borders**. You can create a table in a document by using the Insert Table button on the Standard toolbar or the Insert command on the Table menu. Once you have created a table, you can add text and graphics to it. ▰▰▰ You begin by inserting a blank table into the document and then adding text to it.

STEPS

1. **Start Word, close the** Getting Started task pane, **click the** Print Layout View button 🔲 **on the horizontal scroll bar if it is not already selected, click the** Zoom list arrow **on the Standard toolbar, then click** Page Width

   A blank document appears in Print Layout view.

2. **Click the** Insert Table button 🔡 **on the Standard toolbar**

   A grid opens below the button. You move the pointer across this grid to select the number of columns and rows you want the table to contain. If you want to create a table with more than five columns or more than four rows, then expand the grid by dragging the lower-right corner.

3. **Point to the** second box **in the fourth row to select 4x2 Table, then click**

   A table with two columns and four rows is inserted in the document, as shown in Figure E-1. Black borders surround the table cells. The insertion point is in the first cell in the first row.

4. **Type** Location, **then press** [Tab]

   Pressing [Tab] moves the insertion point to the next cell in the row.

5. **Type** Cost, **press** [Tab], **then type** Boston Sunday Globe

   Pressing [Tab] at the end of a row moves the insertion point to the first cell in the next row.

6. **Press** [Tab], **type** 27,600, **press** [Tab], **then type the following text in the table, pressing [Tab] to move from cell to cell**

   | Boston.com | 25,000 |
   | Taxi tops | 18,000 |

7. **Press** [Tab]

   Pressing [Tab] at the end of the last cell of a table creates a new row at the bottom of the table, as shown in Figure E-2. The insertion point is located in the first cell in the new row.

> **TROUBLE**
> If you pressed [Tab] after the last row, click the Undo button 🔄 on the Standard toolbar to remove the new blank row.

8. **Type the following, pressing [Tab] to move from cell to cell and to create new rows**

Boston Herald	18,760
Townonline.com	3,250
Bus stops	12,000
Boston Magazine	12,400

9. **Click the** Save button 🖫 **on the Standard toolbar, then save the document with the filename** Boston Ad Budget **to the drive and folder where your Data Files are located**

   The table is shown in Figure E-3.

FIGURE E-1: Blank table

Column

Table move handle

Insertion point

Row

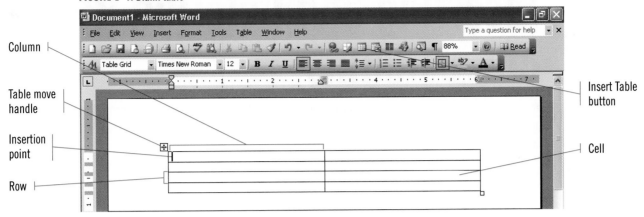

Insert Table button

Cell

FIGURE E-2: New row in table

New row

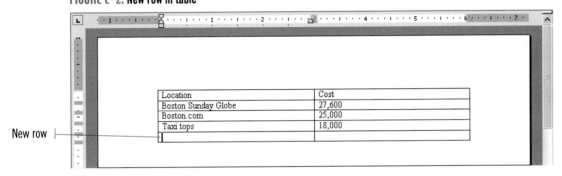

Location	Cost
Boston Sunday Globe	27,600
Boston.com	25,000
Taxi tops	18,000

FIGURE E-3: Text in the table

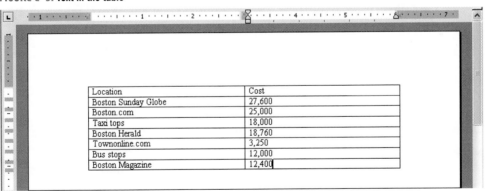

Location	Cost
Boston Sunday Globe	27,600
Boston.com	25,000
Taxi tops	18,000
Boston Herald	18,760
Townonline.com	3,250
Bus stops	12,000
Boston Magazine	12,400

Word 2003

Clues to Use

Converting text to a table and a table to text

Another way to create a table is to convert text that is separated by a tab, a comma, or another separator character into a table. For example, if you want to create a two-column table of last and first names, you could type the names as a list with a comma separating the last and first name in each line, and then convert the text to a table. The separator character—a comma in this example—indicates where you want to divide the table into columns, and a paragraph mark indicates where you want to begin a new row. To convert tabbed or comma-delimited text to a table, select the text, point to

Convert on the Table menu, and then click Text to Table. In the Text to Table dialog box, select from the options for structuring and formatting the table, and then click OK to create the table. You can also select the text and then click the Insert Table button on the Standard toolbar to convert the text to a table.

Conversely, you can convert a table to text that is separated by tabs, commas, or some other character by selecting the table, pointing to Convert on the Table menu, and then clicking Table to Text.

Inserting and Deleting Rows and Columns

You can easily modify the structure of a table by adding and removing rows and columns. First, you must select an existing row or column in the table to indicate where you want to insert or delete information. You can select any element of a table using the Select command on the Table menu, but it is often easier to select rows and columns using the mouse: click in the margin to the left of a row to select the row; click the top border of a column to select the column. Alternatively, you can drag across a row or down a column to select it. To insert rows and columns, use the Insert command on the Table menu or the Insert Rows and Insert Columns buttons on the Standard toolbar. To delete rows and columns, use the Delete command on the Table menu. ▰▰▰ You add a new row to the table and delete an unnecessary row. You also add new columns to the table to provide more detailed information.

STEPS

1. **Click the** Show/Hide ¶ button ¶ **on the Standard toolbar to display formatting marks**
   An end of cell mark appears at the end of each cell and an end of row mark appears at the end of each row.

QUICK TIP
To insert more than one row or column, select the number of rows or columns you want to insert, then click the Insert Rows or Insert Columns button.

2. **Place the pointer in the margin to the left of the** Townonline.com row **until the pointer changes to** ⬧, **then click**
   The entire row is selected, including the end of row mark. If the end of row mark is not selected, you have selected only the text in a row, not the row itself. When a row is selected, the Insert Table button changes to the Insert Rows button.

3. **Click the** Insert Rows button ▤ **on the Standard toolbar**
   A new row is inserted above the Townonline.com row, as shown in Figure E-4.

4. **Click the** first cell **of the new row, type** Boston Phoenix, **press [Tab], then type** 15,300
   Clicking in a cell moves the insertion point to that cell.

QUICK TIP
You can also delete a row or column by using the Delete command on the Table menu or by pressing [Ctrl][X] or [Shift][Delete].

5. **Select the** Boston Herald row, **right-click the selected row, then click** Delete Rows **on the shortcut menu**
   The selected row is deleted. If you select a row and press [Delete], you delete only the contents of the row, not the row itself.

6. **Place the pointer over the top border of the** Location column **until the pointer changes to** ↓, **then click**
   The entire column is selected. When a column is selected, the Insert Table button changes to the Insert Columns button.

QUICK TIP
To select a cell, place the ⬛ pointer over the left border of the cell, then click.

7. **Click the** Insert Columns button ▦ **on the Standard toolbar, then type** Type
   A new column is inserted to the left of the Location column, as shown in Figure E-5.

8. **Click in the** Location column, **click** Table **on the menu bar, point to** Insert, **click** Columns to the Right, **then type** Details **in the first cell of the new column**
   A new column is added to the right of the Location column. You can also use the Insert command to add columns to the left of the active column or to insert rows above or below the active row.

9. **Press [↓] to move the insertion point to the next cell in the Details column, enter the text shown in Figure E-6 in each cell in the Details and Type columns, click** ¶ **to turn off the display of formatting marks, then save your changes**
   You can use the arrow keys to move the insertion point from cell to cell. Notice that text wraps to the next line in the cell as you type. Compare your table to Figure E-6.

FIGURE E-4: Inserted row

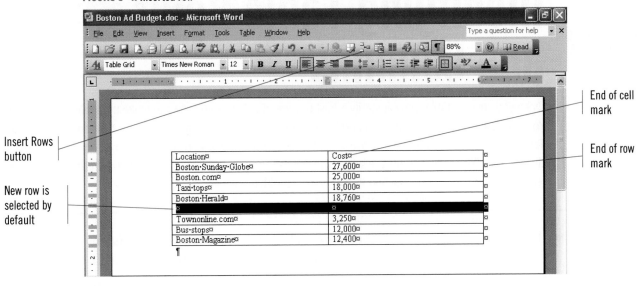

Insert Rows button

New row is selected by default

End of cell mark

End of row mark

FIGURE E-5: Inserted column

New column

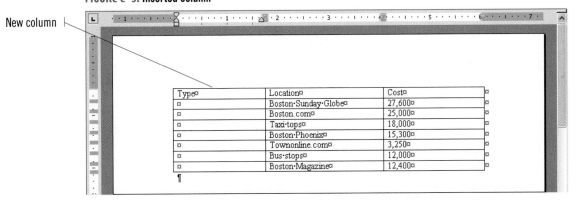

FIGURE E-6: Text in Type and Details columns

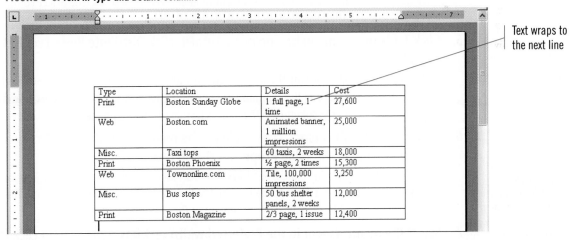

Text wraps to the next line

Clues to Use

Copying and moving rows and columns

You can copy and move rows and columns within a table in the same manner you copy and move text. Select the row or column you want to move, then use the Copy or Cut button to place the selection on the Clipboard. Place the insertion point in the location you want to insert the row or column, then click the Paste button to paste the selection. Rows are inserted above the row containing the insertion point; columns are inserted to the left of the column containing the insertion point. You can also copy or move columns and rows by selecting them and using the ⬚ pointer to drag them to a new location in the table.

Modifying Table Rows and Columns

Once you create a table, you can easily adjust the size of columns and rows to make the table easier to read. You can change the size of columns and rows by dragging a border, by using the AutoFit command on the Table menu, or by setting exact measurements for column width and row height using the Table Properties dialog box. ▓▓▓▓▓ You adjust the size of the columns and rows to make the table more attractive and easier to read. You also center the text vertically in each table cell.

STEPS

QUICK TIP

Press [Alt] as you drag a border to display the column width or row height measurements on the ruler.

1. **Position the pointer over the border between the first and second columns until the pointer changes to ✛‖✛, then drag the border to approximately the ½" mark on the horizontal ruler**

   The dotted line that appears as you drag represents the border. Dragging the column border changes the width of the first and second columns: the first column is narrower and the second column is wider. When dragging a border to change the width of an entire column, make sure no cells are selected in the column. You can also drag a row border to change the height of the row above it.

2. **Position the pointer over the right border of the Location column until the pointer changes to ✛‖✛, then double-click**

   Double-clicking a column border automatically resizes the column to fit the text.

3. **Double-click the right border of the Details column with the ✛‖✛ pointer, then double-click the right border of the Cost column with the ✛‖✛ pointer**

   The widths of the Details and Cost columns are adjusted.

4. **Move the pointer over the table, then click the table move handle ⊞ that appears outside the upper-left corner of the table**

   Clicking the table move handle selects the entire table. You can also use the Select command on the Table menu to select an entire table.

QUICK TIP

Quickly resize a table by dragging the table resize handle to a new location.

5. **Click Table on the menu bar, point to AutoFit, click Distribute Rows Evenly, then deselect the table**

   All the rows in the table become the same height, as shown in Figure E-7. You can also use the commands on the AutoFit menu to make all the columns the same width, to make the width of the columns fit the text, and to adjust the width of the columns so the table is justified between the margins.

QUICK TIP

To change the margins in all the cells in a table, click Options on the Table tab, then enter new margin settings in the Table Options dialog box.

6. **Click in the Details column, click Table on the menu bar, click Table Properties, then click the Column tab in the Table Properties dialog box**

   The Column tab, shown in Figure E-8, allows you to set an exact width for columns. You can specify an exact height for rows and an exact size for cells using the Row and Cell tabs. You can also use the Table tab to set a precise size for the table, to change the alignment of the table on a page, and to wrap text around a table.

7. **Select the measurement in the Preferred width text box, type 3, then click OK**

   The width of the Details column changes to 3".

QUICK TIP

Quickly center a table on a page by selecting the table and clicking the Center button ≡ on the Formatting toolbar.

8. **Click ⊞ to select the table, click Table on the menu bar, click Table Properties, click the Cell tab, click the Center box in the Vertical alignment section, click OK, deselect the table, then save your changes**

   The text is centered vertically in each table cell, as shown in Figure E-9.

FIGURE E-7: **Resized columns and rows**

Table move handle: click to select the table; drag to move the table

Rows are all the same height

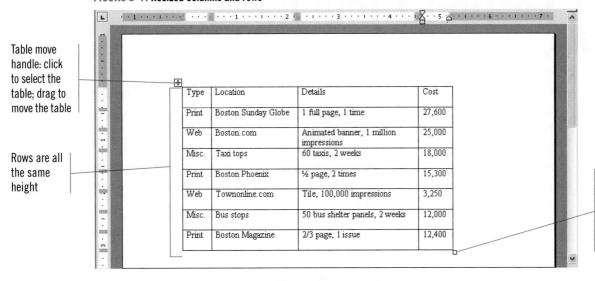

Table resize handle; drag to change the size of all the rows and columns

FIGURE E-8: **Table Properties dialog box**

Width of active column (yours might differ)

Click to change the width of the previous column

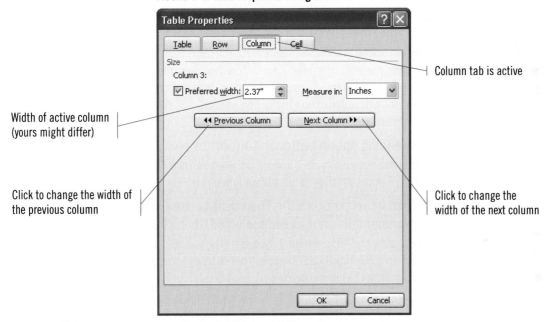

Column tab is active

Click to change the width of the next column

FIGURE E-9: **Text centered vertically in cells**

Text is centered vertically in the cell

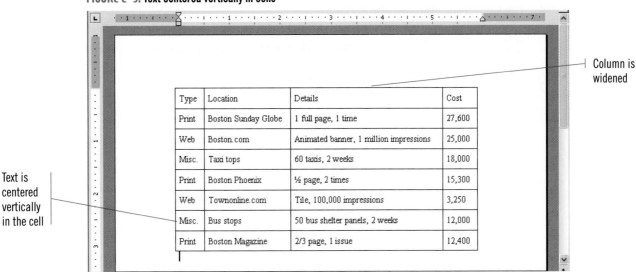

Column is widened

Sorting Table Data

Tables are often easier to interpret and analyze when the data is **sorted**, which means the rows are organized in alphabetical or sequential order based on the data in one or more columns. When you sort a table, Word arranges all the table data according to the criteria you set. You set sort criteria by specifying the column (or columns) by which you want to sort, and indicating the sort order—ascending or descending—you want to use. **Ascending order** lists data alphabetically or sequentially (from A to Z, 0 to 9, or earliest to latest). **Descending order** lists data in reverse alphabetical or sequential order (from Z to A, 9 to 0, or latest to earliest). You can sort using the data in one column or multiple columns. When you sort by multiple columns you must select primary, secondary, and tertiary sort criteria. You use the Sort command on the Table menu to sort a table. ◼◼◼◼ You sort the table so that all ads of the same type are listed together. You also add secondary sort criteria so that the ads within each type are listed in descending order by cost.

STEPS

QUICK TIP

To quickly sort a table by a single column, click in the column, then click the Sort Ascending ↓ or Sort Descending button ↓ on the Tables and Borders toolbar. When you use these buttons, Word does not include the header row in the sort.

1. **Place the insertion point anywhere in the table**

   To sort an entire table, you simply need to place the insertion point anywhere in the table. If you want to sort specific rows only, then you must select the rows you want to sort.

2. **Click Table on the menu bar, then click Sort**

   The Sort dialog box opens, as shown in Figure E-10. You use this dialog box to specify the column or columns by which you want to sort, the type of information you are sorting (text, numbers, or dates), and the sort order (ascending or descending). Column 1 is selected by default in the Sort by list box. Since you want to sort your table first by the information in the first column—the type of ad (Print, Web, or Misc.)—you don't change the Sort by criteria.

3. **Click the Descending option button in the Sort by area**

   The ad type information will be sorted in descending—or reverse alphabetical—order, so that the "Web" ads will be listed first, followed by the "Print" ads, and then the "Misc." ads.

4. **In the first Then by section click the Then by list arrow, click Column 4, click the Type list arrow, click Number if it is not already selected, then click the Descending option button**

   Within the Web, Print, and Misc. groups, the rows will be sorted by the cost of the ad—the information contained in the fourth column, which is numbers, not dates or text. The rows will appear in descending order within each group, with the most expensive ad listed first.

5. **Click the Header row option button in the My list has section to select it**

   The table includes a header row that you do not want included in the sort. A **header row** is the first row of a table that contains the column headings.

6. **Click OK, then deselect the table**

   The rows in the table are sorted first by the information in the Type column and second by the information in the Cost column, as shown in Figure E-11. The first row of the table, which is the header row, is not included in the sort.

7. **Save your changes to the document**

FIGURE E-10: Sort dialog box

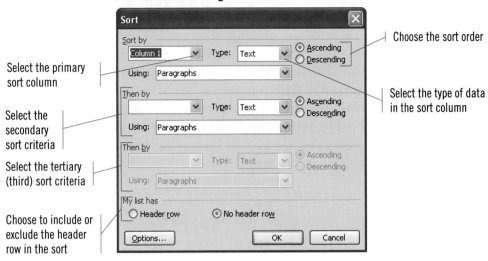

Select the primary sort column

Select the secondary sort criteria

Select the tertiary (third) sort criteria

Choose to include or exclude the header row in the sort

Choose the sort order

Select the type of data in the sort column

FIGURE E-11: Sorted table

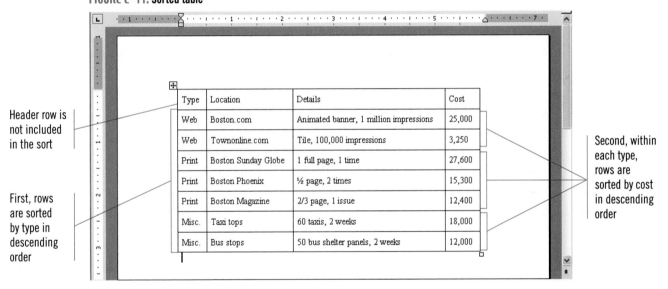

Header row is not included in the sort

First, rows are sorted by type in descending order

Second, within each type, rows are sorted by cost in descending order

Type	Location	Details	Cost
Web	Boston.com	Animated banner, 1 million impressions	25,000
Web	Townonline.com	Tile, 100,000 impressions	3,250
Print	Boston Sunday Globe	1 full page, 1 time	27,600
Print	Boston Phoenix	½ page, 2 times	15,300
Print	Boston Magazine	2/3 page, 1 issue	12,400
Misc.	Taxi tops	60 taxis, 2 weeks	18,000
Misc.	Bus stops	50 bus shelter panels, 2 weeks	12,000

Clues to Use

Sorting lists and paragraphs

In addition to sorting table data, you can use the Sort command on the Table menu to sort lists and paragraphs. For example, you might want to sort a list of names alphabetically. To sort lists and paragraphs, select the items you want included in the sort, click Table on the menu bar, and then click Sort. In the Sort Text dialog box, use the Sort by list arrow to select the sort by criteria (paragraphs or fields), use the Type list arrow to select the type of data (text, numbers, or dates), and then click the Ascending or Descending option button to choose a sort order.

When sorting text information in a document, the term "fields" refers to text or numbers that are separated by a character, such as a tab or a comma. For example, if the names you want to sort are listed in "Last name, First name" order, then last name and first name are each considered a field. You can choose to sort the list in alphabetical order by last name or by first name. Use the Options button in the Sort Text dialog box to specify the character that separates the fields in your lists or paragraphs, along with other sort options.

Splitting and Merging Cells

A convenient way to change the format and structure of a table is to merge and split the table cells. When you **merge** cells, you combine adjacent cells into a single larger cell. When you **split** a cell, you divide an existing cell into multiple cells. You can merge and split cells using the Merge Cells and Split Cells commands on the Table menu, or the Merge Cells and Split Cells buttons on the Tables and Borders toolbar.  You merge cells in the first column to create a single cell for each ad type—Web, Print, and Misc. You also add a new row to the bottom of the table, and split the cells in the row to create three new rows with a different structure.

STEPS

TROUBLE

To move the Tables and Borders toolbar, click its title bar and drag it to a new location.

1. **Click the** Tables and Borders button 🖰 **on the Standard toolbar, then click the** Draw Table button 🖰 **on the Tables and Borders toolbar to turn off the Draw pointer ⁄ if necessary**

   The Tables and Borders toolbar, which includes buttons for formatting and working with tables, opens. See Table E-1.

2. **Select the two** Web cells **in the first column of the table, click the** Merge Cells button 🖰 **on the Tables and Borders toolbar, then deselect the text**

   The two Web cells merge to become a single cell. When you merge cells, Word converts the text in each cell into a separate paragraph in the merged cell.

3. **Select the first** Web **in the cell, then press** [Delete]

4. **Select the three** Print cells **in the first column, click** 🖰, **type** Print, **select the two** Misc. cells, **click** 🖰, **then type** Misc.

   The three Print cells merge to become one cell and the two Misc. cells merge to become one cell.

5. **Click the** Bus stops cell, **click the** Insert Table list arrow 🖰 ▾ **on the Tables and Borders toolbar, then click** Insert Rows Below

   A row is added to the bottom of the table. The Insert Table button on the Tables and Borders toolbar also changes to the Insert Rows Below button. The active buttons on the Tables and Borders toolbar reflect the most recently used commands. You can see a menu of related commands by clicking the list arrow next to a button.

6. **Select the** first three cells **in the new last row of the table, click** 🖰, **then deselect the cell**

   The three cells in the row merge to become a single cell.

QUICK TIP

To split a table in two, click the row you want to be the first row in the second table, click Table on the menu bar, then click Split Table.

7. **Click the** first cell **in the last row, then click the** Split Cells button 🖰 **on the Tables and Borders toolbar**

   The Split Cells dialog box opens, as shown in Figure E-12. You use this dialog box to split the selected cell or cells into a specific number of columns and rows.

8. **Type** 1 **in the Number of columns text box, press** [Tab], **type** 3 **in the Number of rows text box, click** OK, **then deselect the cells**

   The single cell is divided into three rows of equal height. When you split a cell into multiple rows and/or columns, the width of the original column does not change. If the cell you split contains text, all the text appears in the upper-left cell.

9. **Click the** last cell **in the Cost column, click** 🖰, **repeat Step 8, then save your changes**

   The cell is split into three rows, as shown in Figure E-13. The last three rows of the table now have only two columns.

FIGURE E-12: Split Cells dialog box

Tables and Borders button

Insert Rows Below button

Cells created by merging other cells

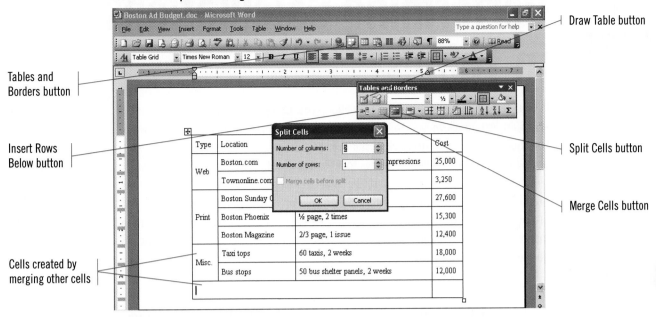

Draw Table button

Split Cells button

Merge Cells button

Word 2003

FIGURE E-13: Cells split into three rows

Cells are split into three rows

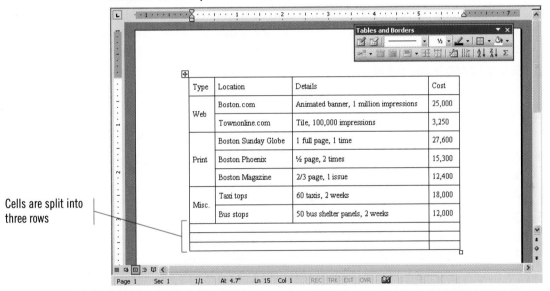

TABLE E-1: Buttons on the Tables and Borders toolbar

button	use to	button	use to
	Draw a table or cells		Divide a cell into multiple cells
	Remove a border between cells		Change the alignment of text in cells
	Change border line style		Make rows the same height
½	Change the thickness of borders		Make columns the same width
	Change the border color		Format the table with a Table AutoFormat table style
	Add or remove individual borders		Change the orientation of text
	Change the shading color of cells		Sort rows in ascending order
	Insert rows, columns, cells, or a table, and AutoFit columns		Sort rows in descending order
	Combine the selected cells into a single cell	Σ	Calculate the sum of values above or to the left of the active cell

Performing Calculations in Tables

If your table includes numerical information, you can perform simple calculations in the table. The Word AutoSum feature allows you to quickly total the numbers in a column or row. In addition, you can use the Formula command to perform other standard calculations, such as averages. When you calculate data in a table using formulas, you use cell references to refer to the cells in the table. Each cell has a unique **cell reference** composed of a letter and a number; the letter represents its column and the number represents its row. For example, the cell in the third row of the fourth column is cell D3. Figure E-14 shows the cell references in a simple table. You use AutoSum to calculate the total cost of the Boston ad campaign. You also add information about the budgeted cost and create a formula to calculate the difference between the actual and budgeted costs.

STEPS

QUICK TIP

If a column or row contains blank cells, you must type a zero in any blank cell before using AutoSum.

1. **Click the first blank cell in column 1, type Total Cost, press [Tab], then click the AutoSum button Σ on the Tables and Borders toolbar**

   Word totals the numbers in the cells above the active cell and inserts the sum as a field. You can use the AutoSum button to quickly total the numbers in a column or a row. If the cell you select is at the bottom of a column of numbers, AutoSum totals the column. If the cell is at the right end of a row of numbers, AutoSum totals the row.

2. **Select 12,000 in the cell above the total, then type 13,500**

   If you change a number that is part of a calculation, you must recalculate the field result.

QUICK TIP

To change a field result to regular text, click the field, then press [Ctrl][Shift][F9].

3. **Press [↓], then press [F9]**

   When the insertion point is in a cell that contains a formula, pressing [F9] updates the field result.

4. **Press [Tab], type Budgeted, press [Tab], type 113,780, press [Tab], type Difference, then press [Tab]**

   The insertion point is in the last cell of the table.

5. **Click Table on the menu bar, then click Formula**

   The Formula dialog box opens, as shown in Figure E-15. The SUM formula appears in the Formula text box. Word proposes to sum the numbers above the active cell, but you want to insert a formula that calculates the difference between the actual and budgeted costs. You can type simple custom formulas using a plus sign (+) for addition, a minus sign (-) for subtraction, an asterisk (*) for multiplication, and a slash (/) for division.

TROUBLE

Cell references are determined by the number of columns in each row, not by the number of columns in the table. Therefore, rows 9 and 10 have only two columns.

6. **Select =SUM(ABOVE) in the Formula text box, then type =B9-B10**

   You must type an equal sign (=) to indicate that the text following it is a formula. You want to subtract the budgeted cost in the second column of row 10 from the actual cost in the second column of row 9; therefore, you type a formula to subtract the value in cell B10 from the value in cell B9.

7. **Click OK, then save your changes**

   The difference appears in the cell, as shown in Figure E-16.

FIGURE E-14: Cell references in a table

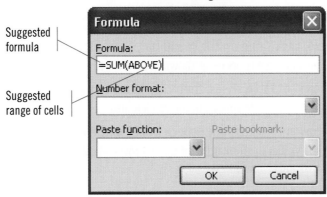

Row 3

Column D
(fourth column)

Cell reference
indicates the cell's
column and row

FIGURE E-15: Formula dialog box

Suggested
formula

Suggested
range of cells

FIGURE E-16: Difference calculated in table

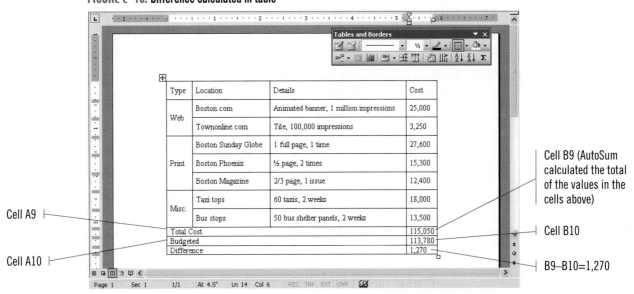

Cell A9

Cell A10

Cell B9 (AutoSum
calculated the total
of the values in the
cells above)

Cell B10

B9–B10=1,270

Word 2003

Clues to Use

Working with formulas

In addition to the SUM function, Word includes formulas for averaging, counting, and rounding data, to name a few. To use a Word formula, click the Paste function list arrow in the Formula dialog box, select a function, and then insert the cell references of the cells you want included in the calculation in parentheses after the name of the function. When entering formulas, you must separate cell references by a comma. For example, if you want to average the values in cells A1, B3, and C4, enter the formula =AVERAGE(A1,B3,C4). You must also separate cell ranges by a colon. For example, to total the values in cells A1 through A9, enter the formula =SUM(A1:A9). To display the result of a calculation in a particular number format, such as a decimal percentage (0.00%), click the Number format list arrow in the Formula dialog box and select a number format. Word inserts the result of a calculation as a field in the selected cell.

Using Table AutoFormat

Adding shading and other design elements to a table can help give it a polished appearance and make the data easier to read. The Word Table AutoFormat feature allows you to quickly apply a table style to a table. Table styles include borders, shading, fonts, alignment, colors, and other formatting effects. You can apply a table style to a table using the Table AutoFormat command on the Table menu or the Table AutoFormat button on the Tables and Borders toolbar. You want to enhance the appearance of the table with shading, borders, and other formats. You use the Table AutoFormat feature to quickly apply a table style to the table.

STEPS

1. **Click in the table, click Table on the menu bar, then click Table AutoFormat**
   The Table AutoFormat dialog box opens, as shown in Figure E-17.

2. **Scroll down the list of table styles, then click Table List 7**
   A preview of the Table List 7 style appears in the Preview area.

3. **Clear the Last row and Last column check boxes in the Apply special formats to section**
   The Preview area shows that the formatting of the last row and column of the table now match the formatting of the other rows and columns in the table.

QUICK TIP
Use the Reveal Formatting task pane to view the format settings applied to tables and cells.

4. **Click Apply**
   The Table List 7 style is applied to the table, as shown in Figure E-18. Because of the structure of the table, this style neither enhances the table nor helps make the data more readable.

5. **With the insertion point in the table, click the Table AutoFormat button ⊠ on the Tables and Borders toolbar, scroll down the list of table styles in the Table AutoFormat dialog box, click Table Professional, then click Apply**
   The Table Professional style is applied to the table. This style works with the structure of the table.

TROUBLE
When you select the Type column, the first column in the last three rows is also selected.

6. **Select the Type column, click the Center button ≡ on the Formatting toolbar, select the Cost column, then click the Align Right button ≡ on the Formatting toolbar**
   The data in the Type column is centered, and the data in the Cost column is right-aligned.

7. **Select the last three rows of the table, click ≡, then click the Bold button B on the Formatting toolbar**
   The text in the last three rows is right-aligned and bold is applied.

8. **Select the first row of the table, click ≡, click the Font Size list arrow on the Formatting toolbar, click 16, deselect the row, then save your changes**
   The text in the header row is centered and enlarged, as shown in Figure E-19.

Clues to Use

Using tables to lay out a page

Tables are often used to display information for quick reference and analysis, but you can also use tables to structure the layout of a page. You can insert any kind of information in the cell of a table—including graphics, bulleted lists, charts, and other tables (called **nested tables**). For example, you might use a table to lay out a resume, a newsletter, or a Web page. When you use a table to lay out a page, you generally remove the table borders to hide the table structure from the reader. After you remove borders, it can be helpful to display the table gridlines onscreen while you work. **Gridlines** are light gray lines that show the boundaries of cells, but do not print. If your document will be viewed online—for example, if you are planning to e-mail your resume to potential employers—you should turn off the display of gridlines before you distribute the document so that it looks the same online as it looks when printed. To turn gridlines off or on, click the Hide Gridlines or Show Gridlines command on the Table menu.

FIGURE E-17: Table AutoFormat dialog box

List of table styles

Preview of the selected style

Options for customizing the application of style settings

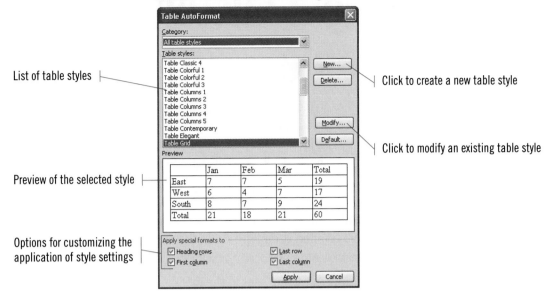

Click to create a new table style

Click to modify an existing table style

FIGURE E-18: Table List 7 style applied to table

The shading applied to the merged cells is confusing

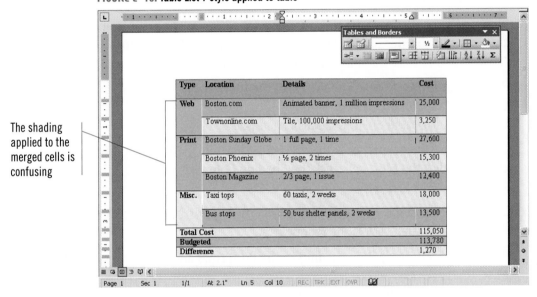

FIGURE E-19: Table Professional style applied to table

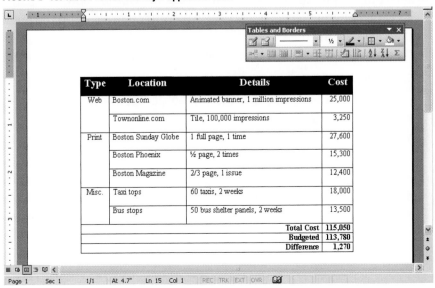

Creating a Custom Format for a Table

You can also use the buttons on the Tables and Borders toolbar to create your own table designs. For example, you can add or remove borders and shading, vary the line style, thickness, and color of borders, change the orientation of text from horizontal to vertical, and change the alignment of text in cells. ▰▰▰▰ You adjust the text direction, shading, and borders in the table to make it easier to understand at a glance.

STEPS

1. **Select the Type and Location cells in the first row, click the Merge Cells button ▦ on the Tables and Borders toolbar, then type Ad Location**

   The two cells are combined into a single cell containing the text "Ad Location."

2. **Select the Web, Print, and Misc. cells in the first column, click the Change Text Direction button ▥ on the Tables and Borders toolbar twice, then deselect the cells**

   The text is rotated 270 degrees.

3. **Position the pointer over the right border of the Web cell until the pointer changes to +‖+, then drag the border to approximately the ¼" mark on the horizontal ruler**

   The width of the column containing the vertical text narrows.

QUICK TIP
In cells with vertical text, the I-beam pointer is rotated 90 degrees.

4. **Place the insertion point in the Web cell, then click the Shading Color list arrow ▨▾ on the Tables and Borders toolbar**

   The Shading Color palette opens, as shown in Figure E-20.

5. **Click Gold on the palette, click the Print cell, click the Shading Color list arrow ▨▾, click Pink, click the Misc. cell, click the Shading Color list arrow ▨▾, then click Aqua**

   Shading is applied to each cell.

6. **Drag to select the six white cells in the Web rows (rows 2 and 3), click the Shading Color list arrow ▨▾, then click Light Yellow**

7. **Repeat Step 6 to apply Rose shading to the Print rows and Light Turquoise shading to the Misc. rows**

   Shading is applied to all the cells in rows 1–8.

TROUBLE
If gridlines appear, click Table on the menu bar, then click Hide Gridlines.

8. **Select the last three rows of the table, click the Outside Border list arrow ▦▾ on the Tables and Borders toolbar, click the No Border button ▦ on the menu that appears, then deselect the rows**

   The top, bottom, left, and right borders are removed from each cell in the selected rows.

QUICK TIP
On the Borders button menu, click the button that corresponds to the border you want to add or remove.

9. **Select the Total Cost row, click the No Border list arrow ▦▾, click the Top Border button ▦, click the 113,780 cell, click the Top Border list arrow ▦▾, then click the Bottom Border button ▦**

   A top border is added to each cell in the Total Cost row, and a bottom border is added below 113,780. The completed table is shown in Figure E-21.

10. **Press [Ctrl][Home], press [Enter], type your name, save your changes, print a copy of the document, close the document, then exit Word**

    Press [Enter] at the beginning of a table to move the table down one line in a document.

Merged cell

Text is rotated in the cell

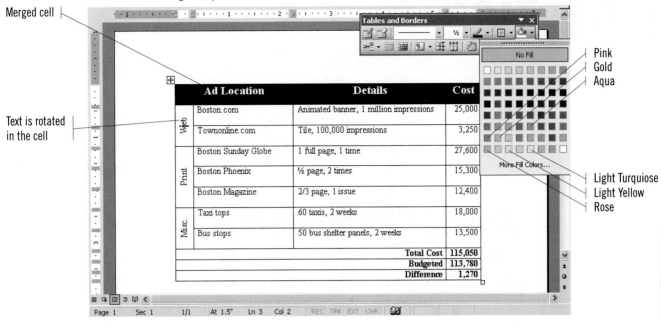

Pink
Gold
Aqua

Light Turquiose
Light Yellow
Rose

No Fill

More Fill Colors...

FIGURE E-21: Completed table

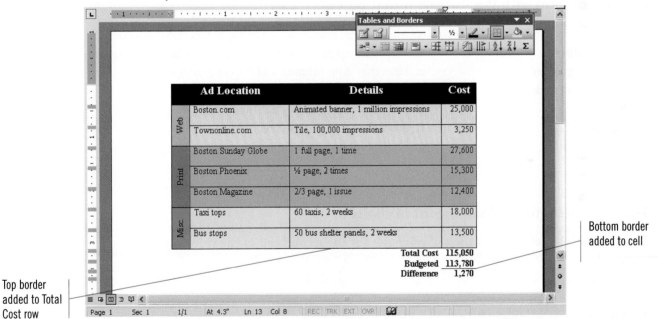

Bottom border added to cell

Top border added to Total Cost row

Clues to Use

Drawing a table

The Word Draw Table feature allows you to draw table cells exactly where you want them. To draw a table, click the Draw Table button on the Tables and Borders toolbar to turn on the Draw pointer, and then click and drag to draw a cell. Using the same method, you can draw borders within the cell to create columns and rows, or draw additional cells attached to the first cell. Click the Draw Table button to turn off the draw feature.

If you want to remove a border from a table, click the Eraser button on the Tables and Borders toolbar to activate the Eraser pointer, and then click the border you want to remove. Click the Eraser button to turn off the erase feature. You can use the Draw pointer and the Eraser pointer to change the structure of any table, not just the tables you draw from scratch.

Practice

Label each element of the Tables and Borders toolbar shown in Figure E-22.

FIGURE E-22

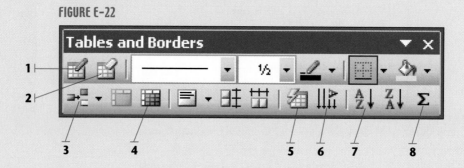

Match each term with the statement that best describes it.

 9. Cell
10. Nested table
11. Ascending order
12. Descending order
13. Borders
14. Gridlines
15. Cell reference

a. A cell address composed of a column letter and a row number
b. Lines that separate columns and rows in a table and that print
c. Lines that show columns and rows in a table, but do not print
d. An object inserted in a table cell
e. Sort order that organizes text from A to Z
f. Sort order that organizes text from Z to A
g. The box formed by the intersection of a column and a row

Select the best answer from the list of choices.

16. **Which of the following is the cell reference for the second cell in the third column?**
    a. C2
    b. 2C
    c. 3B
    d. B3

17. **Which of the following is *not* a valid way to add a new row to the bottom of a table?**
    a. Click in the bottom row, then click the Insert Rows Below button on the Tables and Borders toolbar
    b. Click in the bottom row, point to Insert on the Table menu, then click Rows Below
    c. Place the insertion point in the last cell of the last row, then press [Tab]
    d. Click in the bottom row, then click the Insert Rows button on the Standard toolbar

18. **Which button do you use to change the orientation of text in a cell?**
    a. ▢
    b. ▯
    c. ▢
    d. ▢

19. Which of the following is *not* a correct formula for adding the values in cells A1, A2, and A3?

  a. =SUM(A1:A3)

  b. =SUM(A1, A2, A3)

  c. =SUM(A1~A3)

  d. =A1+A2+A3

20. What happens when you double-click a column border?

  a. A new column is added to the left

  b. The column width is adjusted to fit the text

  c. The columns in the table are distributed evenly

  d. A new column is added to the right

▼ SKILLS REVIEW

1. Insert a table.

  a. Start Word, close the Getting Started task pane, then save the new blank document as **Mutual Funds** to the drive and folder where your Data Files are located.

  b. Type your name, press [Enter] twice, type **Mutual Fund Performance**, then press [Enter].

  c. Insert a table that contains four columns and four rows.

  d. Type the text shown in Figure E-23, pressing [Tab] to add rows as necessary.

  e. Save your changes.

FIGURE E-23

Fund Name	1 Year	5 Year	10 Year
Computers	16.47	25.56	27.09
Europe	-6.15	13.89	10.61
Natural Resources	19.47	12.30	15.38
Health Care	32.45	24.26	23.25
Financial Services	22.18	21.07	24.44
500 Index	9.13	15.34	13.69

2. Insert and delete rows and columns.

  a. Insert a row above the Health Care row, then type the following text in the new row:

    Canada 8.24   8.12   8.56

  b. Delete the Europe row.

  c. Insert a column to the right of the 10 Year column, type **Date Purchased** in the header row, then enter a date in each cell in the column using the format MM/DD/YY (for example, 11/27/98).

  d. Move the Date Purchased column to the right of the Fund Name column, then save your changes.

3. Modify table rows and columns.

  a. Double-click the border between the first and second columns to resize the columns.

  b. Drag the border between the second and third columns to the 2¼" mark on the horizontal ruler.

  c. Double-click the right border of the 1 Year, 5 Year, and 10 Year columns.

  d. Select the 1 Year, 5 Year, and 10 Year columns, then distribute the columns evenly.

  e. Select rows 2–7, use the Table Properties dialog box to set the row height to exactly .3", then save your changes.

4. Sort table data.

  a. Sort the table data in descending order by the information in the 1 Year column.

  b. Sort the table data in ascending order by date purchased.

  c. Sort the table data by fund name in alphabetical order, then save your changes.

5. **Split and merge cells.**
   a. Insert a row above the header row.
   b. Merge the first cell in the new row with the Fund Name cell.
   c. Merge the second cell in the new row with the Date Purchased cell.
   d. Merge the three remaining blank cells in the first row into a single cell, then type **Average Annual Returns** in the merged cell.
   e. Add a new row to the bottom of the table.
   f. Merge the first two cells in the new row, then type **Average Return** in the merged cell.
   g. Select the first seven cells in the first column (from Fund Name to Natural Resources), open the Split Cells dialog box, clear the Merge cells before split check box, then split the cells into two columns.
   h. Type **Trading Symbol** as the heading for the new column, then enter the following text in the remaining cells in the column: **FINX, CAND, COMP, FINS, HCRX, NARS.**
   i. Double-click the right border of the first column to resize the column, double-click the right border of the last column, then save your changes.

6. **Perform calculations in tables.**
   a. Place the insertion point in the last cell in the 1 Year column, then open the Formula dialog box.
   b. Delete the text in the Formula text box, type **=average(above)**, click the Number Format list arrow, click 0.00%, then click OK.
   c. Repeat Step b to insert the average return in the last cell in the 5 Year and 10 Year columns.
   d. Change the value of the 1-year average return for the Natural Resources fund to **10.35.**
   e. Use [F9] to recalculate the average return for 1 year, then save your changes.

7. **Using Table AutoFormat.**
   a. Open the Table AutoFormat dialog box, select an appropriate table style for the table, then apply the style to the table. Was the style you chose effective?
   b. Using Table AutoFormat, apply the Table List 3 style to the table.
   c. Change the font of all the text in the table to 10-point Arial. (*Hint*: Select the entire table.)
   d. Apply bold to the 1 Year, 5 Year, and 10 Year column headings, and to the bottom row of the table.
   e. Center the table between the margins, center the table title **Mutual Fund Performance**, format the title in 14-point Arial, apply bold, then save your changes.

8. **Create a custom format for a table.**
   a. Select the entire table, then use the Align Center button on the Tables and Borders toolbar to center the text in every cell vertically and horizontally.
   b. Right-align the dates in column 3 and the numbers in columns 4–6.
   c. Left-align the fund names and trading symbols in columns 1 and 2.
   d. Right-align the text in the bottom row. Make sure the text in the header row is still centered.
   e. Select all the cells in the header row, including the 1 Year, 5 Year, and 10 Year column headings, change the shading color to indigo, then change the font color to white.
   f. Apply rose shading to the cells containing the fund names and trading symbols.
   g. Apply pale blue, light yellow, and lavender shading to the cells containing the 1 Year, 5 Year, and 10 Year data, respectively. Do not apply shading to the bottom row of the table.
   h. Remove all the borders in the table.
   i. Add a ½-point white bottom border to the Average Annual Returns cell. (*Hint*: Use the Tables and Borders toolbar.)
   j. Add a 2¼-point black border around the outside of the table. Also add a top border to the last row of the table.
   k. Examine the table, make any necessary adjustments, then save your changes.
   l. Preview the table in Print Preview, print a copy, close the file, then exit Word.

▼ INDEPENDENT CHALLENGE 1

You are the director of sales for a publishing company with branch offices in six cities around the globe. In preparation for the upcoming sales meeting, you create a table showing your sales projections for the fiscal year 2006.

a. Start Word, then save the new blank document as **2006 Sales** to the drive and folder where your Data Files are located.

b. Type the table heading **Projected Sales in Millions, Fiscal Year 2006** at the top of the document, then press [Enter] twice.

c. Insert a table with five columns and four rows, then enter the data shown in Figure E-24 into the table, adding rows as necessary.

d. Resize the columns to fit the text.

e. Sort the table rows in alphabetical order by Office.

f. Add a new row to the bottom of the table, type **Total** in the first cell, then enter a formula in each remaining cell in the new row to calculate the sum of the cells above it.

FIGURE E-24

Office	Q1	Q2	Q3	Q4
Paris	9500	5800	3900	9800
Tokyo	6700	8900	4500	4900
Berlin	8800	8500	6800	7400
Shanghai	5800	7200	4700	8200
New York	8500	7800	9800	9400
Melbourne	7900	6800	3800	6200

g. Add a new column at the right end of the table, type **Total** in the first cell, then enter a formula in each remaining cell in the new column to calculate the sum of the cells to the left of it. (*Hint*: Make sure the formula you insert in each cell sums the cells to the left, not the cells above.)

h. Using Table AutoFormat, apply a table style to the table. Select a style that enhances the information contained in the table.

i. Center the text in the header row, left-align the remaining text in the first column, then right-align the numerical data in the table.

j. Enhance the table with fonts, font colors, shading, and borders to make the table attractive and easy to read at a glance.

k. Increase the font size of the table heading to 18 points, then center the table heading and the table on the page.

l. Press [Ctrl][End], press [Enter], type your name, save your changes, print the table, close the file, then exit Word.

▼ INDEPENDENT CHALLENGE 2

You have been invited to speak to your local board of realtors about the economic benefits of living in your city. To illustrate some of your points, you want to distribute a handout comparing the cost of living and other economic indicators in the U.S. cities that offer features similar to your city. You decide to format the data as a table.

a. Start Word, open the file WD E-1.doc, then save it as **US Cities** to the drive and folder where your Data Files are located.

b. Format the table heading in 18-point Arial, apply bold, then center the heading.

c. Turn on formatting marks, select the tabbed text in the document, then convert the text to a table.

d. Add a row above the first row in the table, then enter the following column headings in the new header row: **City, Cost of Living, Median Income, Average House Cost, Bachelor Degree Rate**.

e. Format the table text in 10-point Arial.

f. Apply an appropriate Table AutoFormat style to the table. Apply bold to the header row if necessary.

g. Adjust the column widths so that the table is attractive and readable. (*Hint*: Put the column headings on two lines.)

h. Make the height of each row at least .25".

i. Center Left align the text in each cell in the first column, including the column head.

j. Center Right align the text in each cell in the remaining columns, including the column heads.

k. Center the entire table on the page.

l. Sort the table by cost of living in descending order. (*Hint*: Use the Sort dialog box.)

▼ INDEPENDENT CHALLENGE 2 (CONTINUED)

Advanced Challenge Exercise

- Add a new row to the bottom of the table, then type **Average** in the first cell in the new row.
- In each subsequent cell in the Average row, insert a formula that calculates the averages of the cells above it. (*Hint:* For each cell, replace SUM with AVERAGE in the Formula text box, but do not make other changes.)
- Change the font color of the text in the Average row to a color of your choice.

m. On the blank line below the table, type **Note: The average cost of living in the United States is 100.**, italicize the text, then use a tab stop and indents to align the text with the left side of the table if it is not aligned.

n. Enhance the table with borders, shading, fonts, and other formats, if necessary to make it attractive and readable.

o. Type your name at the bottom of the document, save your changes, print a copy of the table, close the document, then exit Word.

▼ INDEPENDENT CHALLENGE 3

You work in the advertising department at a magazine. Your boss has asked you to create a fact sheet on the ad dimensions for the magazine. The fact sheet should include the dimensions for each type of ad. As a bonus, you could also add a visual representation of the different ad shapes and sizes, shown in Figure E-25. You'll use tables to lay out the fact sheet, present the dimension information, and, if you are performing the ACE steps, illustrate the ad shapes and sizes.

a. Start Word, open the file WD E-2.doc from the drive and folder where your Data Files are located, then save it as **Ad Dimensions**. Read the document to get a feel for its contents.

b. Drag the border between the first and second column to approximately the 2¾" mark on the horizontal ruler, resize the second and third columns to fit the text, then use the Table Properties dialog box to make each row in the table at least .5".

c. Change the alignment of the text in the first column to center left, then change the alignment of the text in the second and third columns to center right.

d. Remove all the borders from the table, then apply a 2¼-point, red, dotted line, inside horizontal border to the entire table. This creates a red dotted line between each row.

e. In the second blank paragraph under the table heading, insert a new table with three columns and four rows, then merge the cells in the third column of the new blank table.

f. Drag the border between the first and second columns of the new blank table to the 1¼" mark on the horizontal ruler. Drag the border between the second and third columns to the 1½" mark.

g. Select the table that contains text, cut it to the Clipboard, then paste it in the merged cell in the blank table. The table with text is now a nested table in the main table.

h. Split the nested table above the Unit Size (Bleed) row. (*Hint:* Place the insertion point in the Unit Size (Bleed) row, then use the Split Table command on the Table menu.)

i. Scroll up, merge the four cells in the first column of the main table, then merge the four cells in the second column.

j. Split the first column into one column and seven rows.

k. Using the Row tab in the Table Properties dialog box, change the row height of each cell in the first column so that the rows alternate between exactly 1.8" and .25" in height. Make the height of the first, third, fifth, and seventh rows 1.8".

l. Add red shading to the first, third, fifth, and seventh cells in the first column, then remove all the borders from the main table.

▼ INDEPENDENT CHALLENGE 3 (CONTINUED)

Advanced Challenge Exercise

- In the first red cell, type **Full Page**, change the font color to white, then center the text vertically in the cell.
- On the Tables and Borders toolbar, change the Line Style to a single line, change the Line Weight to 1, then change the Border Color to white.
- Activate the Draw Table pointer, then, referring to Figure E-25, draw a vertical border that divides the second red cell into ⅔ and ⅓. (*Hint:* You can also divide the cell using the Split Cells and Merge Cells buttons.)
- Label the cells and align the text as shown in the figure. (*Hint:* Change the text direction and alignment before typing text. Take care not to change the size of the cells when you type. If necessary, press [Enter] to start a new line of text in a cell, or reduce the font size of the text.)
- Referring to Figure E-25, divide the third and fourth red cells, then label the cells as shown in the figure.

m. Examine the document for errors, then make any necessary adjustments.

n. Press [Ctrl][End], type your name, save your changes to the document, preview it, print a copy, close the file, then exit Word.

FIGURE E-25

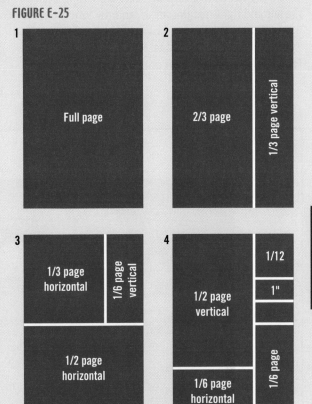

▼ INDEPENDENT CHALLENGE 4

A well-written and well-formatted resume gives you a leg up on getting a job interview. In a winning resume, the content and format support your career objective and effectively present your background and qualifications. One simple way to create a resume is to lay out the page using a table. In this exercise you research guidelines for writing and formatting resumes. You then create your own resume using a table for its layout.

a. Use your favorite search engine to search the Web for information on writing and formatting resumes. Use the keywords **resume templates**.

b. Print helpful advice on writing and formatting resumes from at least two Web sites.

c. Think about the information you want to include in your resume. The header should include your name, address, telephone number, and e-mail address. The body should include your career objective and information on your education, work experience, and skills. You may want to add additional information.

d. Sketch a layout for your resume using a table as the underlying grid. Include the table rows and columns in your sketch.

e. Start Word, open a new blank document, then save it as **My Resume** to the drive and folder where your Data Files are located.

f. Set appropriate margins, then insert a table to serve as the underlying grid for your resume. Split and merge cells and adjust the size of the table columns as necessary.

g. Type your resume in the table cells. Take care to use a professional tone and keep your language to the point.

h. Format your resume with fonts, bullets, and other formatting features. Adjust the spacing between sections by resizing the table columns and rows.

i. When you are satisfied with the content and format of your resume, remove the borders from the table, then hide the gridlines if they are visible.

j. Check your resume for spelling and grammar errors.

k. Save your changes, preview your resume, print a copy, close the file, then exit Word.

▼ VISUAL WORKSHOP

Create the calendar shown in Figure E-26 using a table to lay out the entire page. (*Hints*: The top and bottom margins are .7", the left and right margins are 1", and the font is Century Gothic. The clip art image is inserted in the table. The clip art image is found using the keyword **beach**. Use a different clip art image or font if the ones shown in the figure are not available.) Type your name in the last table cell, save the calendar with the filename **August 2006** to the drive and folder where your Data Files are located, then print a copy.

FIGURE E-26

August 2006

Sunday	Monday	Tuesday	Wednesday	Thursday	Friday	Saturday
		1	2	3	4	5
6	7	8	9	10	11	12
13	14	15	16	17	18	19
20	21	22	23	24	25	26
27	28	29	30	31		

Illustrating Documents with Graphics

OBJECTIVES

Add graphics
Resize graphics
Position graphics
Create text boxes
Create AutoShapes
Use the drawing canvas
Format WordArt
Create charts

If you have a SAM user profile, you may have access to hands-on instruction, practice, and assessment of the skills covered in this unit. Log in to your SAM account and go to your assignments page to see what your instructor has assigned.

Graphics can help illustrate the ideas in your documents, provide visual interest on a page, and give your documents punch and flair. In addition to clip art, you can add graphics created in other programs to a document, or you can use the drawing features of Word to create your own images. In this unit, you learn how to insert, modify, and position graphics, how to draw your own images, and how to illustrate a document with WordArt and charts. ▰▰▰ You are preparing materials for a workshop for new members of the MediaLoft marketing staff. You use the graphic features of Word to illustrate three handouts on marketing issues of interest to MediaLoft.

Adding Graphics

Graphic images you can insert in a document include the clip art images that come with Word, photos taken with a digital camera, scanned art, and graphics created in other graphics programs. When you first insert a graphic it is an **inline graphic**—part of the line of text in which it is inserted. You move an inline graphic just as you would move text. To be able to move a graphic independently of text, you must apply a text-wrapping style to it to make it a **floating graphic**, which can be moved anywhere on a page. To insert clip art or another graphic file into a document, you use the Picture command on the Insert menu. You have written a handout containing tips for writing and designing ads. You want to illustrate the handout with the MediaLoft logo, a graphic created in another graphics program. You use the Picture, From File command to insert the logo in the document, and then wrap the text around the logo.

STEPS

1. **Start Word, open the file** WD F-1.doc **from the drive and folder where your Data Files are located, save it as** Ad Tips, **then read the document to get a feel for its contents**

   The document opens in Print Layout view.

QUICK TIP
The Drawing button is a toggle button that you can use to display and hide the Drawing toolbar.

2. **Click the** Show/Hide ¶ **button** ¶ **on the Standard toolbar to display formatting marks, then click the** Drawing **button** 🖌 **on the Standard toolbar to display the Drawing toolbar if it is not already displayed**

   The Drawing toolbar, located below the document window, includes buttons for inserting, creating, and modifying graphics.

3. **Click before the heading** Create a simple layout, **click** Insert **on the menu bar, point to** Picture, **then click** From File

   The Insert Picture dialog box opens. You use this dialog box to locate and insert graphic files. Most graphic files are **bitmap graphics**, which are composed of a series of small dots, called **pixels**, that define color and intensity. Bitmap graphics are often saved with a .bmp, .png, .jpg, .wmf, .tif, or .gif file extension. To view all the graphic files in a particular location, use the Files of type list arrow to select All Pictures. To view a particular type of graphic, use the Files of type list arrow to select the graphic type.

4. **Click the** Files of type list arrow, **click** All Pictures **if it is not already selected, use the** Look in list arrow **to navigate to the drive and folder where your Data Files are located, click the file** MLoft.jpg, **then click** Insert

   The logo is inserted as an inline graphic at the location of the insertion point. Unless you want a graphic to be part of a line of text, usually the first thing you do after inserting it is to wrap text around it so it becomes a floating graphic. To be able to position a graphic anywhere on a page, you must apply a text-wrapping style to it even if there is no text on the page.

TROUBLE
If your Picture toolbar does not open, click View on the menu bar, point to Toolbars, then click Picture.

5. **Click the** logo graphic **to select it**

   Squares, called **sizing handles**, appear on the sides and corners of the graphic when it is selected, as shown in Figure F-1. The Picture toolbar also opens. The Picture toolbar includes buttons for modifying graphics.

6. **Click the** Text Wrapping button 🖼 **on the Picture toolbar**

   A menu of text-wrapping styles opens.

7. **Click** Tight

   The text wraps around the sides of the graphic, as shown in Figure F-2. Notice that the sizing handles change to circles, indicating the graphic is a floating graphic, and an anchor and a green rotate handle appear. The anchor indicates the floating graphic is **anchored** to the nearest paragraph, so that the graphic moves with the paragraph if the paragraph is moved. The anchor symbol appears only when formatting marks are displayed.

8. **Click** ¶, **deselect the graphic, then click the** Save button 🖫 **on the Standard toolbar to save your changes**

FIGURE F-1: Inline graphic

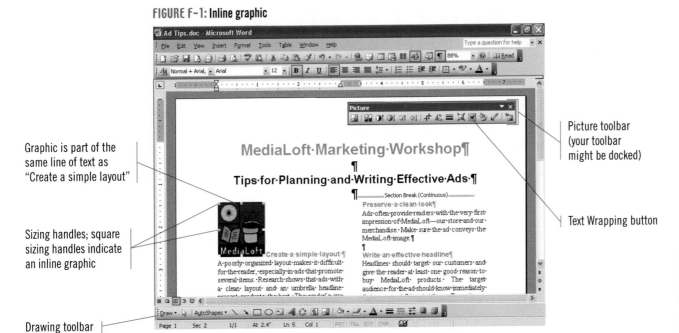

Graphic is part of the same line of text as "Create a simple layout"

Sizing handles; square sizing handles indicate an inline graphic

Drawing toolbar

Picture toolbar (your toolbar might be docked)

Text Wrapping button

FIGURE F-2: Floating graphic

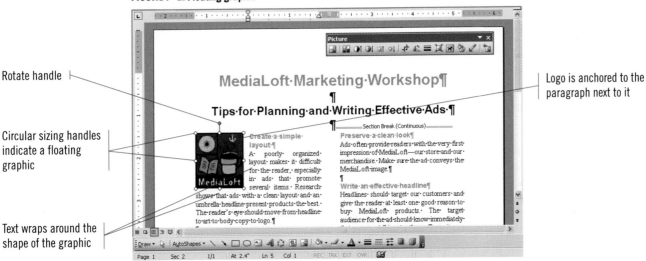

Rotate handle

Circular sizing handles indicate a floating graphic

Text wraps around the shape of the graphic

Logo is anchored to the paragraph next to it

Clues to Use

Narrowing a search for clip art

Searching for clip art with an active Internet connection gives you access to the thousands of clips available on the Microsoft Office Online Web site. With so many clips to choose from, your search can be more productive if you set specific search criteria. To perform an initial search for a clip, type a word or words that describe the clip you want to find in the Search text box in the Clip Art task pane, shown in Figure F-3, and then click Go. If the clips returned in the Results box are too numerous or don't match the criteria you set, you can try using more keywords. For example, rather than "family," you might type "mother father baby" to return only clips associated with all three keywords. You can also narrow your search by reducing the number of collections to search, or by limiting your search to a specific media type, such as photographs. To search specific collections, click the Search in list arrow in the task pane, and then deselect the check box next to each collection you want to omit from the search. To search a specific media type, click the Results should be list arrow, and then deselect the check box next to each type of clip you want to omit from the search. In both lists, you can click a plus sign next to a collection name or media type to expand the list of options. To read more hints on searching for clips, click the Tips for finding clips hyperlink in the Clip Art task pane.

FIGURE F-3: Clip Art task pane

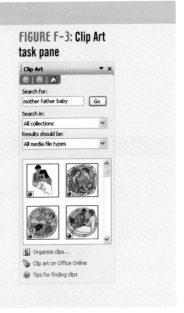

Word 2003

Resizing Graphics

Once you insert a graphic into a document, you can change its shape or size by using the mouse to drag a sizing handle or by using the Picture command on the Format menu to specify an exact height and width for the graphic. Resizing a graphic with the mouse allows you to see how the image looks as you modify it. Using the Picture command to alter a graphic's shape or size allows you to set precise measurements. ▓▓▓▓ You enlarge the MediaLoft logo.

STEPS

QUICK TIP
Click Ruler on the View menu to display the rulers.

1. **Click the logo graphic to select it, place the pointer over the middle-right sizing handle, when the pointer changes to ↔, drag to the right until the graphic is about 1¾" wide**

   As you drag, the dotted outline indicates the size and shape of the graphic. You can refer to the ruler to gauge the measurements as you drag. When you release the mouse button, the image is stretched to be wider. Dragging a side, top, or bottom sizing handle changes only the width or height of a graphic.

QUICK TIP
If you enlarge a bitmap graphic too much, the dots that make up the picture become visible and the graphic is distorted.

2. **Click the Undo button ↺ on the Standard toolbar, place the pointer over the upper-right sizing handle, when the pointer changes to ↗ drag up and to the right until the graphic is about 2" tall and 1¾" wide as shown in Figure F-4, then release the mouse button**

   The image is enlarged. Dragging a corner sizing handle resizes the graphic proportionally so that its width and height are reduced or enlarged by the same percentage. Table F-1 describes other ways to resize objects using the mouse.

3. **Double-click the logo graphic**

   The Format Picture dialog box opens. It includes options for changing the coloring, size, scale, text wrapping, and position of a graphic. You can double-click any graphic object or use the Picture command on the Format menu to open the Format Picture dialog box.

4. **Click the Size tab**

   The Size tab, shown in Figure F-5, allows you to enter precise height and width measurements for a graphic or to scale a graphic by entering the percentage by which you want to reduce or enlarge it. When a graphic is sized to **scale**, its height to width ratio remains the same.

TROUBLE
Your height measurement might differ slightly.

5. **Select the measurement in the Width text box in the Size and rotate section, type 1.5, then click the Height text box in the Size and rotate section**

   The height measurement automatically changes to 1.68". When the Lock aspect ratio check box is selected, you need to enter only a height or width measurement. Word calculates the other measurement so that the resized graphic is proportional.

6. **Click OK, then save your changes**

   The logo is resized to be precisely 1.5" wide and approximately 1.68" tall.

TABLE F-1: Methods for resizing an object using the mouse

do this	to
Drag a corner sizing handle	Resize a clip art or bitmap graphic proportionally from a corner
Press [Shift] and drag a corner sizing handle	Resize a drawing object, such as an AutoShape or a WordArt object, proportionally from a corner
Press [Ctrl] and drag a side, top, or bottom sizing handle	Resize any graphic object vertically or horizontally while keeping the center position fixed
Press [Ctrl] and drag a corner sizing handle	Resize any graphic object diagonally while keeping the center position fixed
Press [Shift][Ctrl] and drag a corner sizing handle	Resize any graphic object proportionally while keeping the center position fixed

FIGURE F-4: Dragging to resize an image

Dotted outline shows the size of the graphic as you drag

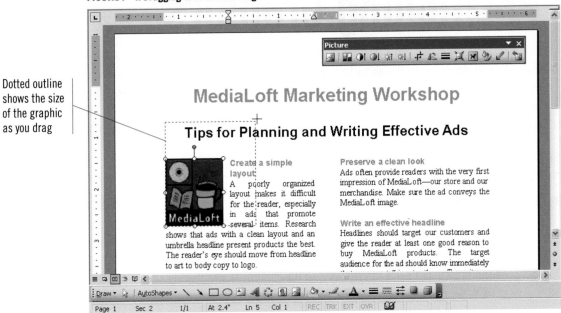

FIGURE F-5: Size tab in the Format Picture dialog box

Set specific height and width measurements (yours might differ)

Change the scale of an object

Select to keep height and width proportional

Select to make scaled measurements relative to the original size

Click to reset image to its original size

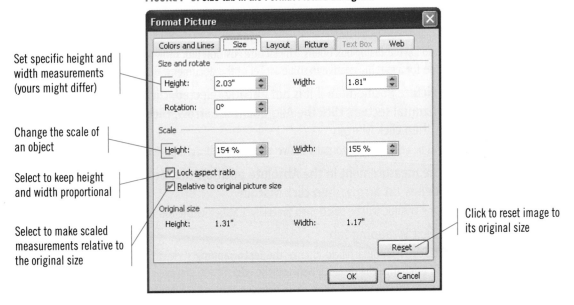

Clues to Use

Cropping graphics

If you want to use only part of a picture in a document, you can crop the graphic to trim the parts you don't want to use. To crop a graphic, select it, then click the Crop button ⬚ on the Picture toolbar. The pointer changes to the cropping pointer ⬚, and cropping handles (solid black lines) appear on all four corners and sides of the graphic. To crop one side of a graphic, drag a side cropping handle inward to where you want to trim the graphic. To crop two adjacent sides at once, drag a corner cropping handle inward to the point where you want the corner of the cropped image to be. When you drag a cropping handle, the shape of the cropping pointer changes to correspond to the shape of the cropping handle you are dragging. When you finish adjusting the parameters of the graphic, click the Crop button again to turn off the crop feature. You can also crop a graphic by entering precise crop measurements on the Picture tab in the Format Picture dialog box.

Positioning Graphics

Once you insert a graphic into a document and make it a floating graphic, you can move it by dragging it with the mouse, nudging it with the arrow keys, or setting an exact location for the graphic using the Picture command on the Format menu. Dragging an object with the mouse or using the arrow keys allows you to position a graphic visually. Using the Picture command to position a graphic allows you to place an object precisely on a page. You experiment with different positions for the MediaLoft logo to determine which position enhances the document the most.

STEPS

QUICK TIP
To move an object only horizontally or vertically, press [Shift] as you drag.

1. **Select the** logo graphic **if it is not already selected, move the pointer over the graphic, when the pointer changes to ⬚, drag the graphic down and to the right as shown in Figure F-6 so its top aligns with the top of the** Create a simple layout **heading**

   As you drag, the dotted outline indicates the position of the graphic. When you release the mouse button, the graphic is moved and the text wraps around the graphic. Notice that the Create a simple layout heading is now above the graphic.

2. **With the graphic selected, press [◄] four times, then press [▲] three times**

   Each time you press an arrow key the graphic is **nudged**—moved a small amount—in that direction. You can also press [Ctrl] and an arrow key to nudge an object in even smaller (one pixel) increments. Nudging the graphic did not position it exactly where you want it to be.

QUICK TIP
You can place a floating graphic anywhere on a page, including outside the margins.

3. **Double-click the** graphic, **click the** Layout tab **in the Format Picture dialog box, then click** Advanced

   The Advanced Layout dialog box opens. The Picture Position tab, shown in Figure F-7, allows you to specify an exact position for a graphic relative to some aspect of the document, such as a margin, column, or paragraph.

4. **Click the** Picture Position tab **if it is not already selected, click the** Alignment option button **in the Horizontal section, click the** Alignment list arrow, **click** Centered, **click the** relative to list arrow, **then click** Margin

   The logo will be centered horizontally between the left and right page margins.

5. **Change the measurement in the Absolute position text box in the Vertical section to** 1.5, **click the** below list arrow, **then click** Margin

   The top of the graphic will be positioned precisely 1.5" below the top margin.

6. **Click the** Text Wrapping tab

   You use the Text Wrapping tab to change the text-wrapping style, to wrap text around only one side of a graphic, and to change the distance between the edge of the graphic and the edge of the wrapped text. You want to increase the amount of white space between the sides of the graphic and the wrapped text.

7. **Select** Square, **select** 0.13 **in the Left text box, type** .3, **press [Tab], then type** .3 **in the Right text box**

   The distance between the graphic and the edge of the wrapped text will be .3" on either side.

TROUBLE
If the Picture toolbar remains open after you deselect the graphic, close the toolbar.

8. **Click** OK **to close the Advanced Layout dialog box, click** OK **to close the Format Picture dialog box, deselect the graphic, then save your changes**

   The logo is centered between the margins, the top of the graphic is positioned 1.5" below the top margin, and the amount of white space between the left and right sides of the graphic and the wrapped text is increased to .3", as shown in Figure F-8.

FIGURE F-6: Dragging a graphic to move it

Top of graphic aligns with the top of the text

Dotted outline shows the position as you drag

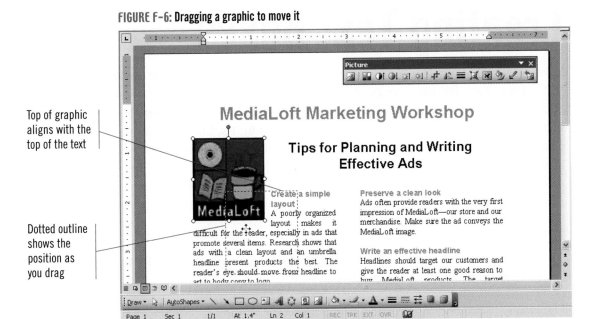

FIGURE F-7: Picture Position tab in the Advanced Layout dialog box

Select to horizontally align a graphic relative to an aspect of the document

Select to position a graphic a precise distance from an aspect of the document (your measurements might differ)

Select the aspect of the document you want to position the graphic relative to

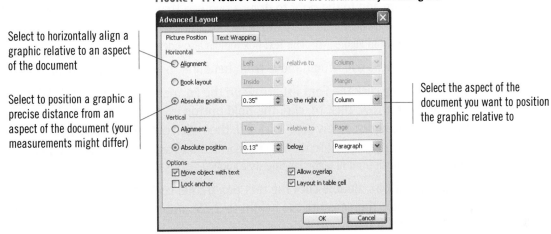

FIGURE F-8: Repositioned logo

Logo is centered and its top is 1.5" from the top margin

1.5" mark on the ruler

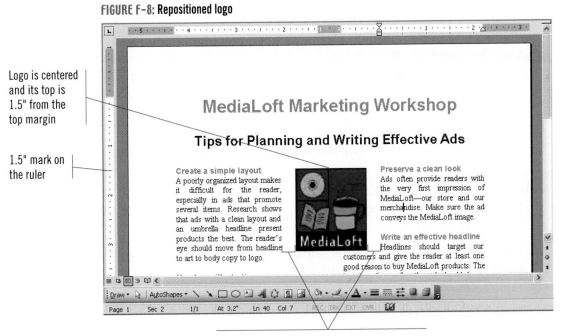

Space between the graphic and the text is increased

Creating Text Boxes

When you want to illustrate your documents with text, you can create a text box. A **text box** is a container that you can fill with text and graphics. Like other drawing objects, text boxes can be resized, formatted with colors, lines, and text-wrapping, and positioned anywhere on a page. You create a text box using the Text Box button on the Drawing toolbar or the Text Box command on the Insert menu. When you insert a text box or another drawing object, a drawing canvas opens in the document. A **drawing canvas** is a workspace for creating your own graphics. You can choose to draw the text box directly in the document, or to draw it in the drawing canvas.  You want to add a pull quote to call attention to the main point of the handout. You draw a text box, add the pull quote text to it, format the text, and then position the text box on the page.

STEPS

QUICK TIP
To draw a text box around existing text, select the text, then click the Text Box button.

1. **Scroll down, click before the** Use large illustrations **heading, then click the** Text Box button ▣ **on the Drawing toolbar**

   A drawing canvas opens in the document, as shown in Figure F-9, and the pointer changes to ╋. You'll draw a text box outside the drawing canvas.

2. **Move the** ╋ **pointer directly under the lower-left corner of the MediaLoft logo, then click and drag down and to the right to draw a text box that is about 1½" wide and 2¾" tall**

   When you release the mouse button, the drawing canvas disappears and the insertion point is located in the text box, as shown in Figure F-10. The Text Box toolbar also opens.

3. **Type** The reader's eye should move from headline to art to body copy to logo

TROUBLE
If the text does not fit in the text box, drag the bottom sizing handle down to enlarge the text box.

4. **Select the text, click the** Font list arrow **on the Formatting toolbar, click** Arial, **click the** Font Size list arrow, **click** 14, **click the** Bold button ▣, **click the** Center button ▤, **click the** Line Spacing list arrow ▤▾, **click** 2.0, **then click outside the text box**

   The text is formatted. Notice that the body text does not wrap around the text box. By default, text boxes are inserted with the In front of text-wrapping style applied.

QUICK TIP
Use the Text Box tab to change the margins in a text box.

5. **Click the** text box, **double-click the** text box frame, **click the** Size tab **in the Format Text Box dialog box, then change the height to** 2.75" **and the width to** 1.5" **in the Size and rotate section, if necessary**

   When you click a text box with the I pointer, the insertion point moves inside the text box and sizing handles appear. Clicking the frame of a text box with the ╀ pointer selects the text box object itself. Double-clicking the frame opens the Format Text Box dialog box.

6. **Click the** Layout tab, **click** Advanced, **click the** Picture Position tab, **click the** Alignment option button **in the Horizontal section, click the** Alignment list arrow, **click** Centered, **click the** relative to list arrow, **click** Margin, **make sure the** Absolute position option button **in the Vertical section is selected, change the measurement in the Absolute position text box to** 3.4, **click the** below list arrow, **then click** Margin

   The text box will be centered between the left and right margins, and its top will be precisely 3.4" below the top margin.

7. **Click the** Text Wrapping tab, **click** Square, **change the Top, Bottom, Left, and Right measurements to** .3" **in the Distance from text section, click** OK **twice, then deselect the text box**

   The text is wrapped in a square around the text box.

8. **Click inside the text box, click the** Line Color list arrow ▨▾ **on the Drawing toolbar, click** No Line, **then deselect the text box**

   The thin black border around the text box is removed, as shown in Figure F-11.

9. **Press** [Ctrl][End], **type your name, save your changes, print, then close the file**

FIGURE F-9: Drawing canvas

Drawing canvas

Drawing Canvas toolbar

FIGURE F-10: Text box

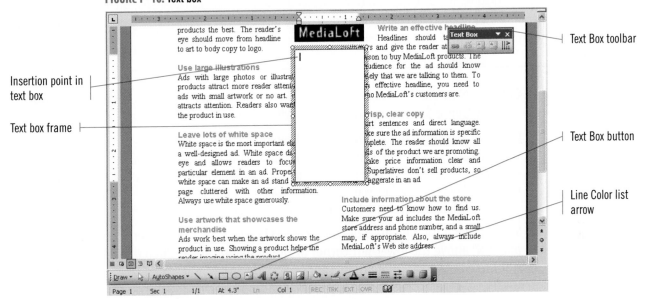

Insertion point in text box

Text box frame

Text Box toolbar

Text Box button

Line Color list arrow

FIGURE F-11: Completed handout with text box

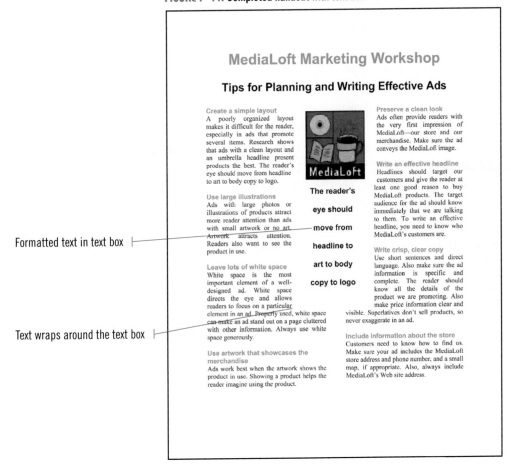

Formatted text in text box

Text wraps around the text box

Creating AutoShapes

One way you can create your own graphics in Word is to use AutoShapes. **AutoShapes** are the rectangles, ovals, triangles, lines, block arrows, stars, banners, lightning bolts, hearts, suns, and other drawing objects you can create using the tools on the Drawing toolbar. The Drawing toolbar also includes tools for adding colors, shadows, fills, and three-dimensional effects to your graphics. Table F-2 describes the buttons on the Drawing toolbar. You can choose to draw a line or shape exactly where you want it in a document, or you can create a graphic in a drawing canvas. It's helpful to use a drawing canvas if your graphic includes multiple items. ▓▓▓ Your second handout needs to illustrate MediaLoft book sales by genre. You use AutoShapes to create a picture of a stack of books, and then add the text to the picture.

STEPS

1. **Click the** New Blank Document button 🗋 **on the Standard toolbar, then save the document as** Genre Sales **to the drive and folder where your Data Files are located**

2. **Click the** Rectangle button 🔲 **on the Drawing toolbar**
   When you click an AutoShape button, a drawing canvas opens and the pointer changes to ╋. Depending on your computer settings, the Drawing Canvas toolbar might also open. The Drawing Canvas toolbar contains buttons for sizing the graphics you create in the drawing canvas, and for wrapping text around the drawing canvas. You'll learn more about resizing and positioning the drawing canvas in the next lesson.

QUICK TIP

To draw a square, click the Rectangle button, then press [Shift] while you drag the pointer. Similarly, to draw a circle, click the Oval button, then press [Shift] while you drag the pointer.

3. **Scroll down until the entire drawing canvas is visible on your screen, place the pointer about ¾" above the lower-left corner of the drawing canvas, then drag down and to the right to create a rectangle that is about 5" wide and ½" tall**
   You do not need to be exact in your measurements as you drag. When you release the mouse button, sizing handles appear around the rectangle to indicate it is selected. Cropping handles also appear around the edges of the drawing canvas.

4. **Click** AutoShapes **on the Drawing toolbar, point to** Basic Shapes**, then click the** Sun
   The AutoShapes menu contains categories of shapes and lines that you can draw.

5. **Place the ╋ pointer in the upper-left corner of the drawing canvas, then drag down and to the right to create a sun that is about ½" wide**
   The sun shape includes a yellow diamond-shaped adjustment handle. You can drag an **adjustment handle** to change the shape, but not the size, of many AutoShapes.

6. **Position the pointer over the adjustment handle until it changes to ▷, drag the handle to the right about ¼", click the** Fill Color list arrow 🎨▾ **on the Drawing toolbar, click** Gold**, click the** rectangle **to select it, click** 🎨▾**, then click** Rose
   The sun shape becomes narrower and the shapes are filled with color. Notice that when you select a color, the active color changes on the Fill Color button.

7. **Refer to Figure F-12 to draw three more rectangles, then fill the rectangles with color**
   After all four rectangles are drawn, use the sizing handles to resize the rectangles if necessary.

QUICK TIP

Double-click the Rectangle, Oval, Line, or Arrow button to activate the ╋ pointer and draw more than one shape or line. When you are finished drawing, click the button again.

8. **Press and hold [Shift], click each** rectangle **to select it, click the** 3-D Style button 🔳 **on the Drawing toolbar, then click** 3-D Style 1 **(the first style in the top row)**
   The rectangles appear three-dimensional, making the group look like a stack of books.

QUICK TIP

To edit text in an AutoShape, right-click it, then click Edit Text.

9. **Deselect the books, right-click the** top book**, click** Add Text**, click the** Font Size list arrow **on the Formatting toolbar, click** 20**, then type** Children's - 17%
   The 3-D rectangle changes to a text box. You can convert any shape to a text box by right-clicking it and clicking Add Text.

10. **Add the 20-point text as shown in Figure F-13, then save your changes**

FIGURE F-12: AutoShapes in the drawing canvas

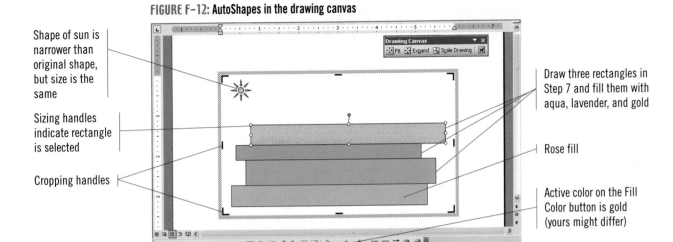

Shape of sun is narrower than original shape, but size is the same

Sizing handles indicate rectangle is selected

Cropping handles

Draw three rectangles in Step 7 and fill them with aqua, lavender, and gold

Rose fill

Active color on the Fill Color button is gold (yours might differ)

FIGURE F-13: Text added to AutoShapes

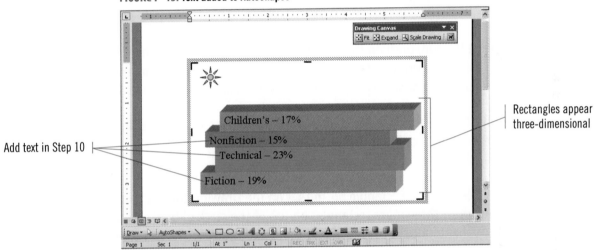

Add text in Step 10

Children's – 17%
Nonfiction – 15%
Technical – 23%
Fiction – 19%

Rectangles appear three-dimensional

TABLE F-2: Buttons on the Drawing toolbar

button	use to	button	use to
Draw ▾	Open a menu of commands for grouping, positioning, rotating, and wrapping text around graphics, and for changing an AutoShape to a different shape	(clip art)	Insert a clip art graphic
		(picture)	Insert a picture from a file
(select)	Select graphic objects	(fill) ▾	Fill a shape with a color, a texture, a gradient, or a pattern
AutoShapes ▾	Open a menu of drawing options for lines, shapes, and callouts	(line color) ▾	Change the color of a line, an arrow, or a line around a shape
(line)	Draw a straight line	A ▾	Change the color of text
(arrow)	Draw a straight line with an arrowhead	(line style)	Change the style and weight of a line, an arrow, or a line around a shape
(rectangle)	Draw a rectangle or square	(dash style)	Change the dash style of a line, an arrow, or a line around a shape
(oval)	Draw an oval or circle	(arrow style)	Change a line to an arrow; change the style of an arrow
(text box)	Insert a text box	(shadow)	Add a shadow to a graphic object
(WordArt)	Insert a WordArt graphic	(3-D)	Make a graphic object three-dimensional
(diagram)	Insert a diagram or an organization chart		

Using the Drawing Canvas

When multiple shapes are contained in a drawing canvas, you can resize and move them as a single graphic object. The Drawing Canvas toolbar includes buttons for sizing a drawing canvas and for wrapping text around it. Once you apply a text-wrapping style to a drawing canvas, you can position it anywhere in a document. ▨▨▨▨ You want to add another three books to the stack. You enlarge the drawing canvas, add the shapes, size the drawing as a single object, and then move it to the bottom of the page.

STEPS

1. **Click the Zoom list arrow on the Standard toolbar, click 75%, then click the stack of books graphic to make the drawing canvas visible if it is not visible**
   Cropping handles appear around the edges of the drawing canvas.

2. **Place the pointer over the top-middle cropping handle, when the pointer changes to ⊥, drag the handle to the top of the page, then release the mouse button**
   The drawing canvas is enlarged from the top, but the size of the graphic does not change. Dragging a cropping handle resizes the drawing canvas, but not the graphic.

3. **Select the sun, position the pointer over it until the pointer changes to ⬚, drag the sun on top of the right end of the Technical book, then release the mouse button**
   The sun shape is moved to the spine of the book, but is hidden beneath the rectangle shape.

> **TROUBLE**
> If the sun is not selected, click Undo Move Object on the Edit menu, and then repeat Step 3.

4. **With the sun shape selected, click the Draw button on the Drawing toolbar, point to Order, then click Bring to Front**
   The sun shape is moved on top of the rectangle shape.

5. **Double-click the Rectangle button ▢ on the Drawing toolbar to activate the rectangle tool, draw three more rectangles on top of the stack of books, click ▢ to turn off the tool, then right-click each rectangle and add the 20-point text shown in Figure F-14**

6. **Select each rectangle, fill it with any color, then apply the 3-D Style 1**

> **TROUBLE**
> If your Drawing Canvas toolbar is not open, right-click the drawing canvas frame, then click Show Drawing Canvas toolbar on the shortcut menu.

7. **Click the Fit Drawing to Contents button ⊡Fit on the Drawing Canvas toolbar**
   The drawing canvas is automatically resized to fit the graphic within it.

8. **Click the Zoom list arrow, click Whole Page, then click the Scale Drawing button ⊞ Scale Drawing on the Drawing Canvas toolbar**
   The cropping handles on the drawing canvas change to sizing handles. You can now use the drawing canvas frame to resize the contents of the drawing canvas as a single graphic.

> **QUICK TIP**
> To precisely size or position a drawing canvas, double-click the drawing canvas frame to open the Format Drawing Canvas dialog box.

9. **Drag the bottom-middle sizing handle down until the graphic is about 6" tall**
   Resizing the drawing canvas resizes all the shapes within it. Dragging a top, bottom, or side handle stretches the graphic. Dragging a corner handle resizes the graphic proportionally.

10. **Click the Text Wrapping button ⊠ on the Drawing Canvas toolbar, click Square, place the pointer over the drawing canvas frame so it changes to ⬚, drag the drawing canvas down and position it so it is centered in the bottom part of the page, deselect the drawing canvas, then save your changes**
    Compare your document to Figure F-15. You must wrap text around a drawing canvas to be able to position it anywhere on a page.

FIGURE F-14: New rectangles in drawing canvas

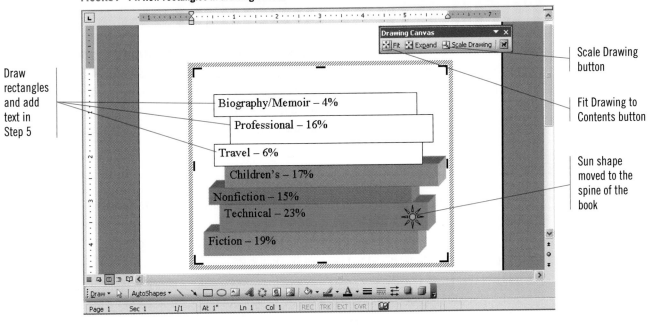

Draw rectangles and add text in Step 5

Scale Drawing button

Fit Drawing to Contents button

Sun shape moved to the spine of the book

FIGURE F-15: Resized and repositioned graphic

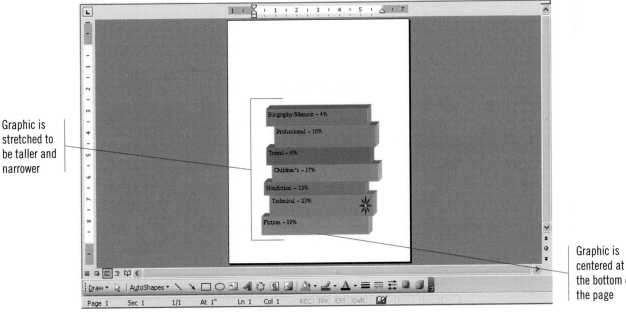

Graphic is stretched to be taller and narrower

Graphic is centered at the bottom of the page

Clues to Use

Drawing lines

In addition to drawing straight lines and arrows, you can use the Lines tools on the AutoShapes menu to draw curved, freeform, and scribble lines. Click AutoShapes on the Drawing toolbar, point to Lines, then select the type of line you want to draw. Choose Curve ⌇ to draw an object with smooth curves, choose Freeform ⌕ to draw an object with both freehand and straight-line segments, or choose Scribble ✑ to draw a freehand object that looks like it was drawn with a pencil. The lines you draw include vertexes—a **vertex** is either a point where two straight lines meet or the highest point in a curve. To create a curve or freeform line, click the location you

want the line to begin, move the mouse, click to insert a vertex, move the mouse, and so on. Double-click to end a curve or freeform line or click near the starting point to close a shape, if that's what you have drawn. Drawing scribble lines is similar to drawing with a pencil: drag the pointer to draw the line, and then release the mouse button when you are finished. The best way to learn about drawing curve, freeform, and scribble lines is to experiment. Once you draw a line, you can modify its shape by right-clicking it, clicking Edit Points, and then dragging a vertex to a different location.

Formatting WordArt

Another way to give your documents punch and flair is to use WordArt. **WordArt** is a drawing object that contains text formatted with special shapes, patterns, and orientations. You create WordArt using either the WordArt button on the Drawing toolbar or the Picture, WordArt command on the Insert menu. Once you have created a WordArt object, you can use the buttons on the WordArt toolbar to format it with different shapes, fonts, colors, and other effects to create the impact you desire. You use WordArt to create a fun heading for your handout.

STEPS

1. **Press [Ctrl][Home], press [Enter], click the Zoom list arrow on the Standard toolbar, click Page Width, then click the Insert WordArt button ⊿ on the Drawing toolbar**
   The WordArt Gallery opens. It includes the styles you can choose for your WordArt.

2. **Click the first style in the third row, then click OK**
   The Edit WordArt Text dialog box opens. You type the text you want to format as WordArt in this dialog box and, if you wish, change the font and font size of the WordArt text.

3. **Type Genre Sales, then click OK**
   The WordArt object appears at the location of the insertion point. Like other graphic objects, the WordArt object is an inline graphic until you wrap text around it.

> **QUICK TIP**
> You can use the Text Wrapping button on the WordArt toolbar to convert the object to a floating graphic.

4. **Click the WordArt object to select it**
   The WordArt toolbar opens when a WordArt object is selected. It includes buttons for editing and modifying WordArt.

> **TROUBLE**
> If your page goes blank, click the Undo button on the Standard toolbar and repeat Step 5. Take care not to make the WordArt object taller than 2".

5. **Drag the lower-right corner sizing handle down and to the right to make the object about 2" tall and 6" wide**
   The WordArt is enlarged to span the page between the left and right margins, as shown in Figure F-16.

6. **Click the WordArt Character Spacing button 🗛 on the WordArt toolbar, click Tight, click the WordArt Shape button 🅰 on the WordArt toolbar, then click the Can Up shape (the third shape in the third row)**
   The spacing between the characters is decreased and the shape of the WordArt text changes.

7. **Click the Format WordArt button 🦋 on the WordArt toolbar, then click the Colors and Lines tab**
   The Format WordArt dialog box opens. You use the Colors and Lines tab to change the fill color of WordArt, to change the transparency of the fill color, and to change the color or style of the line surrounding the WordArt characters.

> **QUICK TIP**
> To fill AutoShapes with fill effects, click the Fill Color list arrow on the Drawing toolbar, then click Fill Effects.

8. **Click the Color list arrow in the Fill section, then click Fill Effects**
   The Fill Effects dialog box opens, as shown in Figure F-17. You use this dialog box to change the fill colors and effects of the WordArt object. Using the Gradient tab, you can select a preset gradient effect or choose colors and shading styles to create your own gradient effect. You can also apply a preset texture using the Texture tab, design a two-color pattern using the Pattern tab, or fill the object with a graphic using the Picture tab.

9. **Make sure the Two colors option button is selected in the Colors section on the Gradient tab, click the Color 1 list arrow, click Indigo, click the Color 2 list arrow, click Pink, click the Diagonal up option button in the Shading styles section, click the lower-right box in the Variants section, then click OK twice**
   The new fill effects are applied to the WordArt. The completed handout is shown in Figure F-18.

10. **Press [Ctrl][Home], type your name, save your changes, print the document, then close the file**

FIGURE F-16: Resized WordArt

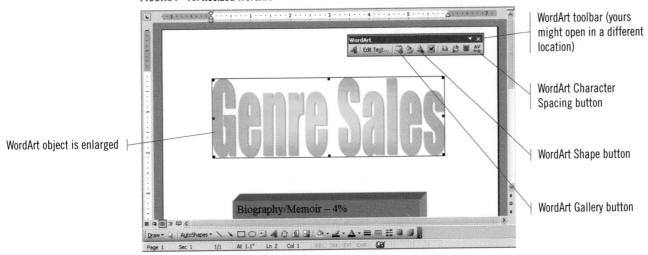

WordArt toolbar (yours might open in a different location)

WordArt Character Spacing button

WordArt object is enlarged

WordArt Shape button

WordArt Gallery button

FIGURE F-17: Fill Effects dialog box

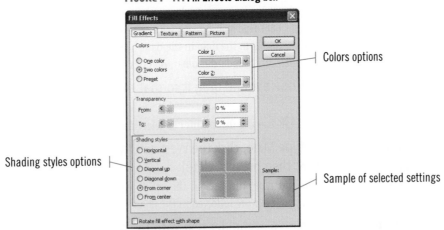

Colors options

Shading styles options

Sample of selected settings

FIGURE F-18: Completed handout with WordArt

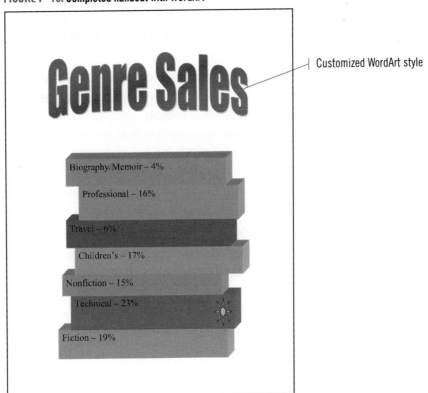

Customized WordArt style

Creating Charts

Adding a chart can be an attractive way to illustrate a document that includes numerical information. A **chart** is a visual representation of numerical data and usually is used to illustrate trends, patterns, or relationships. The Word chart feature allows you to create many types of charts, including bar, column, pie, area, and line charts. You can add a chart to a document using the Picture, Chart command on the Insert menu. ▓▓▓▓ You create a handout that includes a chart showing the distribution of MediaLoft customers by age and gender.

STEPS

1. **Open the file** WD F-2.doc **from the drive and folder where your Data Files are located, save it as** Age and Gender, **then press** [Ctrl][End]
   The insertion point is centered under the title.

QUICK TIP
To show the toolbars on two rows, click the Toolbar Options button at the end of the Formatting toolbar, then click Show Buttons on Two Rows.

2. **Click** Insert **on the menu bar, point to** Picture, **then click** Chart
   A table opens in a datasheet window and a column chart appears in the document. The datasheet and the chart contain placeholder data that you replace with your own data. The chart is based on the data in the datasheet. Any change you make to the data in the datasheet is made automatically to the chart. Notice that when a chart object is open, the Standard toolbar includes buttons for working with charts.

3. **Click the** datasheet title bar **and drag it so that the chart is visible, then move the pointer over the** datasheet
   The pointer changes to ✛. You use this pointer to select the cells in the datasheet.

QUICK TIP
Click the Chart Type list arrow ▦ ▾ on the Standard toolbar to change the type of chart.

4. **Click the** East cell, **type** Male, **click the** West cell, **type** Female, **click the gray** 3 cell **to select the third row, then press** [Delete]
   When you click a cell and type, the data in the cell is replaced with the text you type. As you edit the datasheet, the changes you make are reflected in the chart.

5. **Replace the remaining placeholder text with the data shown in Figure F-19, then click outside the chart to deselect it**

6. **Click the** chart **to select the object, press** [Ctrl], **then drag the** lower-right corner sizing handle **down and to the right until the outline of the chart is approximately 7" wide**
   The chart is enlarged and still centered.

QUICK TIP
Point to any part of a chart to see a ScreenTip that identifies the part. You can also use the Chart Objects list arrow on the Standard toolbar to select a part of a chart.

7. **Double-click the** chart **to open it, click the** View Datasheet button ▦ **on the Standard toolbar to close the datasheet, click the** legend **to select it, then click the** Format Legend button ▥ **on the Standard toolbar**
   The Format Legend dialog box opens. It includes options for modifying the legend. Select any part of a chart object and use ▥ to open a dialog box with options for formatting that part of the chart. In this case, the name of the button is Format Legend because the legend is selected.

8. **Click the** Placement tab, **click the** Bottom option button, **then click** OK
   The legend moves below the chart.

9. **Click the** Value Axis (the y-axis), **click** ▥, **click the** Number tab **in the Format Axis dialog box, click** Percentage **in the Category list, click the** Decimal places down arrow **twice so** 0 **appears, click** OK, **then deselect the chart**
   Percent signs are added to the y-axis. The completed handout is shown in Figure F-20.

10. **Type** Prepared by **followed by your name centered in the document footer, save your changes, print the handout, close the document, then exit Word**

FIGURE F-19: Datasheet and chart object

Format button

Datasheet window

Chart reflects data in datasheet after all data is entered

Value axis (y-axis)

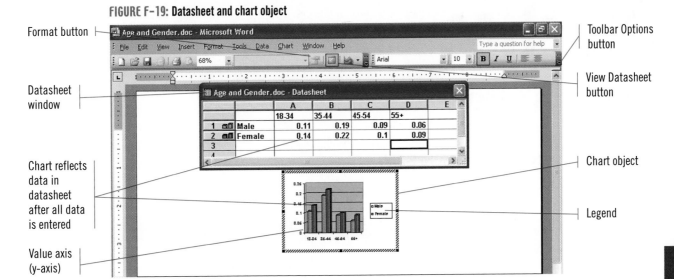

Toolbar Options button

View Datasheet button

Chart object

Legend

FIGURE F-20: Completed handout with chart

Percent signs added to the value axis

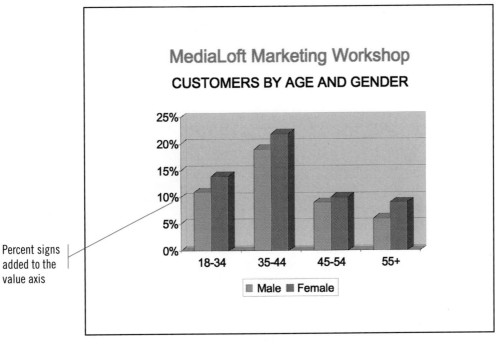

Clues to Use

Creating diagrams and organization charts

Diagrams are another way to illustrate concepts in your documents. Word includes a diagram feature that allows you to quickly create and format several types of diagrams, including pyramid, Venn, target, cycle, and radial diagrams, as well as organization charts. To insert a diagram or an organization chart, click the Insert Diagram or Organization Chart button 🔅 on the Drawing toolbar or use the Diagram command on the Insert menu to open the Diagram Gallery, shown in Figure F-21. Select a diagram type in the Diagram Gallery, then click OK. The diagram appears in a drawing canvas with placeholder text, and the Diagram toolbar opens. The Diagram toolbar contains buttons for customizing and formatting the diagram, and for sizing and positioning the drawing canvas. Use the AutoFormat button on the Diagram toolbar to apply colors and shading to your diagram.

FIGURE F-21: Diagram Gallery

Diagram Gallery

Select a diagram type:

Organization Chart
Used to show hierarchical relationships

OK   Cancel

Practice

▼ CONCEPTS REVIEW

Label the elements shown in Figure F-22.

FIGURE F-22

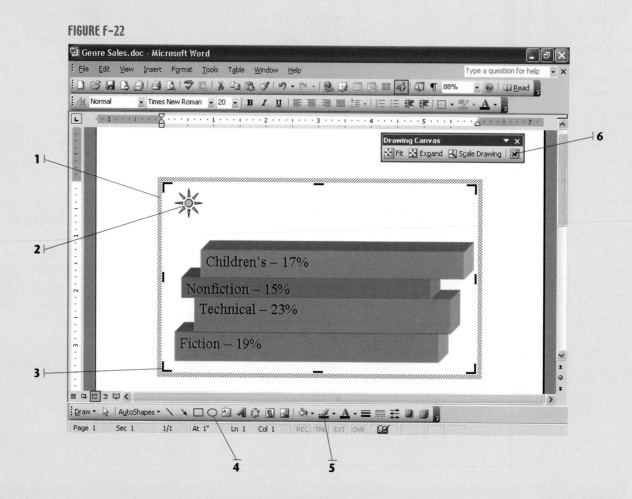

Match each term with the statement that best describes it.

7. **Text box**
8. **Drawing canvas**
9. **AutoShape**
10. **Bitmap graphic**
11. **Chart**
12. **WordArt**
13. **Pixels**
14. **Vertex**

a. A graphic object drawn using the tools on the Drawing toolbar
b. A workspace for creating graphics
c. A graphic that is composed of a series of small dots
d. A graphic object that is a container for text and graphics
e. Dots that define color and intensity in a graphic
f. A visual representation of numerical data
g. A graphic object composed of specially formatted text
h. The intersection of two line sections or the highest point on a curve

Select the best answer from the list of choices.

15. Which button can be used to create a text box?

a. [icon]

b. [icon]

c. [icon]

d. [icon]

16. What must you do to a drawing canvas before moving it to a different location?

a. Scale the drawing canvas.

b. Enter a precise position for the drawing canvas in the Format Drawing Canvas dialog box.

c. Fit the drawing canvas to the contents.

d. Wrap text around the drawing canvas.

17. What do you drag to change an AutoShape's shape, but not its size or dimensions?

a. Sizing handle

b. Rotate handle

c. Cropping handle

d. Adjustment handle

18. Which method do you use to nudge a picture?

a. Select the picture, then press an arrow key.

b. Select the picture, then drag a top, bottom, or side sizing handle.

c. Select the picture, then drag a corner sizing handle.

d. Select the picture, then drag it to a new location.

19. If you want to create an oval that contains formatted text, what kind of graphic object would you create?

a. A text box

b. WordArt

c. A pie chart

d. An AutoShape

20. What style of text wrapping is applied to a text box by default?

a. Square

b. In line with text

c. In front of text

d. Tight

▼ SKILLS REVIEW

1. Add graphics.

a. Start Word, open the file WD F-3.doc from the drive and folder where your Data Files are located, then save it as **Farm Flyer**.

b. Press [Ctrl][End], then insert the file **Farm.jpg** from the drive and folder where your Data Files are located.

c. Select the photo, apply the Square text-wrapping style to it, then save your changes.

2. Resize graphics.

a. Scroll down so that the graphic is at the top of your screen.

b. Drag the lower-right sizing handle to enlarge the graphic proportionally so that it is about 4" wide and 3" high.

c. Click the Crop button on the Picture toolbar.

d. Drag the bottom-middle cropping handle up approximately 1", then click the Crop button again.

e. Double-click the photo, click the Size tab, then change the width of the photo to 6". (*Hint*: Make sure the Lock aspect ratio check box is selected.)

f. Save your changes.

3. Position graphics.

   a. Drag the photo up so that its top is aligned with the top margin.

   b. Double-click the photo, click the Layout tab, then click Advanced.

   c. On the Picture Position tab, change the horizontal alignment to centered relative to the margins.

   d. In the Vertical section, change the absolute position to 2" below the margin.

   e. On the Text Wrapping tab, change the wrapping style to Top and bottom, change the Top measurement to 2", then change the Bottom measurement to .3".

   f. Click OK to close the Advanced Layout and Format Picture dialog boxes, then save your changes.

4. Create text boxes.

   a. Change the zoom level to Whole Page, then draw a 1.5" x 6" text box at the bottom of the page. (*Note:* Do not draw the text box in the drawing canvas if it opens.)

   b. Change the zoom level to Page Width, type **Mountain Realty** in the text box, format the text in 18-point Arial, bold, then center it in the text box.

   c. Press [Enter], type **603-555-3466**, press [Enter], type **www.mountainrealty.com**, then format the two lines of text in 11-point Arial, bold.

   d. Resize the text box to be 1" high and 4" wide, then move it to the lower-left corner of the page, aligned with the left and bottom margin.

   e. Fill the text box with Blue-Gray, change the font color of the text to White, then remove the line from around the text box.

   f. With the text box selected, click Draw on the Drawing toolbar, point to Change AutoShape, point to Basic Shapes, then click the Oval. (*Note:* Adjust the text size or oval size if necessary.)

   g. Deselect the text box, then save your changes.

5. Create AutoShapes.

   a. Place the insertion point in the paragraph of text above the oval, click AutoShapes on the Drawing toolbar, point to Basic Shapes, then click the Isosceles Triangle shape.

   b. Draw an isosceles triangle in the drawing canvas, then fill it with Violet. (*Note:* The drawing canvas appears on a new page 2. You resize and position the drawing canvas after you finish drawing in it.)

   c. Draw three more isosceles triangles in the drawing canvas, then fill them with Lavender, Blue-Gray, and Indigo.

   d. Drag the triangles to position them so they overlap each other to look like mountains.

   e. Draw a sun shape in the drawing canvas, fill it with Gold, then position it so it overlaps the tops of the mountains. Resize the sun if necessary.

   f. Select the sun, click Draw on the Drawing toolbar, point to Order, then click Send to Back.

   g. Use the Order commands to change the order of the triangles and the sun so that the shapes look like a mountain range with the sun setting behind it. Resize and reposition the shapes as necessary to create a mountain effect, then save your changes.

6. Use the drawing canvas.

   a. Fit the drawing canvas to the mountain range graphic. (*Hint:* You might need to scroll the document to locate the drawing canvas after you fit the drawing canvas to it.)

   b. Apply the Square text-wrapping style to the drawing canvas.

   c. Click the Scale Drawing button, then resize the drawing canvas so the graphic is approximately 1.5" wide and 1" tall. Adjust the shapes in the drawing canvas if the graphic looks awkward after resizing it.

   d. Change the zoom level to Whole Page, move the drawing canvas to the lower-right corner of the page, aligned with the right and bottom margins, then deselect the drawing canvas.

   e. Save your changes, then press [Ctrl][Home] to move the insertion point to the top of the document (the beginning of the text).

7. **Format WordArt.**
   a. Insert a WordArt object, select any horizontal WordArt style, type **Farmhouse**, then click OK.
   b. Apply Square text wrapping to the WordArt object, then move it above the photograph if necessary.
   c. Resize the WordArt object to be 6" wide and 1.25" tall, then position it so it is centered between the margins and 1" below the top of the page.
   d. Open the WordArt Gallery, then change the style to the fifth style in the second row.
   e. Open the Format WordArt dialog box, open the Fill Effects dialog box, select the Preset color Nightfall, select any Shading style and Variant, then apply the settings to the WordArt object.
   e. Type **Contact** followed by your name in the document footer, center the text, then format it in 12-point Arial.
   f. Save your changes to the flyer, print a copy, then close the file.

8. **Create charts.**
   a. Open a new, blank document, then save it as **Realty Sales** to the drive and folder where your Data Files are located.
   b. Click the Center button, type **Mountain Realty 2006 Sales**, then format the text in 26-point Arial, bold.
   c. Press [Enter] twice, then insert a chart.
   d. Click the Chart Type list arrow on the Standard toolbar, then click Pie Chart. (*Hint*: Use the Toolbar Options button as needed to locate the Chart Type button.)
   e. Select the second and third rows in the datasheet, then press [Delete].
   f. Replace the data in the datasheet with the data shown in Figure F-23, then close the datasheet. (*Hint*: If the label in your datasheet is East, replace it with **Pie 1**.)
   g. Select the legend, click the Format Legend button, then change the placement of the legend to Bottom.
   h. Use the Chart Objects list arrow to select the Plot Area, open the Format Plot Area dialog box, then change the Border and Area patterns to None.

FIGURE F-23

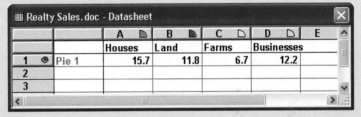

   i. Use the Chart Objects list arrow to select Series "Pie 1," open the Format Data Series dialog box, click the Data Labels tab, then make the data labels show the percentage.
   j. Resize the chart object proportionally so it is about 5" wide and 3" tall.
   k. Type **Prepared by** followed by your name centered in the document footer, save your changes, print the document, close the file, then exit Word.

▼ INDEPENDENT CHALLENGE 1

You are starting a business and need to design a letterhead. Your letterhead needs to include a logo, which you design using AutoShapes, as well as your name and contact information. Figure F-24 shows a sample letterhead.

   a. Start Word, open a new blank document, then save it as **Letterhead** to the drive and folder where your Data Files are located.
   b. Identify the nature of your business, then examine the shapes available on the AutoShapes menus and decide what kind of logo to create.
   c. Using pencil and paper, sketch a design for your letterhead. Determine the positions for your logo, name, address, and any other design elements you want to include. You will create and organize all the elements of your letterhead in a drawing canvas.

FIGURE F-24

Word 2003

▼ INDEPENDENT CHALLENGE 1 (CONTINUED)

d. Using AutoShapes, create your logo in a drawing canvas. Use the buttons on the Drawing toolbar to enhance the logo with color, text, lines, shadows, and other effects.

e. Resize the logo and position it in the drawing canvas.

f. In the drawing canvas, create a text box that includes your name, address, and other important contact information. Format the text and the text box using the buttons on the Formatting and Drawing toolbars.

g. Resize the text box as necessary and position it in the drawing canvas.

h. Add to the drawing canvas any other design elements you want to include.

i. When you are satisfied with the layout of your letterhead in the drawing canvas, fit the drawing canvas to its contents, then resize the drawing canvas as necessary.

j. Wrap text around the drawing canvas, then position it on the page.

k. Save your changes, preview the letterhead, print a copy, close the file, then exit Word.

▼ INDEPENDENT CHALLENGE 2

You design ads for GoTroppo.com, a company that specializes in discounted travel to tropical destinations. Your next assignment is to design a full-page ad for a travel magazine. Your ad needs to contain a photograph of a vacation scene, shown in Figure F-25, the text "Your vacation begins here and now," and the Web address "www.gotroppo.com." If you are performing the ACE steps, your ad will also include a company logo.

FIGURE F-25

a. Start Word, open a new, blank document, then save it as **GoTroppo Ad** to the drive and folder where your Data Files are located.

b. Change all four page margins to .7".

c. Insert the file **Vacation.jpg** from the drive and folder where your Data Files are located, then examine the photo. Think about how you can use this photo effectively in your ad.

d. Using pencil and paper, sketch the layout for your ad. You can use AutoShapes, lines, text boxes, WordArt, and any other design elements in your ad to make it powerful and eye-catching.

e. Apply a text-wrapping style to the photograph to make it a floating graphic, then format the photograph as you planned. You can crop it, resize it, move it, and combine it with other design elements.

f. Using text boxes or WordArt, add the text **Your vacation begins here and now** and the Web address **www.gotroppo.com** to the ad.

g. Use the buttons on the Drawing and Formatting toolbars to format the graphic objects.

Advanced Challenge Exercise

■ Using AutoShapes and a text box in a drawing canvas, create a logo that includes a sun setting over the ocean and the company name **gotroppo.com**. Figure F-26 shows a sample logo.

■ Using the Fill Effects dialog box, fill the AutoShapes with color, gradients, patterns, or textures.

■ Resize the drawing canvas to suit your needs, then move the logo to where you want it in the ad.

FIGURE F-26

h. Adjust the layout and design of the ad: adjust the colors, add or remove design elements, and resize and reposition the objects as necessary.

i. When you are satisfied with your ad, type your name in the document header, save your changes, print a copy, close the document, then exit Word.

▼ INDEPENDENT CHALLENGE 3

You are a graphic designer. The public library has hired you to design a bookmark for Literacy Week. Their only request is that the bookmark includes the words Literacy Week. You'll create three different bookmarks for the library.

a. Start Word, open a new, blank document, then save it as **Bookmarks** to the drive and folder where your Data Files are located.

b. Change all four page margins to .7", change the page orientation to landscape, and change the zoom level to Whole Page.

c. Draw three rectangles in a drawing canvas. Resize the rectangles to be 2.5" x 6.5" and move them so they do not overlap. Each rectangle will become a bookmark. (*Hint*: If you use the Format AutoShape dialog box to resize the rectangles, make sure the Lock aspect ratio check box is not selected.)

d. In the first rectangle, design a bookmark using AutoShapes.

e. In the second rectangle, design a bookmark using WordArt.

f. In the third rectangle, design a bookmark using clip art.

Advanced Challenge Exercise

■ Fill one bookmark with a gradient, one with a texture, and one with a pattern. You might need to revise some aspects of the bookmarks you created in the previous steps.

■ To one bookmark, add a photograph.

■ To one bookmark, add curved, scribble, or freeform lines.

g. Use the buttons on the Drawing toolbar to format the bookmarks with fills, colors, lines, and other effects. Be sure to add the words Literacy Week to each bookmark.

h. Type your name in the document header, save your changes, print, close the document, then exit Word.

▼ INDEPENDENT CHALLENGE 4

One way to find graphic images to use in your documents is to download them from the Web. Many Web sites feature images that are in the public domain, which means they have no copyright restrictions and permission is not required to use the images. You are free to download these images and use them in your documents, although you must acknowledge the artist or identify the source. Other Web sites include images that are copyrighted and require written permission, and often payment, to use. Before downloading and using graphics from the Web, it's important to research and establish their copyright status and permission requirements. In this exercise you download photographs from the Web and research their copyright restrictions.

a. Start Word, open the file WD F-4.doc from the drive and folder where your Data Files are located, then save it as **Copyright Info**. This document contains a table that you will fill with the photos you find on the Web and the copyright restrictions for those photos.

b. Use your favorite search engine to search the Web for photographs. Use the keywords **photo archives** to conduct your search.

c. Find at least three Web sites that contain photos you could use in a document. Save a photo from each Web site to your computer, and note the URL and copyright restrictions. To save an image from a Web page, right-click the image, then click the appropriate command on the shortcut menu.

d. Insert the photos you saved from the Web in the Photo column of the table. Resize the photos proportionally so that they are no more than 1.5" tall or 1.5" wide. Wrap text around the photos and center them in the table cells.

e. For each photo, enter the URL and the copyright restrictions for the photo in the table. In the Copyright Restrictions column, indicate if the photo is copyrighted or in the public domain, and note the requirements for using that photo in a document.

f. Type your name in the document header, save your changes, print a copy, close the file, then exit Word.

Using the files WD F-5.doc and Surfing.jpg (found in the drive and folder where your Data Files are located), create the flyer shown in Figure F-27. Type your name in the header, save the flyer as **Surf Safe**, then print a copy.

FIGURE F-27

Surf Safe

NEVER SURF ALONE

Follow the rules
All beginning surfers need to follow basic safety rules before heading into the waves. The key to safe surfing is caution and awareness.

Wear sunscreen
Sunscreen helps prevent skin cancer and aging of the skin. 30+ SPF broad spectrum sunscreen screens out both UVA and UVB rays and provides more than 30 times your natural sunburn protection. Apply sunscreen at least 15 minutes before exposing yourself to the sun, and reapply it every two hours or after swimming, drying with a towel, or excessive perspiration. Zinc cream also helps prevent sunburn and guards against harmful UV rays.

Dress appropriately
Wear a wet suit or a rash vest. Choose a wet suit that is appropriate for the water temperature. Rash vests help protect against UV rays.

Use a safe surfboard
A safe surfboard is a surfboard that suits your ability. Beginners need a big, thick surfboard for stability.

Learn how to escape rips
A rip current is a volume of water moving out to sea: the bigger the surf, the stronger the rips associated with it. Indicators of rips include:

- Brown water caused by stirred up sand
- Foam on the surface of the water that trails past the break
- Waves breaking on both sides of a rip current
- A rippled appearance between calm water
- Debris floating out to sea

If you are dragged out by a rip, don't panic! Stay calm and examine the rip conditions before trying to escape the current. Poor swimmers should ride the rip out from the beach and then swim parallel to the shore for 30 or 40 meters. Once you have escaped the rip, swim toward the shore where the waves are breaking. You can also probe with your feet to see if a sand bar has formed near the edge of the rip. Strong swimmers should swim at a 45 degree angle across the rip.

Study the surf
Always study the surf before going in. Select a safe beach with waves under 1 meter, and pick waves that are suitable for your ability.

Creating a Web Page

OBJECTIVES

Plan a Web page
Create a Web page
Format a Web page with themes
Illustrate a Web page with graphics
Save a document as a Web page
Add hyperlinks
Modify hyperlinks
Preview a Web page in a browser

If you have a SAM user profile, you may have access to hands-on instruction, practice, and assessment of the skills covered in this unit. Log in to your SAM account and go to your assignments page to see what your instructor has assigned.

Creating a Web page and posting it on the World Wide Web or an intranet is a powerful way to share information with other people. The Web page formatting features of Word allow you to easily create professional looking Web pages from scratch or to save an existing document in HTML format so it can be viewed using a browser. In this unit, you learn how to create a new Web page and how to save an existing document as a Web page. You also learn how to edit and format Web pages, create and modify hyperlinks, and preview a Web page in a browser. MediaLoft is sponsoring the Seattle Writers Festival, a major public event featuring prominent writers from around the world. You need to create a Web site for the Seattle Writers Festival to promote the event and provide information to the public. You plan to post the Web site on the World Wide Web.

Planning a Web Page

A **Web page** is a document that can be stored on a computer called a Web server and viewed on the World Wide Web or on an intranet using a **browser**, a software program used to access and display Web pages. A **Web site** is a group of associated Web pages that are linked together with hyperlinks. Before creating a Web page or a Web site, it's important to plan its content and organization. The **home page** is the main page of a Web site, and the first Web page viewers see when they visit a site. Usually, it is the first page you plan and create. ▰▰▰▰ The Seattle Writers Festival Web site will include a home page that serves both as an introduction to the festival and as a table of contents for the other Web pages in the site. Before creating the home page, you identify the content you want to include, plan the organization of the Web site, and sketch the design for each Web page.

DETAILS

- ### Identify the goal of the Web site
  A successful Web site has a clear purpose. For example, it might promote a product, communicate information, or facilitate a transaction. Your Web site will communicate information about the Seattle Writers Festival to the public.

QUICK TIP

Take care to limit the text and graphics on each Web page to those that help you meet your specific goal.

- ### Sketch the Web site
  Identify the information you want to include on each Web page, sketch the layout and design of each Web page, and map the links between the pages in the Web site. A well-designed Web site is visually interesting and easy for viewers to use. Figure G-1 shows a sketch of the Seattle Writers Festival Web site.

- ### Create each Web page and save it in HTML format
  You can create a Web page from scratch in Word or convert an existing document to a Web page. When you create a Web page in Word, you save it in HTML format. **HTML** (Hypertext Markup Language) is the programming language used to describe how each element of a Web page should appear when viewed with a browser. You will use a blank Web page template to create the home page. You will create the Program of Events Web page by saving an existing document in HTML format. Files saved in HTML format can be recognized by their .htm, .html, .mht, or .mhtml file extension.

QUICK TIP

If you intend to publish to the Web, filenames should use all lowercase letters and include no special characters or blank spaces. Valid characters include letters, numbers, and the underscore character.

- ### Determine the file-naming convention to use
  Different operating systems place various restrictions on Web site filenames. Many Web page designers follow the standard eight-dot-three file-naming convention, which specifies that a filename have a maximum of eight characters followed by a period and a three-letter file extension—mypage.htm or chap_1.htm, for example. You will use the eight-dot-three naming convention for your Web pages.

- ### Format each Web page
  You can use the standard Word formatting features to enhance Web pages with fonts, backgrounds, graphics, lines, tables, and other format effects. Word also includes visual themes that you can apply to Web pages to format them quickly. The look of a Web page has as much of an impact on the viewer as its content, so it's important to select fonts, colors, and graphics that complement the goal of your Web site. You plan to apply a theme that expresses the spirit of the writers festival to each Web page. A consistent look between Web pages is an important factor in Web site design.

- ### Create the hyperlinks between Web pages
  Hyperlinks are text or graphics that viewers can click to open a file, another Web page, or an e-mail message, or that viewers can click to jump to a specific location in the same file. Hyperlinks are commonly used to link the pages of a Web site to each other. You will add hyperlinks that link the home page to other Web pages in your Web site. You will also add links from the home page to other Web sites on the Internet and to an e-mail message to MediaLoft.

- ### View the Web site using a browser
  Before publishing your Web site to the Web or an intranet, it's important to view your Web pages in a browser to make sure they look and work as you intended. You will use the Web Page Preview feature to check the formatting of each Web page in your browser and to test the hyperlinks.

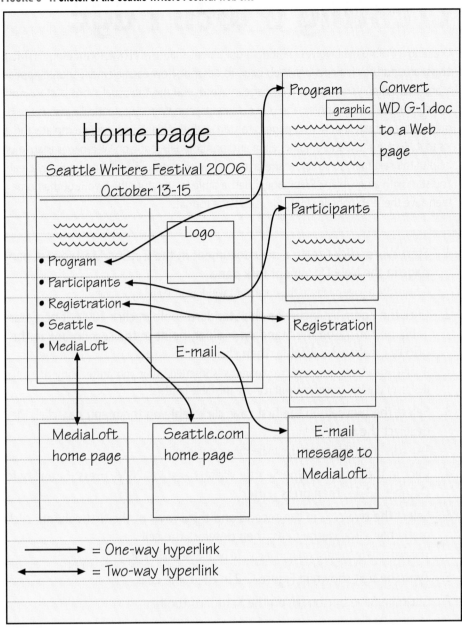

Clues to Use

Choosing a Web page file format

When you save a document as a Web page in Word, you save it in one of several HTML formats, which ensures the HTML codes are embedded in the file. You have the option of saving the document in Single File Web Page (.mht or .mhtml) format or in Web Page (.htm or .html) format. In a single file Web page, all the elements of the Web page, including the text and graphics, are saved together in a single MIME encapsulated aggregate HTML (MHTML) file, making it simple to publish your Web page or send it via e-mail. By contrast, if you choose to save a Web page as an .htm file, Word automatically creates a supporting folder in the same location as the .htm file. This folder has the same name as the .htm file plus the suffix _files, and it houses the supporting files associated with the Web page. For example, when you create a new Web page or save an existing document as an .htm file, each graphic—including the bullets, background textures, horizontal lines, and other graphics included on the Web page—is automatically converted to a GIF or JPEG format file and saved in the supporting folder. Be aware that if you copy or move a Web page saved in .htm format to a different location, it's important that you copy or move the supporting folder (and all the files in it) along with the .htm file, otherwise the links between the .htm file and the supporting files may be broken. If a browser cannot locate the graphic files associated with a Web page, the browser displays a placeholder (often a red X) instead of a graphic. By default, Word saves a Web page as a single file Web page using the .mht file extension.

Creating a Web Page

Creating a Web page involves creating a document that uses HTML formatting. HTML places codes, called **tags**, around the elements of a Web page to describe how each element should appear when viewed with a browser. When you create a Web page in Word, you use the usual Word buttons and commands to edit and format the text, graphics, and other elements, and Word automatically inserts the HTML tags for you. A quick way to create a new Web page is to start with the blank Web page template and add text and graphics to it. Because text and graphics align and position differently on Web pages than in Word documents, it's helpful to use a table to structure the layout of a Web page. ▀▀▀ You begin by creating the home page. You start with a new blank Web page, insert a table to structure the layout of the home page, add text, and then save the Web page in single file Web Page format.

STEPS

QUICK TIP
Web Layout view shows a Web page as it appears when viewed in a Web browser.

1. **Start Word, click Create a new document in the Getting Started task pane, then click Web page in the New Document task pane**
   A blank Web page opens in the document window in Web Layout view.

2. **Click the Zoom list arrow on the Standard toolbar, click 100% if necessary, click the Insert Table button ▦ on the Standard toolbar, point to the second box in the third row of the grid to create a 3 x 2 Table, then click**
   A table with three rows and two columns is inserted. After you finish using the table to help lay out the design of the Web page, you will remove the table borders.

3. **Select the two cells in the first row, click Table on the menu bar, click Merge Cells, then deselect the row**
   Two cells in the first row merge to become a single cell.

4. **Click in the first row, type Seattle Writers Festival 2006, press [Enter] twice, type October 13-15, then press [Enter]**

5. **Select the two cells in the second and third rows of the first column, click Table on the menu bar, click Merge Cells, then deselect the cell**
   The two cells in the first column merge to become a single cell.

QUICK TIP
There are no margins in Web Layout view and text wraps to fit the window.

6. **Type the text shown in Figure G-2 in the table cells**

7. **Click the Save button ▦ on the Standard toolbar**
   The Save As dialog box opens. Word assigns a default page title and filename for the Web page and indicates Single File Web Page (*.mht; *mhtml) as the Save as type. If you prefer to save the Web page as an .htm file with a supporting folder for the associated files, click the Save as type list arrow, and then click Web Page (*.htm, *.html).

QUICK TIP
To edit a page title, click Properties on the File menu, click the Summary tab, then type a new title in the Title text box.

8. **Click Change Title, type Seattle Writers Festival - Home (Your Name) in the Set Page Title dialog box, then click OK**
   The page title appears in the title bar when the Web page is viewed with a browser. It's important to assign a page title that describes the Web page for visitors.

9. **Drag to select Seattle Writers Festival 2006.mht in the File name text box, type swfhome, use the Save in list arrow to navigate to the drive and folder where your Data Files are located, then compare your Save As dialog box with Figure G-3**
   The filename appears in the title bar when the Web page is viewed in Word.

10. **Click Save**
    The filename swfhome.mht appears in the title bar. Depending on your Windows settings, the file extension may or may not appear after the filename.

New Web Page button

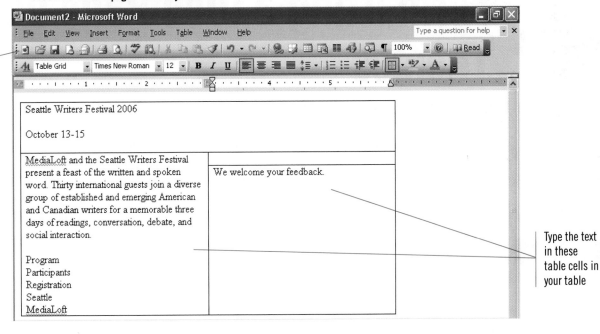

Type the text in these table cells in your table

Word 2003

FIGURE G-3: Save As dialog box

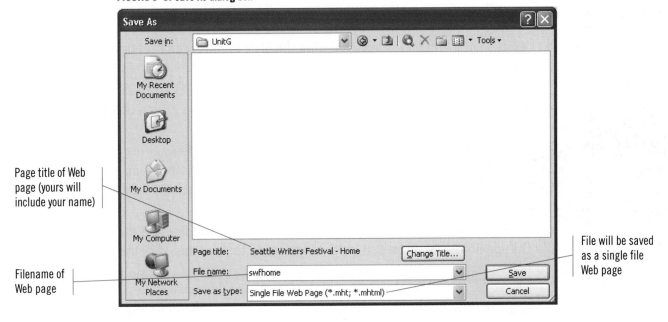

Page title of Web page (yours will include your name)

Filename of Web page

File will be saved as a single file Web page

Clues to Use

Adding frames to a Web page

Many Web pages you visit on the Internet include frames for display-ing fixed information. A **frame** is a section of a Web page window in which a separate Web page can be displayed. Frames commonly contain hyperlinks and other navigation elements that help visitors browse a Web site. A header that remains at the top of the screen while visitors browse a Web site is one example of a frame; a left col-umn that contains hyperlinks to each page in the Web site and stays on the screen while readers visit different pages is another example. You can add a frame to a Web page by pointing to Frames on the Format menu, and then clicking the type of frame you want to add.

Click New Frames Page to open the Frames toolbar, which you can use to select a location (left, right, above, or below) for a new, empty frame. Alternately, if you have applied heading styles to text in the current Web page, you can click Table of Contents in Frame to create a frame that includes hyperlinks to each heading in the Web page. Once you have created a frames page, you can resize the frames by dragging a frame border. To hide or show the frame bor-ders or specify which page first appears in a frame, point to Frames on the Format menu, click Frame Properties, and then change the settings in the Frame Properties dialog box.

Formatting a Web Page with Themes

Word includes a multitude of themes that you can apply to Web pages to quickly give them an attractive and consistent look. A **theme** is a set of complementary design elements that you can apply to Web pages, e-mail messages, and other documents that are viewed on screen. Themes include Web page backgrounds, styles for headings and hyperlinks, picture bullets, horizontal lines, table borders, and other specially designed formats that work well together. To apply a theme to a Web page, you use the Theme command on the Format menu. █████ You apply a theme to the Web page, format the text using the theme styles, and add a horizontal line and bullets. You then experiment with alternate themes to find a design that more closely matches the character of the Writers Festival.

STEPS

1. **Click Format on the menu bar, click Theme, then click Blends in the Choose a Theme list box**
   A preview of the Blends theme appears in the Theme dialog box, as shown in Figure G-4. The theme includes a background and styles for text, hyperlinks, bullet characters, and horizontal lines.

> **QUICK TIP**
>
> To create a custom background, point to Background on the Format menu. For a solid color background, select a standard color or click More Colors. For a background with a gradient, texture, pattern, or picture, click Fill Effects.

2. **Click OK**
   The theme background is added to the Web page and the Normal style that comes with the theme is applied to the text.

3. **Select Seattle Writers Festival 2006, click the Style list arrow on the Formatting toolbar, click Heading 1 in the Style list, then click the heading to deselect the text**
   The Heading 1 style—16-point Trebuchet MS bold—is applied to the heading text.

4. **Select October 13-15, click the Style list arrow, click Heading 2, then click the date to deselect the text**
   The Heading 2 style—14-point Trebuchet MS—is applied to the date text.

5. **Select the heading and the date, click the Center button ▤ on the Formatting toolbar, move the pointer over the table, click the table move handle ⊞ to select the table, then click ▤**
   The heading, date, and table are centered on the Web page.

> **QUICK TIP**
>
> To change the size or alignment of a line, double-click the line to open the Format Horizontal Line dialog box, then adjust the settings on the Horizontal Line tab.

6. **Place the insertion point in the blank line between the heading and the date, click the Outside Border list arrow ▦▾ on the Formatting toolbar, then click the Horizontal Line button ▤**
   A horizontal line formatted in the theme design is added below the heading.

7. **Select the five-line list at the bottom of the first column, then click the Bullets button ☰ on the Formatting toolbar**
   The list is formatted using bullets from the Blends theme design.

> **QUICK TIP**
>
> Backgrounds are visible only in Web Layout view and do not print.

8. **Click Format on the menu bar, click Theme, scroll down the Choose a Theme list box, click Pixel, then click OK**
   The background and the text, line, and bullet styles applied to the Web page change to the designs used in the Pixel theme. You do not need to reapply the styles to a Web page when you change its theme.

9. **Select Seattle Writers Festival 2006, click the Font Size list arrow on the Formatting toolbar, click 26, click the Font Color list arrow ▲▾ on the Formatting toolbar, click Indigo, deselect the text, then save your changes**
   The font size of the heading is increased and the color changes to Indigo. Once you have applied styles to text you can customize the format to suit your purpose. Compare your Web page with Figure G-5.

FIGURE G-4: Blends theme in the Theme dialog box

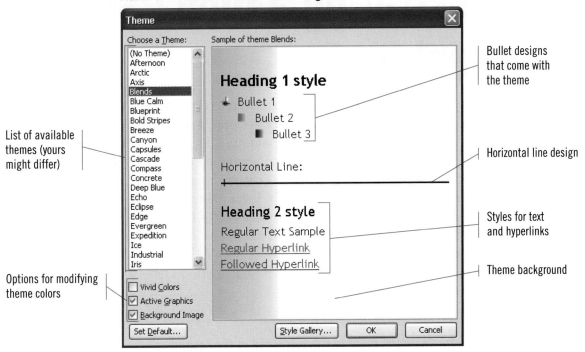

List of available themes (yours might differ)

Bullet designs that come with the theme

Horizontal line design

Styles for text and hyperlinks

Theme background

Options for modifying theme colors

FIGURE G-5: Pixel theme applied to the Web page

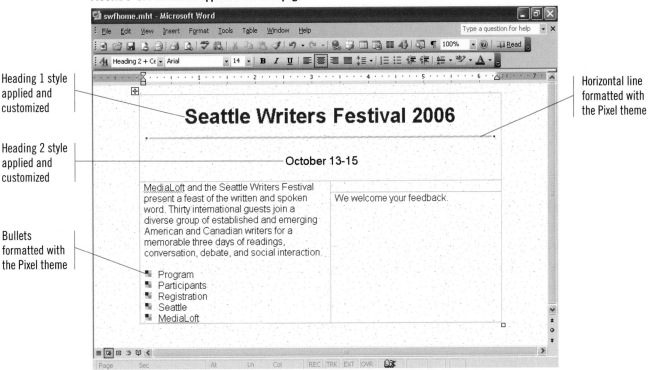

Heading 1 style applied and customized

Heading 2 style applied and customized

Bullets formatted with the Pixel theme

Horizontal line formatted with the Pixel theme

Illustrating a Web Page with Graphics

You can illustrate your Web pages with pictures, clip art, WordArt, text boxes, AutoShapes, and other graphic objects. When you insert a graphic on a Web page, it is inserted as an inline graphic and you must apply text wrapping to be able to move it independently of the line of text. Floating graphics align and position differently on Web pages than in Word documents, however, because browsers do not support the same graphic-formatting options as Word. For example, a floating graphic with square text wrapping can only be left- or right-aligned on a Web page, whereas you can position a floating graphic anywhere in a Word document. For this reason, it's important to use Web Layout view to position graphics on a Web page. If you want to position floating graphics or text precisely on a Web page, you can create a table and then insert the text or graphics in the table cells.  You want the MediaLoft logo to appear to the right of center on the Web page. You insert the logo in the blank cell in the table, and then adjust the table formatting to make the Web page attractive.

STEPS

QUICK TIP

To insert a text file in a table cell, click Insert on the menu bar, click File, select the file, then click Insert.

1. **Place the insertion point in the blank cell in the second column of the table, click Insert on the menu bar, point to Picture, then click From File**
   The Insert Picture dialog box opens.

2. **Use the Look in list arrow to navigate to the drive and folder where your Data Files are located, click the file mloft.jpg, then click Insert**
   The logo is inserted in the cell as an inline graphic.

QUICK TIP

To resize a graphic, crop it, or change the text wrapping style, double-click the graphic to open the Format Picture dialog box.

3. **Click the logo to select it, click the Center button ☰ on the Formatting toolbar, press [→], then press [Enter]**
   The graphic is centered in the table cell and a blank line is inserted under the logo.

4. **Position the pointer over the border between the first and second columns until the pointer changes to +‖+, then drag the border to approximately the 4 ¼" mark on the horizontal ruler**
   The first column widens and the second column narrows. The logo remains centered in the table cell.

5. **Select We welcome your feedback., click ☰, then click in the table to deselect the text**
   The text is centered in the table cell, as shown in Figure G-6. In Web Layout view, text and graphics are positioned as they are in a Web browser.

TROUBLE

If gridlines appear on your Web page after you remove the borders, click Table on the menu bar, then click Hide Gridlines.

6. **Click the table move handle ⊞ to select the table, click the Horizontal Line list arrow ⊞ ▾ on the Formatting toolbar, click the No Border button ⊞, deselect the table, then save your changes**
   Removing the table borders masks that the underlying structure of the Web page is a table, as shown in Figure G-7. The text on the left is now a wide column and the logo and text under the logo are positioned to the right of center. By inserting text and graphics in a table, you can position them exactly where you want.

FIGURE G-6: Logo and text centered in the second column

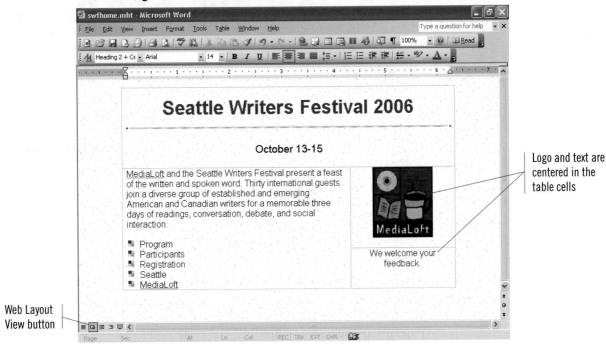

Logo and text are centered in the table cells

Web Layout View button

FIGURE G-7: Web page with table borders removed

Table move handle

Clues to Use

Adding alternate text for graphics

Graphics can take a long time to appear on a Web page. Some people turn off the display of graphics in their browsers so that they can download and view Web pages more quickly. If you don't want visitors to your Web page to see empty space in place of a graphic, you can add alternate text to appear on the Web page instead of the graphic. Alternate text appears in some browsers while the graphic is loading, and is used by search engines to find Web pages. To add alternate text to a Web page, select the graphic, and then click the Picture command on the Format menu. On the Web tab in the Format Picture dialog box, type the text you want to appear in lieu of the graphic, and then click OK.

Saving a Document as a Web Page

When you save an existing document as a Web page, Word converts the content and formatting of the Word file to HTML and displays the Web page as it will appear in a browser. Any formatting that is not supported by Web browsers is either converted to similar supported formatting or removed from the Web page. For example, if you save a document that contains a floating graphic in HTML format, the graphic will be left- or right-aligned on the Web page. Table G-1 describes several common formatting elements that are not supported by Web browsers. To save a document as a Web page, you use the Save as Web Page command on the File menu. ██████ You want to add a Web page that includes the festival program of events to your Web site. Rather than create the Web page from scratch, you convert an existing document to HTML format. You then adjust the formatting of the new Web page and apply the Pixel theme.

STEPS

QUICK TIP

To create a Web page that is compatible with a specific browser, click Tools on the menu bar, click Options, click the General tab, click Web Options, then select from the options on the Browsers tab in the Web Options dialog box.

1. **Open the file WD G-1.doc from the drive and folder where your Data Files are located, click the Zoom list arrow on the Standard toolbar, then click Two Pages**

   The document opens in Print Layout view, as shown in Figure G-8. Notice that the document is two pages long, the text is formatted in three columns, and the graphic on the first page is centered.

2. **Click File on the menu bar, click Save as Web Page, click Change Title, type Seattle Writers Festival – Program of Events (Your Name) in the Set Page Title dialog box, click OK, select WD G-1.mht in the Filename text box, type swfevent, then click Save**

   A dialog box opens and informs you that browsers do not support some of the formatting features of the document, including that the floating graphic will be left- or right-aligned in the Web page.

TROUBLE

If the Web page appears in a different view, click the Web Layout View button on the horizontal scroll bar.

3. **Click Continue**

   A copy of the document is saved in HTML format with the filename "swfevent" and the page title "Seattle Writers Festival – Program of Events (Your Name)." The Web page appears in Web Layout view. Notice that the graphic is now left-aligned on the Web page.

4. **Click the Zoom list arrow on the Standard toolbar, click 100% if necessary, then scroll to the bottom of the Web page**

   The text is now formatted in a single column, there are no margins on the Web page, and the document is one long page.

5. **Press [Ctrl][Home], double-click the graphic to open the Format Picture dialog box, click the Size tab, select 3.76 in the Height text box, type 2, then click OK**

   The size of the graphic is reduced.

QUICK TIP

To be able to position a graphic precisely on a Web page, you must insert the graphic in a table or make it an inline graphic.

6 **Drag the graphic to the upper-right corner of the Web page, then deselect the graphic**

   The graphic jumps into place in the upper-right corner when you release the mouse button.

7. **Click Format on the menu bar, click Theme, click Pixel in the Choose a Theme list box, click OK, then save your changes**

   The Pixel theme is applied to the Web page, giving it a look that is consistent with the home page. Notice that the bullet characters change to the bullet design included with the theme. The font of the body text also changes to the Normal style font used in the theme (12-point Arial). Compare your Web page with Figure G-9.

FIGURE G-8: Word document in Print Layout view

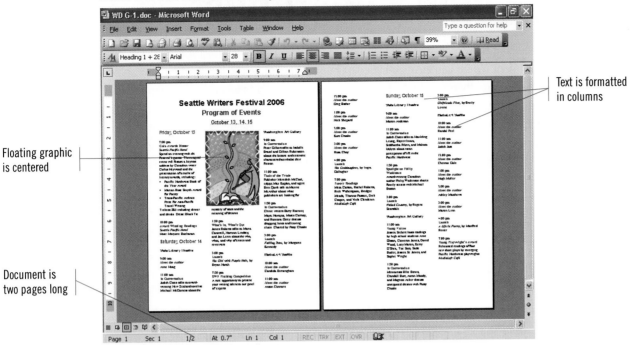

Text is formatted in columns

Floating graphic is centered

Document is two pages long

FIGURE G-9: Web page in Web Layout view

Graphic is moved to the upper-right corner

Body text changes to Pixel theme Normal style

Bullets change to Pixel theme bullets

TABLE G-1: Word features that are not supported by Web browsers

feature	result when viewed with a browser
Character formatting	Shadow text becomes bold; small caps become all caps; embossed, engraved, and outline text becomes solid; character scale changes to 100%; and drop caps are removed
Paragraph formatting	Indents are removed, tabs might not align correctly, and border and shading styles might change
Page layout	Margins, columns, page numbers, page borders, and headers and footers are removed; all footnotes are moved to the end of the document
Graphics	Floating graphics, including pictures, AutoShapes, text boxes, and WordArt, are left- or right-aligned
Tables	Decorative cell borders become box borders, diagonal borders are removed, vertical text is changed to horizontal

Adding Hyperlinks

Hyperlinks allow readers to link (or "jump") to a Web page, an e-mail address, a file, or a specific location in a document. When you create a hyperlink in a document, you select the text or graphic you want to use as a hyperlink and then specify the location you want to jump to when the hyperlink is clicked. You create hyperlinks using the Insert Hyperlink button on the Standard toolbar. Text that is formatted as a hyperlink appears as colored, underlined text. ████ To make navigating the Events Web page easier, you create hyperlinks that jump from the dates in the third line of the Web page to the schedule for those dates farther down the Web page. You then insert several hyperlinks on your home page: one to link to the Events Web page, one to link to the Seattle.com Web site on the Internet, and one to link to an e-mail message to MediaLoft.

STEPS

1. **Select 15 in the third line of the Events Web page, then click the Insert Hyperlink button 🖳 on the Standard toolbar**

   The Insert Hyperlink dialog box opens. You use this dialog box to specify the location of the Web page, file, e-mail address, or position in the current document you want to jump to when the hyperlink—in this case, the text "15"—is clicked.

2. **Click Place in This Document in the Link to section**

   All the headings in the Web page are displayed in the dialog box, as shown in Figure G-10. In this context, a "heading" is any text to which a heading style has been applied.

   > **QUICK TIP**
   > Press [Ctrl] and click any hyperlink in Word to follow the hyperlink.

3. **Click Sunday, October 15 in the Select a place in this document section, then click OK**

   The selected text, "15", is formatted in blue and underlined, the hyperlink style when the Pixel theme is applied. When the Web page is viewed in a browser, clicking the 15 hyperlink jumps the viewer to the heading "Sunday, October 15" farther down the Web page.

4. **Select 14, click 🖳, click Saturday, October 14 in the Insert Hyperlink dialog box, click OK, select 13, click 🖳, click Friday, October 13, click OK, save your changes, then close the file**

   The numbers 14 and 13 are formatted as hyperlinks to the headings for those dates in the Web page. After you save and close the file, the home page appears in the document window.

5. **Select Program in the bulleted list, click 🖳, click Existing File or Web Page in the Link to section, use the Look in list arrow to navigate to the drive and folder where your Data Files are located, then click swfevent.mht**

   The filename swfevent.mht appears in the Address text box, as shown in Figure G-11.

   > **QUICK TIP**
   > To create a ScreenTip that appears in a browser, click ScreenTip in the Insert Hyperlink dialog box, then in the Set Hyperlink ScreenTip dialog box, type the text you want to appear.

6. **Click OK**

   "Program" is formatted as a hyperlink to the Program of Events Web page. If you point to a hyperlink in Word, the address of the file or Web page it links to appears in a ScreenTip.

7. **Select Seattle in the list, click 🖳, type www.seattle.com in the Address text box in the Insert Hyperlink dialog box, then click OK**

   As you type the Web address, Word automatically adds "http://" in front of "www." A Web address is also called a **URL**, which stands for Uniform Resource Locator. The word "Seattle" is formatted as a hyperlink to the Seattle.com Web site on the Internet.

   > **QUICK TIP**
   > By default, Word automatically creates a hyperlink to an e-mail address or URL when you type the address or URL in a document or Web page.

8. **Select feedback under the logo, click 🖳, then click E-mail Address in the Link to section of the Insert Hyperlink dialog box**

   The Insert Hyperlink dialog box changes so you can create a link to an e-mail message.

9. **Type swf@media-loft.com in the E-mail address text box, type Seattle Writers Festival in the Subject text box, click OK, then save your changes**

   The word "feedback" is formatted as a hyperlink, as shown in Figure G-12.

FIGURE G-10: **Creating a hyperlink to a heading**

Create a hyperlink to a Web page or file

Create a hyperlink to a location in the current file

Create a hyperlink to a new blank document

Create a hyperlink to an e-mail address

Text selected to be formatted as a hyperlink

These headings in the document are formatted with heading styles

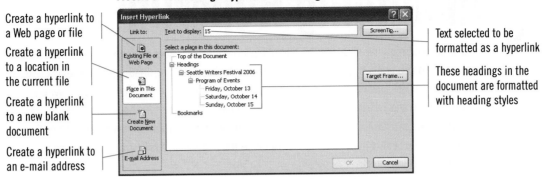

FIGURE G-11: **Creating a hyperlink to a file**

Click to change the default ScreenTip for the hyperlink

Click to browse the Internet for a specific URL to link to

File to jump to when the hyperlink is clicked

Files in the active drive or folder (yours might differ)

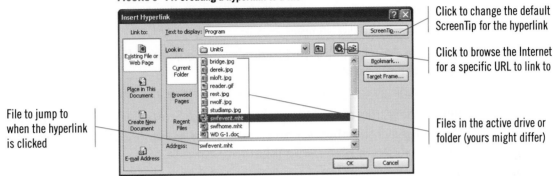

FIGURE G-12: **Hyperlinks in the Web page**

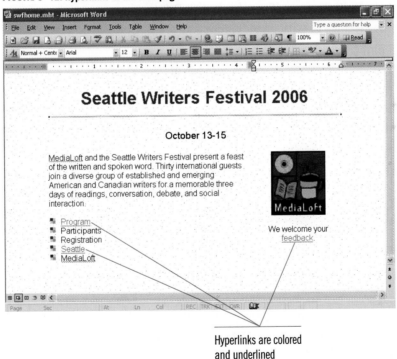

Hyperlinks are colored and underlined

Word 2003

Clues to Use

Pasting text as a hyperlink

You can quickly create a hyperlink to a specific location in any document by copying text from the destination location and pasting it as a hyperlink. To copy and paste text as a hyperlink, select the text you want to jump to, copy it to the Clipboard, place the insertion point in the location you want to insert the hyperlink, click Edit on the menu bar, then click Paste as Hyperlink. The text you copied is pasted and formatted as a hyperlink.

Modifying Hyperlinks

Over time, you might need to edit the hyperlinks on your Web pages with new information or remove them altogether. When you edit a hyperlink, you can change the hyperlink destination, the hyperlink text, or the ScreenTip that appears when a viewer points to the hyperlink. You can easily update or remove a hyperlink by right-clicking it and selecting the Edit Hyperlink or Remove Hyperlink command on the shortcut menu. ▓▓▓▓ You change the hyperlink text for the Program and Seattle hyperlinks to make them more descriptive. You also add a ScreenTip to the Seattle hyperlink so that visitors to the Seattle Writers Festival 2006 home page will better understand what the link offers.

STEPS

1. **Right-click Program, then click Edit Hyperlink on the shortcut menu**
   The Edit Hyperlink dialog box opens.

2. **Click after Program in the Text to display text box, press [Spacebar], type of Festival Events, then click OK**
   The hyperlink text changes to "Program of Festival Events" on the Web page.

3. **Right-click Seattle, click Edit Hyperlink, then click ScreenTip in the Edit Hyperlink dialog box**
   The Set Hyperlink ScreenTip dialog box opens, as shown in Figure G-13. Any text you type in this dialog box appears as a ScreenTip when a viewer points to the hyperlink.

4. **Type Hotels, dining, and entertainment in Seattle in the ScreenTip text box, then click OK**

5. **Click in front of Seattle in the Text to display text box in the Edit Hyperlink dialog box, type Visiting, press [Spacebar], click OK, then save your changes**
   The hyperlink text changes to "Visiting Seattle."

6. **Point to Visiting Seattle**
   The ScreenTip you added appears, as shown in Figure G-14.

Clues to Use

E-mailing a document from Word

Another way to share information online is to e-mail a Word document to others. Using the Send To command on the File menu, you can send a document directly from Word, either as an e-mail message or as an attachment to an e-mail message. To e-mail a document as a message, open the document, point to Send To on the File menu, and then click Mail Recipient. A message header opens above the document window. You can also click the E-mail button ▢ on the Standard toolbar to open a message header. Type the e-mail address(es) of the recipient(s) in the To and Cc text boxes in the message header, separating multiple addresses with a comma or a semicolon. When you are ready to send the file, click Send a Copy on the e-mail header toolbar.

To send a file as an attachment to an e-mail message, open the file, point to Send To on the File menu, and then click Mail Recipient (for Review) or Mail Recipient (as Attachment). When you select Mail Recipient (for Review), a message window opens that includes the request "Please review the attached document" in the body of the message. When you click Mail Recipient (as Attachment), a blank message window opens. Type the e-mail addresses in the To and Cc text boxes, any message you want in the message window, and then click the Send button on the message window toolbar to send the message. When you send a document from Word, your default e-mail program sends a copy of the document to each recipient.

FIGURE G-13: Set Hyperlink ScreenTip dialog box

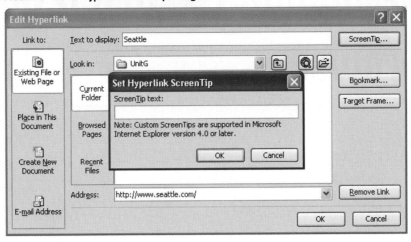

FIGURE G-14: ScreenTip and edited hyperlinks

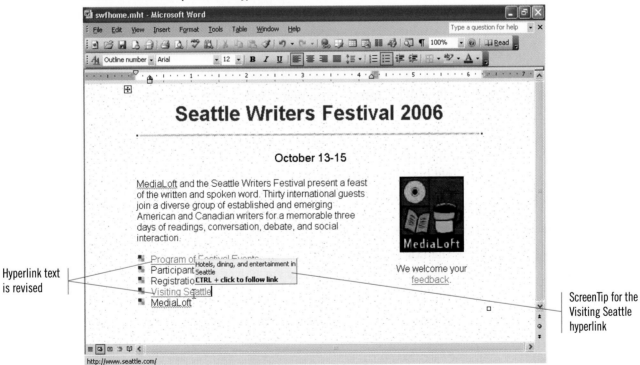

Hyperlink text is revised

ScreenTip for the Visiting Seattle hyperlink

Previewing a Web Page in a Browser

Before you publish Web pages to the Web or an intranet, it's important to preview the pages in a browser to make sure they look as you intended. You can use the Web Page Preview command on the File menu to open a copy of a Web page in your default browser. When previewing a Web page, you should check for formatting errors and test each hyperlink. To complete this lesson, you must have a Web browser installed on your computer. ██████ You preview the Web pages in your browser and test the hyperlinks. After viewing the Program Web page, you use Word to adjust its formatting.

STEPS

1. **Click File on the menu bar, click Web Page Preview, then click the Maximize button on the browser title bar if necessary**
   The browser opens and the home page is displayed in the browser window, as shown in Figure G-15. Notice that the page title—Seattle Writers Festival - Home—appears in the browser title bar. Your page title will also include your name.

   TROUBLE
   If the hyperlink does not work, click File on the browser menu bar, click Open, click Browse, navigate to the swfevent.mht file, click Open, then continue with Step 3.

2. **Click the Program of Festival Events hyperlink**
   The Seattle Writers Festival – Program of Events Web page opens in the browser window.

3. **Click the 15 hyperlink**
   The browser jumps down the page and displays the program for Sunday, October 15 in the browser window.

4. **Click the Back button ⊘ Back on the browser toolbar**
   The top of the Program of Events Web page is displayed in the browser window. The browser toolbar includes buttons for navigating between Web pages, searching the Internet, and printing and editing the current Web page.

   TROUBLE
   If the Edit with Microsoft Office Word button is not available in your browser, click the Word Program button on the taskbar to switch to Word, and then open swfevent.mht.

5. **Click the Edit with Microsoft Office Word button 🅦 on the browser toolbar**
   The Program of Events Web page appears in a Word document window.

6. **Click the Zoom list arrow on the Standard toolbar, click 100% if necessary, select Tickets under the bulleted list, press and hold [Ctrl], select Dress in the same line, release [Ctrl], click the Bold button 🅑 on the Formatting toolbar, save your changes, then close the file**
   The home page appears in the Word document window. You want to check that your changes to the Program of Events Web page will preview correctly in the browser.

   TROUBLE
   If the hyperlink does not work, open the swfevent.mht file in the browser, then click the Refresh button.

7. **Click File on the menu bar, click Web Page Preview, click the Program of Festival Events hyperlink, then click the Refresh button 🗊 on the browser toolbar**
   The revised Program of Events Web page appears in the browser, as shown in Figure G-16.

8. **Click the Print button 🖨 on the browser toolbar to print a copy of the swfevent Web page, click ⊘ Back, then point to the Visiting Seattle hyperlink**
   The ScreenTip you created for the hyperlink appears. The URL of the Seattle.com Web site also appears in the status bar. If you are connected to the Internet you can click the Visiting Seattle hyperlink to open the Seattle.com Web site in your browser window. Click the Back button on the browser toolbar to return to the Seattle Writers Festival home page when you are finished.

   TROUBLE
   If an e-mail message does not open, continue with Step 10.

9. **Click the feedback hyperlink**
   An e-mail message that is automatically addressed to swf@media-loft.com with the subject "Seattle Writers Festival" opens in your default e-mail program.

10. **Close the e-mail message, click 🖨 to print the swfhome Web page, exit your browser, then exit Word**

FIGURE G-15: Home page in Internet Explorer

Page title (yours will include your name)

If your default browser is not Internet Explorer 6, your screens might differ

Edit with Microsoft Office Word button

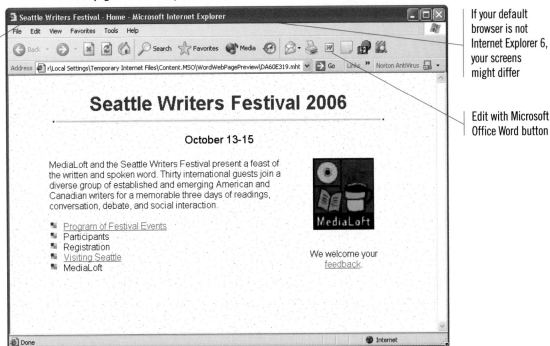

FIGURE G-16: Revised Program of Events page in Internet Explorer

Print button

Text is bold

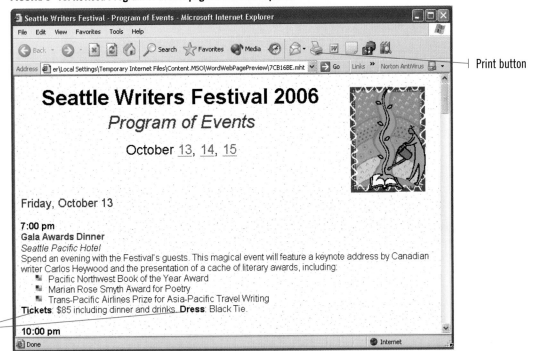

Clues to Use

Posting a Web site to the World Wide Web or an intranet

To make your Web site available to others, you must post (or publish) it to the Web or to a local intranet. Publishing a Web site involves copying the HTML files and any supporting folders and files to a Web server—either your Internet service provider's (ISPs) server, if you want to publish it to the Internet, or the server for your local intranet. Check with your ISP or your network administrator for instructions on how to post your Web pages to the correct server.

Practice

▼ CONCEPTS REVIEW

Label each element shown in Figure G-17.

FIGURE G-17

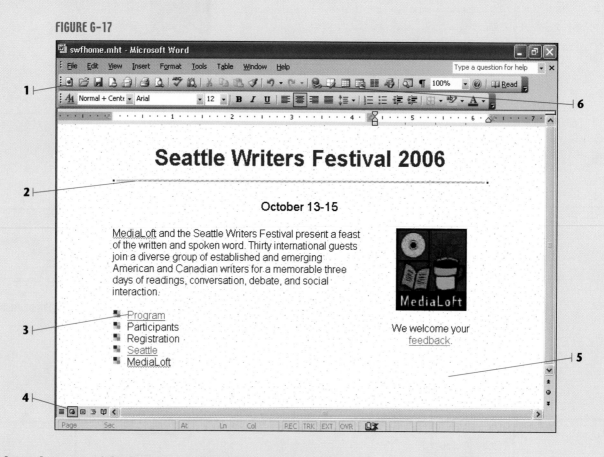

Match each term with the statement that best describes it.

7. **Hyperlink**
8. **Web page**
9. **Home page**
10. **HTML**
11. **Theme**
12. **Web site**
13. **Browser**
14. **URL**

a. A document that can be viewed using a browser
b. A group of associated Web pages
c. The address of a Web page on the World Wide Web
d. A programming language used to create Web pages
e. Text or a graphic that jumps the viewer to a different location when clicked
f. A set of common design elements that can be applied to a Web page
g. The main page of a Web site
h. A software program used to access and display Web pages

Select the best answer from the list of choices.

15. Which of the following is *not* a design element included in a theme?

   a. Bullet design

   b. Frame design

   c. Horizontal line style

   d. Web page background

16. Which of the following *cannot* be opened using a hyperlink?

   a. Files

   b. E-mail messages

   c. Web pages

   d. Support folders

17. Which of the following formats is supported by Web browsers?

   a. Inline graphics

   b. Columns of text

   c. Page numbers

   d. Headers and footers

18. What does using the Save as Web Page command accomplish?

   a. Converts the current file to HTML format

   b. Opens the current file in a browser

   c. Converts floating graphics to inline graphics

   d. Applies a Web theme to the current file

19. Where does the page title of a Web page appear?

   a. In the Word title bar

   b. On the home page

   c. In the browser title bar

   d. In the name of the supporting folder

20. Which of the following statements is false?

   a. A Web page saved as an .mht file does not need a supporting folder.

   b. When you save a document as a Web page, Word adds HTML tags to the file.

   c. You can use the Center button to center a floating graphic in Web Layout view.

   d. Hyperlink text is underlined.

▼ SKILLS REVIEW

1. Create a Web page.

   a. Study the sketch for the Web site devoted to literacy issues shown in Figure G-18.

   b. Start Word and create a blank Web page.

   c. Create a table with two columns and three rows, select the table, then AutoFit the table to fit the window. (*Hint:* Click Table on the menu bar, point to AutoFit, then click AutoFit to Window.)

   d. Type **Literacy Facts** in column 2, cell 1.

   e. Merge cells 2 and 3 in column 2, click Insert on the menu bar, click File, navigate to the drive and folder where your Data Files are located, select WD G-2.doc, then click Insert.

   f. In column 1, cell 3, type the following three-item list: **What you can do, ProLiteracy Worldwide, Contact us**.

   g. Save the file as a single file Web page to the drive and folder where your Data Files are located with the page title **Literacy Facts – Home** and the filename **literacy**.

2. Format a Web page with themes.

   a. Apply the Network theme to the Web page. (*Note:* Select a different theme if Network is not available to you.)

   b. Format Literacy Facts in the Heading 1 style, center the text, then press [Enter].

FIGURE G-18

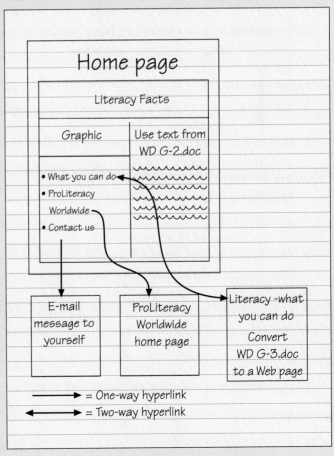

    c. Insert a horizontal line below the heading.

    d. Apply bullets to the list in column 1, cell 3, then save your changes.

3. Illustrate a Web page with graphics.

    a. In the blank cell in the first column, second row, insert the graphic file reader.gif from the drive and folder where your Data Files are located.

    b. Center the graphic in the cell, press [Enter], type **Literacy is not just reading and writing; the ability to perform basic math and solve problems is also important.**, press [Enter], then change the font size of the text to 10.

    c. Click Format on the menu bar, point to Background, click Fill Effects, click the Gradient tab, select the Two colors option button in the Colors section, click the Color 1 list arrow, click Gold, click the Color 2 list arrow, click Light Yellow, select any shading style and variant, then click OK.

    d. Select the table, remove the table borders, hide the gridlines, then save your changes.

4. Save a document as a Web page.

    a. Open the file WD G-3.doc from the drive and folder where your Data Files are located.

    b. Examine the document, then save it as a single file Web page with the page title **Literacy – what you can do** and the filename **whattodo**.

    c. Read the message about formatting changes, then click Continue.

    d. Apply the Network theme (or the theme you used with the Literacy page) to the Web page, then apply the Heading 1 style to the heading.

    e. Double-click the graphic, click the Layout tab, change its text-wrapping style to In line with text, then move it before Literacy in the heading.

    f. Change the background to a gold and light yellow gradient. (*Hint:* See Step 3c.)

    g. Save your changes, then close the file.

5. Add hyperlinks.

    a. In the Literacy Facts file, select What you can do, then format it as a hyperlink to the whattodo.mht file.

    b. Format ProLiteracy Worldwide as a hyperlink to the Web address **www.proliteracy.org**.

    c. Format Contact us as a hyperlink to your e-mail address with the message subject **Literacy information**. (*Note:* If you do not have an e-mail address, skip this step.)

    d. Save your changes.

6. Modify hyperlinks.

    a. Right-click the Contact us hyperlink, click Edit Hyperlink, change the Text to display to your name, click OK, then type **For more information on literacy, contact** in front of your name on the Web page.

    b. Edit the ProLiteracy Worldwide hyperlink so that the ScreenTip says **Information on ProLiteracy Worldwide and links to literacy Web sites**.

    c. Edit the What you can do hyperlink so that the ScreenTip says **Simple actions you can take to help eliminate illiteracy**.

    d. Save your changes.

7. Preview a Web page in a browser.

    a. Preview the Literacy Facts Web page in your browser, test all the hyperlinks, print a copy of the Literacy Facts Web page, then close the browser.

    b. Open the whattodo.mht file in Word.

    c. Press [Ctrl][End], press [Enter], type **For more information, contact** followed by your name and a period, format your name as a hyperlink to your e-mail address with the subject line **Literacy Information**, then save your changes.

    d. Preview the Literacy - what you can do Web page in your browser, test the hyperlink, then print the page.

    e. Close the browser, close all open Word files, then exit Word.

▼ INDEPENDENT CHALLENGE 1

You have written a story about a recent hiking expedition you took and want to share it and some photos with your family and friends. You decide to create a Web page. Figure G-19 shows how you will arrange the photos.

a. Start Word, open a blank Web page, save the Web page as a single file Web page with the page title **Conquering Rising Wolf** and the filename **risewolf** to the drive and folder where your Data Files are located, then change the zoom level to 100% if necessary.

FIGURE G-19

Rising Wolf Mountain (elev. 9513 feet)

Derek enjoying the view

b. Insert a table with two columns and four rows, merge the two cells in the first row, merge the three cells in the second column, select the table, then AutoFit the table to fit the window. (*Hint:* Use the AutoFit command on the Table menu.)

c. Type **Conquering Rising Wolf** in the first row of the table, then press [Enter].

d. Click in the second column, then insert the file WD G-4.doc from the drive and folder where your Data Files are located. (*Hint:* Use the File command on the Insert menu.)

e. Click in the first blank cell in the first column, then insert the graphic file rwolf.jpg from the drive and folder where your Data Files are located.

f. Press [Enter], then type **Rising Wolf Mountain (elev. 9513 feet)**.

g. In the last blank cell in the first column, insert the graphic file Derek.jpg from the drive and folder where your Data Files are located, then resize the photo proportionally to be the same width as the Rising Wolf Mountain photo.

h. Press [Enter], then type **Derek enjoying the view**.

i. Drag the border between the first and second columns left to approximately the 3¼" mark.

j. Apply a theme, then format the Web page using theme elements and other formatting features.

k. Select Glacier National Park in the first paragraph in the second column, format it as a hyperlink to the URL **www.nps.gov/glac/home.htm** with the ScreenTip **Glacier National Park Website Visitor Center**.

l. Press [Ctrl][End], press [Enter], type **E-mail** followed by your name, center the text, then format your name as a hyperlink to your e-mail address, if you have one. Type **Conquering Rising Wolf** as the message subject.

m. Resize the table rows and columns as necessary to make the Web page attractive, remove the borders from the table, save your changes, preview the Web page in your browser, then test the hyperlinks.

n. Switch to Word, make any necessary adjustments, save your changes, preview the Web page in your browser, print a copy, close the browser, close the file in Word, then exit Word.

INDEPENDENT CHALLENGE 2

You and your business partner have just started a mail-order business called Monet's Garden. You create a home page for your business. As your business grows, you plan to add additional pages to the Web site.

a. Start Word, then create a new frames page. (*Hint:* Point to Frames on the Format menu, then click New Frames Page.)

b. Click the New Frame Left button on the Frames toolbar, close the toolbar, then drag the frame border to the left so that the left frame is about one quarter the width of the Web page.

c. Save the frames page as a single file Web Page with the page title **Welcome to Monet's Garden** and the filename **monet**.

d. In the left frame, type **Welcome to Monet's Garden**, press [Enter] four times, then type **1-800-555-2837**.

e. Insert an appropriate clip art graphic between the two lines of text in the left frame. Resize the graphic to fit the frame. (*Hint:* You might need to enlarge the frame temporarily to resize the graphic.)

f. In the right frame, insert the text file WD G-5.doc from the drive and folder where your Data Files are located. (*Hint:* Click File on the Insert menu.)

g. Insert an appropriate clip art graphic in the empty cell in the right frame.

h. Add a solid color background to the right frame, then format the frame with lines, fonts, colors, shading, and any other formatting features.

INDEPENDENT CHALLENGE 2 (CONTINUED)

i. Resize the graphic and table as needed, then remove the table borders. (*Note:* You do not need to remove the borders from the nested table.)

j. At the bottom of the right frame, replace Your Name with your name, then format it as a hyperlink to the e-mail address **info@monetsgarden.com** with the subject **Product Information**.

k. Add a different solid color background to the left frame, then format the frame with lines, fonts, colors, and any other formatting features.

l. Adjust the formatting of the Web page to make it attractive and readable, then save your changes.

Advanced Challenge Exercise

- Place the insertion point in the left frame, then open the Frame Properties dialog box. (*Hint*: Point to Frames on the Format menu.)
- On the Borders tab, click the No borders option button, click the Show scroll bars in browser list arrow, click Never, then click OK.
- Place the insertion point in the right frame, open the Frame Properties dialog box, set the scroll bar to show if needed, then save your changes.

m. Preview the Web page in your browser, test the hyperlink, adjust the formatting of the Web page as needed, then save your changes. (*Note:* Depending on your browser settings, the frames page might not preview correctly in your browser.)

n. Print a copy of the Web page, exit your browser, close the file, then exit Word.

▼ INDEPENDENT CHALLENGE 3

You are in charge of publicity for the Sydney Triathlon 2006 World Cup. One of your responsibilities is to create a Web site to provide details of the event. You have created the content for the Web pages as Word documents, and now need to save and format them as Web pages. Your Web site will include a home page and three other Web pages. One of the Web pages is shown in Figure G-20.

a. Start Word, open the file WD G-6.doc from the drive and folder where your Data Files are located, then save it as a single file Web page with the page title **Sydney Triathlon 2006 World Cup - Home** and the filename **tri_home**.

b. Apply the Slate or Breeze theme. (*Note:* Use a different theme if neither of these themes is available to you.)

FIGURE G-20

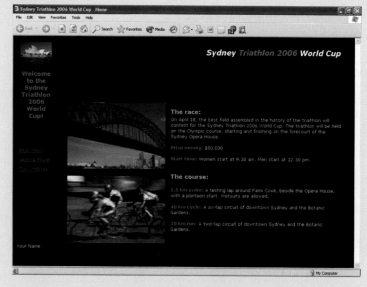

c. Press [Ctrl][A], then change the font size to 10.

d. Apply the Heading 1 style to the heading Sydney Triathlon 2006 World Cup in the first row of the table, right-align the text, apply italic, select Triathlon 2006, then change the font color to a different color.

e. Apply the Heading 3 style to Welcome to the Sydney Triathlon 2006 World Cup! in the upper-left cell of the table, apply bold, then center the text.

f. Read the remaining text on the Web page, then format it with heading styles, fonts, font colors, and other formatting effects to make it look attractive. Preview the Web page in your browser.

g. Remove the table borders, press [Ctrl][End], type your name, save your changes, then close the file.

▼ INDEPENDENT CHALLENGE 3

h. Open each file listed in Table G-2 from the drive and folder where your Data Files are located, save it as a single file Web Page with the page title and file-name listed in the table, follow Steps b–g to format it using the same theme and other formatting features you used to format the home page, then close the file.

TABLE G-2

data file	page title	filename
WD G-7.doc	Sydney Triathlon 2006 World Cup – Best Views	tri_view
WD G-8.doc	Sydney Triathlon 2006 World Cup – Getting There	tri_get
WD G-9.doc	Sydney Triathlon 2006 World Cup – The Athletes	tri_athl

i. In Word, open the tri_home.mht file, then change the zoom level to 100% if necessary.

j. Select Best Views, then format it as a hyperlink to the tri_view.mht file. Format Getting There and The Athletes as hyperlinks to the tri_get.mht and tri_athl.mht files, then save your changes.

k. Open each of the remaining three files—tri_view.mht, tri_get.mht, and tri_athl.mht—and format the text in the left column of each Web page as a hyperlink to the appropriate file. Save your changes, then close each Web page.

l. Be sure tri_home.mht is the active document. Preview the home page in your browser. Test each hyperlink on the home page and on the other Web pages. (If the hyperlinks do not work in your browser, test them in Word.)

m. Examine each Web page in your browser, make any necessary formatting adjustments in Word, print a copy of each Web page from your browser, then close your browser, close all open files, and exit Word.

▼ INDEPENDENT CHALLENGE 4

In this Independent Challenge you will create a Web page that provides information about you and your interests. Your Web page will include text, a graphic, and links to Web sites that you think will be useful to people who visit your Web page.

a. Start Word, open the file WD G-10.doc from the drive and folder where your Data Files are stored, save it as a single file Web page, include your name in the page title, and save it with the filename **my_page**.

b. At the top of the Web page, replace Your Name with your name.

c. Under the heading Contents, format each item in the list as a hyperlink to that heading in the Web page.

d. Under the heading Biographical Information, type at least one paragraph about your background and interests.

e. Under the heading Personal Interests, type a list of your hobbies and interests. Format this list as a bulleted list.

f. Use your favorite search engine to search for Web sites related to your interests. Write down the page titles and URLs of at least three Web sites that you think are worth visiting.

g. Under the heading Favorite Links, type the names of the three Web sites you liked. Format each name as a hyperlink to the Web site, and create a ScreenTip that explains why you think it's a good Web site.

h. Under the heading Contact Information, enter your e-mail address, Web site address, and telephone numbers, if any. Delete any headings that do not apply. Format your e-mail and Web addresses as hyperlinks to those addresses.

i. In each section, format the text Back to top as a hyperlink to your name at the top of the Web page.

j. Illustrate the Web page with a photo of yourself or another graphic. Use a clip art graphic if another graphic is not available to you. Create a table to position the graphic if necessary.

k. Apply a theme, then format the Web page with different formatting features such as bullets and colors.

l. Save your changes, preview the Web page, test each hyperlink, make adjustments, then save again.

Advanced Challenge Exercise

- In Word, send a copy of the Web page to someone in an e-mail message.
- In Word, send a copy of the Web page to someone for review as an attachment to an e-mail message.
- Using the Web Options dialog box, save the Web page for a target browser, then post the Web page to the Web or an intranet if instructed to do so by your instructor.

m. Print a copy of the Web page, close the browser, close the file, then exit Word.

▼ VISUAL WORKSHOP

Create the Web pages shown in Figure G-21 using the graphic files rest.jpg, bridge.jpg, and studlamp.jpg, found on the drive and folder where your Data Files are located. Save the home page with the page title **Gallery Azul Home (Your Name)** and the filename **azulhome.mht**. Save the exhibit page with the page title **Gallery Azul Exhibit (Your Name)** and the filename **azulexhb.mht**. On the home page, create a hyperlink to the exhibit page and a hyperlink to the e-mail address **GalleryAzul@ptown.net**. On the Exhibit page, create a hyperlink to the home page. View the Web pages in your browser, then print a copy of each Web page.

FIGURE G-21

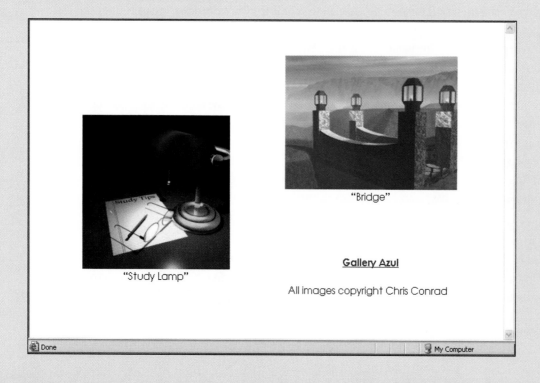

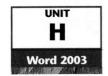
Merging Word Documents

OBJECTIVES

Understand mail merge
Create a main document
Design a data source
Enter and edit records
Add merge fields
Merge data
Create labels
Sort and filter records

If you have a SAM user profile, you may have access to hands-on instruction, practice, and assessment of the skills covered in this unit. Log in to your SAM account and go to your assignments page to see what your instructor has assigned.

A mail merge operation combines a standard document, such as a form letter, with customized data, such as a set of names and addresses, to create a set of personalized documents. You can perform a mail merge to create documents used in mass mailings, such as letters and labels. You also can use mail merge to create documents that include customized information, such as business cards. In this unit you learn how to use the Mail Merge task pane to set up and perform a mail merge. You need to send a welcome letter to the new members of the MediaLoft Coffee Club, a program designed to attract customers to the MediaLoft Café. You also need to send a brochure to all the members of the club. You use mail merge to create a personalized form letter and mailing labels for the brochure.

Understanding Mail Merge

When you perform a mail merge, you merge a standard Word document with a file that contains customized information for many individuals or items. The standard document is called the **main document**. The file with the unique data for individual people or items is called the **data source**. Merging the main document with a data source results in a merged document that contains customized versions of the main document, as shown in Figure H-1. The Mail Merge task pane steps you through the process of setting up and performing a mail merge.  You use the Mail Merge task pane to create your form letters and mailing labels. Before beginning, you explore the steps involved in performing a mail merge.

DETAILS

- **Create the main document**

  The main document contains the text—often called **boilerplate text**—that appears in every version of the merged document. The main document also includes the merge fields, which indicate where the customized information is inserted when you perform the merge. You insert the merge fields in the main document after you have created or selected the data source. You use the Mail Merge task pane to create a main document using either the current document, a template, or an existing document.

- **Create a data source or select an existing data source**

  The data source is a file that contains the unique information for each individual or item. It provides the information that varies in every version of the merged document. A data source is composed of data fields and data records. A **data field** is a category of information, such as last name, first name, street address, city, or postal code. A **data record** is a complete set of related information for an individual or an item, such as one person's name and address. It is easiest to think of a data source file as a table: the header row contains the names of the data fields (the **field names**), and each row in the table is an individual data record. You can use the Mail Merge task pane to create a new data source, or you can merge a main document with an existing data source, such as a data source created in Word, an Outlook contact list, or an Access database.

- **Identify the fields to include in the data source and enter the records**

  When you create a new data source, you must first identify the fields to include. It's important to think of and include all the fields before you begin to enter data. For example, if you are creating a data source that includes addresses, you might need to include fields for a person's middle name, title, department name, or country, even though every address in the data source does not include that information. Once you have identified the fields and set up your data source, you are ready to enter the data for each record.

- **Add merge fields to the main document**

  A merge field is a placeholder that you insert in the main document to indicate where the data from each record should be inserted when you perform the merge. For example, in the location you want to insert a zip code, you insert a zip code merge field. The merge fields in a main document must correspond with the field names in the associated data source. Merge fields must be inserted, not typed, in the main document. The Mail Merge task pane provides access to the dialog boxes you use to insert merge fields.

- **Merge the data from the data source into the main document**

  Once you have established your data source and inserted the merge fields in the main document, you are ready to perform the merge. You can merge to a new file, which contains a customized version of the main document for each record in the data source, or you can merge directly to a printer, fax, or e-mail message.

FIGURE H-1: Mail merge process

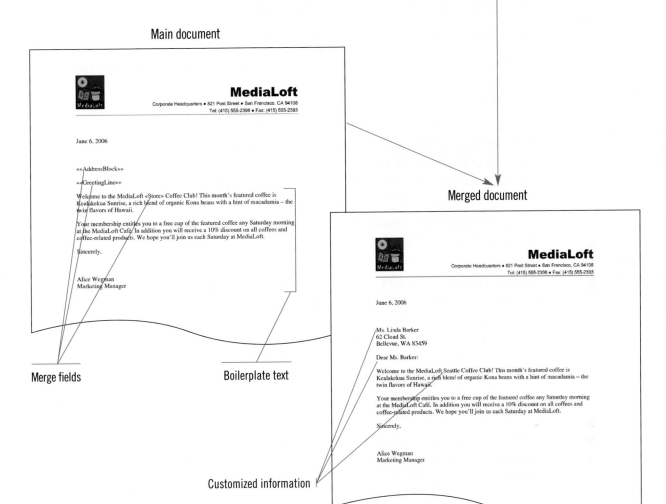

Data source document

Store	Title	First Name	Last Name	Address Line 1	City	State	Zip Code	Country
Seattle	Ms.	Linda	Barker	62 Cloud St.	Bellevue	WA	83459	US
Boston	Mr.	Bob	Cruz	23 Plum St.	Boston	MA	02483	US
Chicago	Ms.	Joan	Yatco	456 Elm St.	Chicago	IL	60603	US
Seattle	Ms.	Anne	Butler	48 East Ave.	Vancouver	BC	V6F 1AH	CANADA
Boston	Mr.	Fred	Silver	56 Pearl St.	Cambridge	MA	02139	US

Field name

Data record

Main document

MediaLoft
Corporate Headquarters ● 821 Post Street ● San Francisco, CA 94108
Tel: (415) 555-2398 ● Fax: (415) 555-2393

June 6, 2006

««AddressBlock»»

««GreetingLine»»

Welcome to the MediaLoft «Store» Coffee Club! This month's featured coffee is Kealakekua Sunrise, a rich blend of organic Kona beans with a hint of macadamia – the twin flavors of Hawaii.

Your membership entitles you to a free cup of the featured coffee any Saturday morning at the MediaLoft Café. In addition you will receive a 10% discount on all coffees and coffee-related products. We hope you'll join us each Saturday at MediaLoft.

Sincerely,

Alice Wegman
Marketing Manager

Merge fields

Boilerplate text

Merged document

MediaLoft
Corporate Headquarters ● 821 Post Street ● San Francisco, CA 94108
Tel: (415) 555-2398 ● Fax: (415) 555-2393

June 6, 2006

Ms. Linda Barker
62 Cloud St.
Bellevue, WA 83459

Dear Ms. Barker:

Welcome to the MediaLoft Seattle Coffee Club! This month's featured coffee is Kealakekua Sunrise, a rich blend of organic Kona beans with a hint of macadamia – the twin flavors of Hawaii.

Your membership entitles you to a free cup of the featured coffee any Saturday morning at the MediaLoft Café. In addition you will receive a 10% discount on all coffees and coffee-related products. We hope you'll join us each Saturday at MediaLoft.

Sincerely,

Alice Wegman
Marketing Manager

Customized information

Creating a Main Document

The first step in performing a mail merge is to create the main document—the file that contains the boiler-plate text. You can create a main document from scratch, save an existing document as a main document, or use a mail merge template to create a main document. The Mail Merge task pane walks you through the process of selecting the type of main document to create. ▓▓▓▓ You use an existing form letter for your main document. You begin by opening the Mail Merge task pane.

STEPS

QUICK TIP

You can click an option button in the task pane to read a description of each type of merge document.

1. **Start Word, click** Tools **on the menu bar, point to** Letters and Mailings, **then click** Mail Merge

   The Mail Merge task pane opens, as shown in Figure H-2, and displays information for the first step in the mail merge process: selecting the type of merge document to create.

2. **Make sure the** Letters option button **is selected, then click** Next: Starting document **to continue with the next step**

   The task pane displays the options for the second step: selecting the main document. You can use the current document, start with a mail merge template, or use an existing file.

QUICK TIP

If you choose "Use the current document" and the current document is blank, you can create a main document from scratch. Either type the boilerplate text at this step, or wait until the task pane prompts you to do so.

3. **Select the** Start from existing document option button, **make sure** More files **is selected in the Start from existing list box, then click** Open

   The Open dialog box opens.

4. **Use the** Look in list arrow **to navigate to the drive and folder where your Data Files are located, select the file** WD H-1.doc, **then click** Open

   The letter that opens contains the boilerplate text for the main document. Notice the filename in the title bar is Document1. When you create a main document that is based on an existing document, Word gives the main document a default temporary filename.

5. **Click the** Save button 🖫 **on the Standard toolbar, then save the main document with the filename** Coffee Letter Main **to the drive and folder where your Data Files are located**

   It's a good idea to include "main" in the filename so that you can easily recognize the file as a main document.

6. **Click the** Zoom list arrow **on the Standard toolbar, click** Text Width, **select** April 9, 2006 **in the letter, type today's date, scroll down, select** Alice Wegman, **type your name, press** [Ctrl][Home], **then save your changes**

   The edited main document is shown in Figure H-3.

7. **Click** Next: Select recipients **to continue with the next step**

   You continue with Step 3 of 6 in the next lesson.

Clues to Use

Using a mail merge template

If you are creating a letter, fax, or directory, you can use a mail merge template to start your main document. Each template includes boiler-plate text, which you can customize, and merge fields, which you can match to the field names in your data source. To create a main document that is based on a mail merge template, click the Start from a template option button in the Step 2 of 6 Mail Merge task pane, then click Select template. In the Select Template dialog box, select a template on the Mail Merge tab, then click OK to create the document. Once you have created the main document, you can customize it with your own information: edit the boilerplate text, change the document format, or add, remove, or modify the merge fields. Before performing the merge, make sure to match the names of the address merge fields used in the template with the field names used in your data source. To match the field names, click the Match Fields button 🔲 on the Mail Merge toolbar, and then use the list arrows in the Match Fields dialog box to select the field name in your data source that corresponds to each address field component in the main document.

FIGURE H-2: Step 1 of 6 Mail Merge task pane

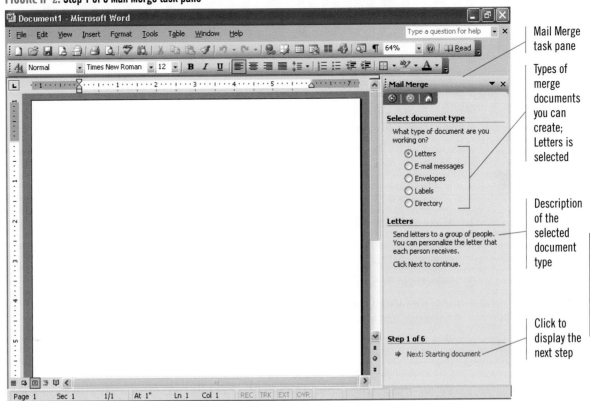

Mail Merge task pane

Types of merge documents you can create; Letters is selected

Description of the selected document type

Click to display the next step

Word 2003

FIGURE H-3: Main document with the Step 2 of 6 Mail Merge task pane

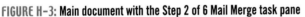
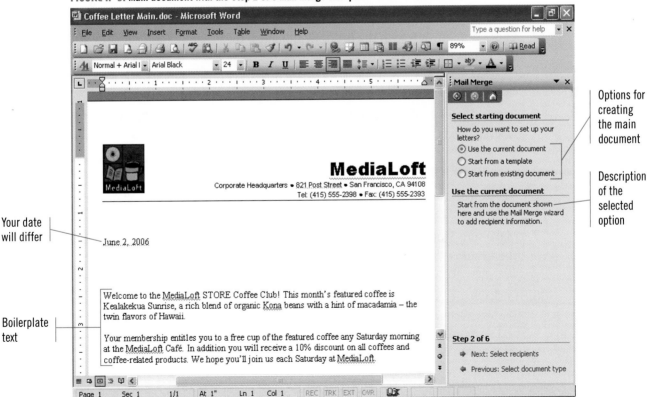

Options for creating the main document

Description of the selected option

Your date will differ

Boilerplate text

Designing a Data Source

Once you have identified the main document, the next step in the mail merge process is to identify the data source, the file that contains the information that differs in each version of the merge document. You can use an existing data source that already contains the records you want to include in your merge, or you can create a new data source. When you create a new data source you must determine the fields to include—the categories of information, such as a first name, last name, city, or zip code—and then add the records. 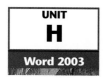 You create a new data source that includes fields for the name, address, and MediaLoft store location of each new member of the Coffee Club.

STEPS

1. **Make sure Step 3 of 6 is displayed at the bottom of the Mail Merge task pane**

   Step 3 of 6 involves selecting a data source to use for the merge. You can use an existing data source, a list of contacts created in Microsoft Outlook, or a new data source.

2. **Select the Type a new list option button, then click Create**

   The New Address List dialog box opens, as shown in Figure H-4. You use this dialog box both to design your data source and to enter records. The Enter Address information section of the dialog box includes fields that are commonly used in form letters, but you can customize your data source by adding and removing fields from this list. A data source can be merged with more than one main document, so it's important to design a data source to be flexible. The more fields you include in a data source, the more flexible it is. For example, if you include separate fields for a person's title, first name, middle name, and last name, you can use the same data source to create an envelope addressed to "Mr. John Montgomery Smith" and a form letter addressed to "Dear John."

3. **Click Customize**

   The Customize Address List dialog box opens, as shown in Figure H-5. You use this dialog box to add, delete, rename, and reorder the fields in the data source.

4. **Click Company Name in the list of field names, click Delete, then click Yes in the warning dialog box that opens**

   Company Name is removed from the list of field names. The Company Name field is no longer a part of the data source.

5. **Repeat Step 4 to delete the Address Line 2, Home Phone, Work Phone, and E-mail Address fields**

   The fields are removed from the data source.

6. **Click Add, type Store in the Add Field dialog box, then click OK**

   A field called "Store," which you will use to indicate the location of the MediaLoft store where the customer joined the Coffee Club, is added to the data source.

7. **Make sure Store is selected in the list of field names, then click Move Up eight times**

   The field name "Store" is moved to the top of the list. Although the order of field names does not matter in a data source, it's convenient to arrange the field names logically to make it easier to enter and edit records.

8. **Click OK**

   The New Address List dialog box shows the customized list of fields, with the Store field first in the list. The next step is to enter each record you want to include in the data source. You add records to the data source in the next lesson.

FIGURE H-4: New Address List dialog box

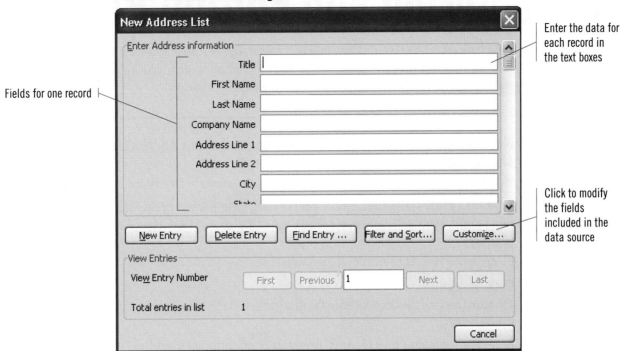

Fields for one record

Enter the data for each record in the text boxes

Click to modify the fields included in the data source

FIGURE H-5: Customize Address List dialog box

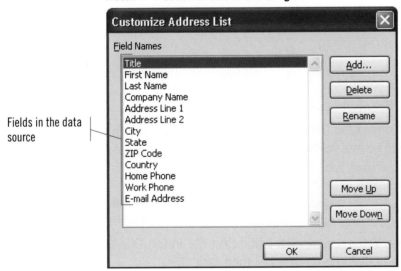

Fields in the data source

Clues to Use

Merging with an Outlook data source

If you maintain lists of contacts in Microsoft Outlook, you can use one of your Outlook contact lists as a data source for a merge. To merge with an Outlook data source, click the Select from Outlook contacts option button in the Step 3 of 6 Mail Merge task pane, then click Choose Contacts Folder to open the Select Contact List Folder dialog box. In this dialog box, select the contact list you want to use as the data source, and then click OK. All the contacts included in the selected folder appear in the Mail Merge Recipients dialog box. Here you can refine the list of recipients to include in the merge by sorting and filtering the records. When you are satisfied, click OK in the Mail Merge Recipients dialog box.

Entering and Editing Records

Once you have established the structure of a data source, the next step is to enter the records. Each record includes the complete set of information for each individual or item you include in the data source. You create a record for each new member of the Coffee Club.

STEPS

QUICK TIP
Be careful not to add spaces or extra punctuation after an entry in a field, or these will appear when the data is merged.

1. **Place the insertion point in the Store text box in the New Address List dialog box, type Seattle, then press [Tab]**

   "Seattle" appears in the Store field and the insertion point moves to the next field in the list, the Title field.

2. **Type Ms., press [Tab], type Linda, press [Tab], type Barker, press [Tab], type 62 Cloud St., press [Tab], type Bellevue, press [Tab], type WA, press [Tab], type 83459, press [Tab], then type US**

   Compare your New Address List dialog box with Figure H-6.

QUICK TIP
It's OK to leave a field blank if you do not need it for a record.

3. **Click New Entry**

   The record for Linda Barker is added to the data source and the dialog box displays empty fields for the next record, record 2.

4. **Enter the following four records, pressing [Tab] to move from field to field, and clicking New Entry at the end of each record except the last:**

Store	Title	First Name	Last Name	Address Line 1	City	State	ZIP Code	Country
Boston	Mr.	Bob	Cruz	23 Plum St.	Boston	MA	02483	US
Chicago	Ms.	Joan	Yatco	456 Elm St.	Chicago	IL	60603	US
Seattle	Ms.	Anne	Butler	48 East Ave.	Vancouver	BC	V6F 1AH	CANADA
Boston	Mr.	Fred	Silver	56 Pearl St.	Cambridge	MA	02139	US

5. **Click Close**

   The Save Address List dialog box opens. Data sources are saved by default in the My Data Sources folder so that you can easily locate them to use in other merge operations. Data sources you create in Word are saved in Microsoft Office Address Lists (*.mdb) format.

TROUBLE
If a check mark appears in the blank record under Fred Silver, click the check mark to eliminate the record from the merge.

6. **Type New Coffee Club Data in the File name text box, use the Save in list arrow to navigate to the drive and folder where your Data Files are located, then click Save**

   The data source is saved, and the Mail Merge Recipients dialog box opens, as shown in Figure H-7. The dialog box shows the records in the data source in table format. You can use the dialog box to edit, sort, and filter records, and to select the recipients to include in the mail merge. You will learn more about sorting and filtering in a later lesson. The check marks in the first column indicate the records that will be included in the merge.

7. **Click the Joan Yatco record, click Edit, select Ms. in the Title text box in the New Coffee Club Data.mdb dialog box, type Dr., then click Close**

   The data in the Title field for Joan Yatco changes from "Ms." to "Dr." and the New Coffee Club Data.mdb dialog box closes.

QUICK TIP
If you want to add new records or modify existing records, click Edit recipient list in the task pane.

8. **Click OK in the Mail Merge Recipients dialog box**

   The dialog box closes. The file type and filename of the data source attached to the main document now appear under Use an existing list in the Mail Merge task pane, as shown in Figure H-8. The Mail Merge toolbar also appears in the program window when you close the data source. You learn more about the Mail Merge toolbar in later lessons.

FIGURE H-6: Record in New Address List dialog box

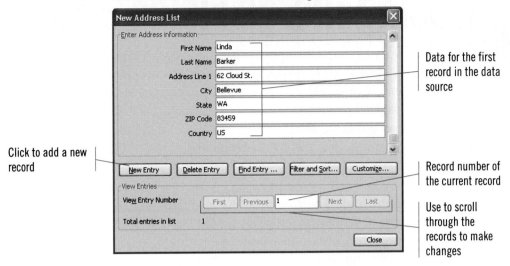

Data for the first record in the data source

Click to add a new record

Record number of the current record

Use to scroll through the records to make changes

FIGURE H-7: Mail Merge Recipients dialog box

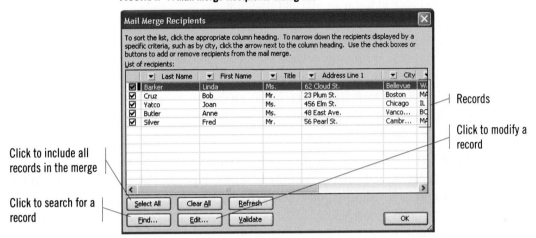

Records

Click to modify a record

Click to include all records in the merge

Click to search for a record

FIGURE H-8: Data source attached to the main document

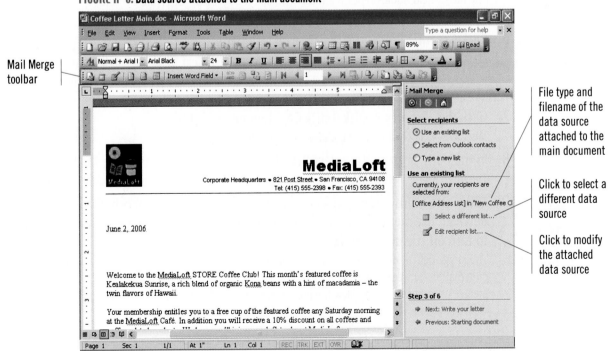

Mail Merge toolbar

File type and filename of the data source attached to the main document

Click to select a different data source

Click to modify the attached data source

Adding Merge Fields

After you have created and identified the data source, the next step is to insert the merge fields in the main document. Merge fields serve as placeholders for text that is inserted when the main document and the data source are merged. The names of merge fields correspond to the field names in the data source. You can insert merge fields using the Mail Merge task pane or the Insert Merge Field button on the Mail Merge toolbar. You cannot type merge fields into the main document. 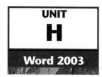 You use the Mail Merge task pane to insert merge fields for the inside address and greeting of the letter. You also insert a merge field for the store location in the body of the letter.

STEPS

1. **Click the Show/Hide ¶ button ¶ on the Standard toolbar to display formatting marks, then click Next: Write your letter in the Mail Merge task pane**

   The Mail Merge task pane shows the options for Step 4 of 6, writing the letter and inserting the merge fields in the main document. Since your form letter is already written, you are ready to add the merge fields to it.

   > **QUICK TIP**
   > You can also click the Insert Address Block button 📄 on the Mail Merge toolbar to insert an address block.

2. **Place the insertion point in the blank line above the first body paragraph, then click Address block in the Mail Merge task pane**

   The Insert Address Block dialog box opens, as shown in Figure H-9. You use this dialog box to specify the fields you want to include in an address block. In this merge, the address block is the inside address of the form letter. An address block automatically includes fields for the street, city, state, and postal code, but you can select the format for the recipient's name and indicate whether to include a company name or country in the address.

3. **Scroll the list of formats for a recipient's name to get a feel for the kinds of formats you can use, then click Mr. Joshua Randall Jr. if it is not already selected**

   The selected format uses the recipient's title, first name, and last name.

4. **Make sure the Only include the country/region if different than: option button is selected, select United States in the text box, type US, then deselect the Format address according to the destination country/region check box**

   You only need to include the country in the address block if the country is different from the United States, so you indicate that all entries in the Country field except "US" should be included in the printed address.

   > **QUICK TIP**
   > You cannot simply type chevrons around a field name. You must insert merge fields using the Mail Merge task pane or the buttons on the Mail Merge toolbar.

5. **Click OK, then press [Enter] twice**

   The merge field AddressBlock is added to the main document. Chevrons (<< and >>) surround a merge field to distinguish it from the boilerplate text.

6. **Click Greeting line in the Mail Merge task pane**

   The Greeting Line dialog box opens. You want to use the format "Dear Mr. Randall:" (the recipient's title and last name, followed by a colon) for a greeting. The default format uses a comma, so you have to change the comma to a colon.

7. **Click the , list arrow, click :, click OK, then press [Enter]**

   The merge field GreetingLine is added to the main document.

   > **QUICK TIP**
   > You can also click the Insert Merge Fields button 📄 on the Mail Merge toolbar to insert a merge field.

8. **In the body of the letter select STORE, then click More items in the Mail Merge task pane**

   The Insert Merge Field dialog box opens and displays the list of field names included in the data source.

9. **Make sure Store is selected, click Insert, click Close, press [Spacebar] to add a space between the merge field and Coffee if there is no space, save your changes, then click ¶ to turn off the display of formatting marks**

   The merge field Store is inserted in the main document, as shown in Figure H-10. You must type spaces and punctuation between merge fields if you want spaces and punctuation to appear between the data in the merged documents. You preview the merged data and perform the merge in the next lesson.

FIGURE H-9: Insert Address Block dialog box

Formats for the
recipient's name

Click to match the
default address field
names to the field
names used in your
data source

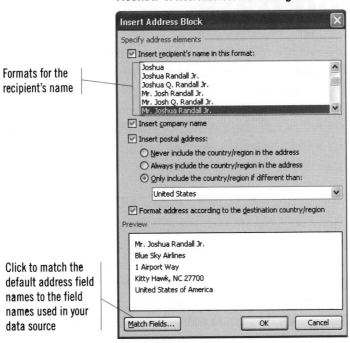

FIGURE H-10: Merge fields in the main document

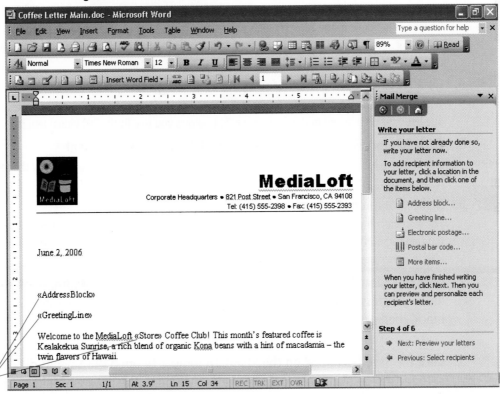

Merge fields

Clues to Use

Matching fields

The merge fields you insert in a main document must correspond
with the field names in the associated data source. If you are using
the Address Block merge field, you must make sure that the default
address field names correspond with the field names used in your
data source. If the default address field names do not match the field

names in your data source, click Match Fields in the Insert Address
Block dialog box, then use the list arrows in the Match Fields dialog
box to select the field name in the data source that corresponds to
each default address field name.

Merging Data

Once you have added records to your data source and inserted merge fields in the main document, you are ready to perform the merge. Before merging, it's a good idea to preview the merged data to make sure the printed documents will appear as you want them to. You can preview the merge using the task pane or the View Merged Data button on the Mail Merge toolbar. When you merge the main document with the data source, you must choose between merging to a new file or directly to a printer. ▗▞▞ Before merging the form letter with the data source, you preview the merge to make sure the data appears in the letter as you intended. You then merge the two files to a new document.

STEPS

QUICK TIP

To adjust the main document, click the View Merged Data button ▣▣ on the Mail Merge toolbar, then make any necessary changes. Click ▣▣ again to preview the merged data.

1. **Click Next: Preview your letters in the Mail Merge task pane**

   The data from the first record in the data source appears in place of the merge fields in the main document, as shown in Figure H-11. Always check the preview document to make sure the merge fields, punctuation, page breaks, and spacing all appear as you intend before you perform the merge.

2. **Click the Next Recipient button ▣▣ in the Mail Merge task pane**

   The data from the second record in the data source appears in place of the merge fields.

3. **Click the Go to Record text box on the Mail Merge toolbar, press [Backspace], type 4, then press [Enter]**

   The data for the fourth record appears in the document window. The non-US country name, in this case Canada, is included in the address block, just as you specified. You can also use the First Record ▣, Previous Record ▣, Next Record ▣, and Last Record ▣ buttons on the Mail Merge toolbar to preview the merged data. Table H-1 describes other buttons on the Mail Merge toolbar.

QUICK TIP

If your data source contains many records, you can merge directly to a printer to avoid creating a large file.

4. **Click Next: Complete the merge in the Mail Merge task pane**

   The options for Step 6 of 6 appear in the Mail Merge task pane. Merging to a new file creates a document with one letter for each record in the data source. This allows you to edit the individual letters.

5. **Click Edit individual letters to merge the data to a new document**

   The Merge to New Document dialog box opens. You can use this dialog box to specify the records to include in the merge.

QUICK TIP

To restore a main document to a regular Word document, click the Main document setup button ▣ on the Mail Merge toolbar, then click Normal Word document. Restoring a main document removes the associated data source from it.

6. **Make sure the All option button is selected, then click OK**

   The main document and the data source are merged to a new document called Letters1, which contains a customized form letter for each record in the data source. You can now further personalize the letters without affecting the main document or the data source.

7. **Click the Zoom list arrow on the Standard toolbar, click Page Width, scroll to the fourth letter (addressed to Ms. Anne Butler), place the insertion point before V6F in the address block, then press [Enter]**

   The postal code is now consistent with the proper format for a Canadian address.

8. **Click the Save button ▣ on the Standard toolbar to open the Save As dialog box, then save the merge document as Coffee Letter Merge to the drive and folder where your Data Files are located**

   You may decide not to save a merged file if your data source is large. Once you have created the main document and the data source, you can create the letters by performing the merge again.

9. **Click File on the menu bar, click Print, click the Current Page option button in the Page range section of the Print dialog box, click OK, then close all open Word files, saving changes if prompted**

   The letter to Anne Butler prints.

FIGURE H-11: Preview of merged data

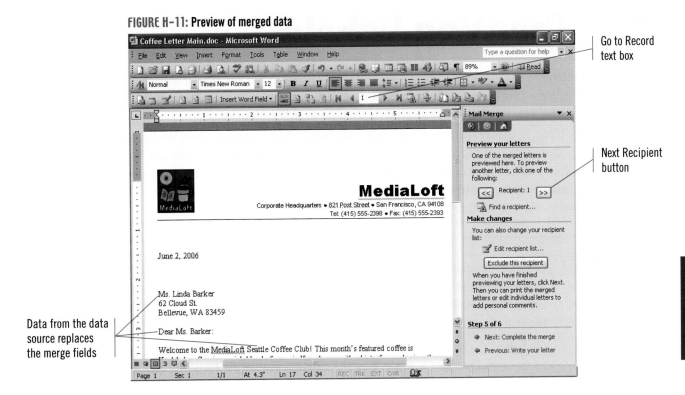

Go to Record text box

Next Recipient button

Data from the data source replaces the merge fields

TABLE H-1: Buttons on the Mail Merge toolbar

button	use to	button	use to
	Change the main document to a different type, or convert it to a normal Word document		Highlight the merge fields in the main document
	Select an existing data source		Match address fields with the field names used in the data source
	Edit, sort, or filter the associated data source		Search for a record in the merged documents
	Insert an Address Block merge field		Check for errors in the merged documents
	Insert a Greeting Line merge field		Merge the data to a new document and display it on screen
	Insert a merge field from the data source		
	Switch between viewing the main document with merge fields and with merged data		Print the merged documents without first reviewing them on screen

UNIT
H
Word 2003

Creating Labels

You can also use the Mail Merge task pane to create mailing labels or print envelopes for a mailing. When you create labels or envelopes, you must select a standard label or envelope size to use as the main document, select a data source, and then insert the merge fields in the main document before performing the merge. In addition to mailing labels, you can use mail merge to create labels for diskettes, CDs, videos, and other items, and to create documents that are based on standard or custom label sizes, such as business cards, nametags, and postcards. ▃▃▃▃ You use the Mail Merge task pane to create mailing labels for a brochure you need to send to all members of the Coffee Club. You create a new label main document and attach an existing data source.

STEPS

1. **Click the** New Blank Document button 🗋 **on the Standard toolbar, click the** Zoom list arrow **on the Standard toolbar, click** Page Width, **click** Tools **on the menu bar, point to** Letters and Mailings, **then click** Mail Merge

   The Mail Merge task pane opens.

> **TROUBLE**
> If your dialog box does not show Avery standard, click the Label products list arrow, then click Avery standard.

2. **Click the** Labels option button **in the Mail Merge task pane, click** Next: Starting document **to move to Step 2 of 6, make sure the** Change document layout option button **is selected, then click** Label options

   The Label Options dialog box opens, as shown in Figure H-12. You use this dialog box to select a label size for your labels and to specify the type of printer you plan to use. The default brand name Avery standard appears in the Label products list box. You can use the Label products list arrow to select other label products or a custom label. The many standard types of Avery labels for mailings, file folders, diskettes, post cards, and other types of labels are listed in the Product number list box. The type, height, width, and paper size for the selected product are displayed in the Label information section.

> **TROUBLE**
> If your gridlines are not visible, click Table on the menu bar, then click Show Gridlines.

3. **Scroll down the Product number list, click** 5161 – Address, **then click** OK

   A table with gridlines appears in the main document, as shown in Figure H-13. Each table cell is the size of a label for the label product you selected.

4. **Save the label main document with the filename** Coffee Labels Main **to the drive and folder where your Data Files are located**

   Next you need to select a data source for the labels.

5. **Click** Next: Select recipients **to move to Step 3 of 6, make sure the** Use an existing list option button **is selected, then click** Browse

   The Select Data Source dialog box opens.

6. **Use the** Look in list arrow **to navigate to the drive and folder where your Data Files are located, then open the file** WD H-2.mdb

   The Mail Merge Recipients dialog box opens and displays all the records in the data source. In the next lesson you sort and filter the records before performing the mail merge.

FIGURE H-12: Label Options dialog box

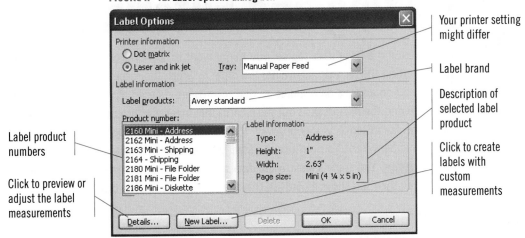

Your printer setting might differ

Label brand

Description of selected label product

Click to create labels with custom measurements

Label product numbers

Click to preview or adjust the label measurements

FIGURE H-13: Label main document

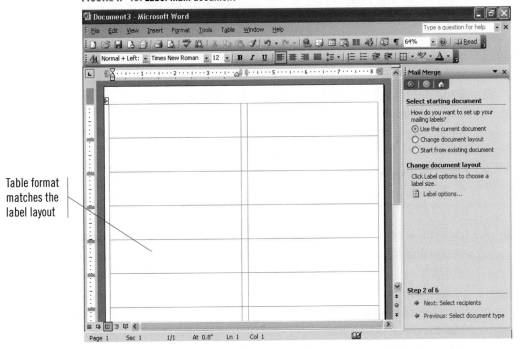

Table format matches the label layout

Clues to Use

Printing individual envelopes and labels

The Mail Merge task pane enables you to easily print envelopes and labels for mass mailings, but you can also quickly format and print individual envelopes and labels using the Envelopes and Labels dialog box. To open the Envelopes and Labels dialog box, point to Letters and Mailings on the Tools menu, then click Envelopes and Labels. On the Envelopes tab, shown in Figure H-14, type the recipient's address in the Delivery address box and the return address in the Return address box. Click Options to open the Envelope Options dialog box, which you can use to select the envelope size, add a postal bar code, change the font and font size of the delivery and return addresses, and change the printing options. When you are ready to print the envelope, click Print in the Envelopes and Labels dialog box. The procedure for printing an individual label is similar to printing an individual envelope: enter the recipient's address on the Labels tab, click Options to select a label product number, click OK, then click Print.

FIGURE H-14: Envelopes and Labels dialog box

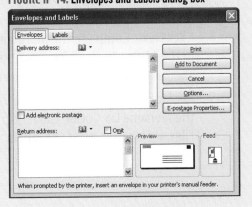

Sorting and Filtering Records

If you are using a large data source, you might want to sort and/or filter the records before performing a merge. Sorting the records determines the order in which the records are merged. For example, you might want to sort an address data source so that records are merged alphabetically by last name or in zip code order. Filtering the records pulls out the records that meet specific criteria and includes only those records in the merge. For instance, you might want to filter a data source to send a mailing only to people who live in the state of New York. You can use the Mail Merge Recipients dialog box both to sort and to filter a data source. ▧▧▧▧ You apply a filter to the data source so that only United States addresses are included in the merge. You then sort those records so that they merge in zip code order.

STEPS

QUICK TIP

For more advanced sort and filter options, click Filter and Sort in the New Address List dialog box when you create or edit the data source.

1. **In the Mail Merge Recipients dialog box, scroll right to display the Country field, click the Country column heading list arrow, then click US on the menu that opens**

   A filter is applied to the data source so that only the records with "US" in the Country field will be merged. The blue arrow in the Country column heading indicates that a filter has been applied to the column. You can filter a data source by as many criteria as you like. To remove a filter, click a column heading list arrow, then click "All."

2. **Scroll right, click the ZIP Code column heading, then scroll right again to see the ZIP Code column**

   The Mail Merge Recipients dialog box now displays only the records with a US address sorted in zip code order, as shown in Figure H-15. If you want to reverse the sort order, you can click a column heading again.

3. **Click OK, then click Next: Arrange your labels in the Mail Merge task pane**

   The sort and filter criteria you set are saved for the current merge, and the options for Step 4 of 6 appear in the task pane.

QUICK TIP

You use the Insert Postal Bar Code dialog box to select the field names for the zip code and street address in your data source. Postal bar codes can be inserted only for U.S. addresses.

4. **Click Postal bar code in the task pane, then click OK in the Insert Postal Bar Code dialog box**

   A merge field for a U.S. postal bar code is inserted in the first label in the main document. When the main document is merged with the data source, a customized postal bar code determined by the recipient's zip code and street address will appear on every label.

5. **Press [→], press [Enter], click Address block in the task pane, then click OK in the Insert Address Block dialog box**

   The Address Block merge field is added to the first label.

6. **Point to the down arrow at the bottom of the task pane to scroll down, then click Update all labels in the task pane**

   The merge fields are copied from the first label to every label in the main document.

QUICK TIP

To change the font or paragraph formatting of merged data, format the merge fields before performing a merge.

7. **Click Next: Preview your labels in the task pane**

   A preview of the merged label data appears in the main document. Only U.S. addresses are included, and the labels are organized in zip code order.

8. **Click Next: Complete the merge in the task pane, click Edit individual labels, then click OK in the Merge to New Document dialog box**

   The merged labels document is shown in Figure H-16.

9. **Replace Ms. Clarissa Landfair with your name in the first label, save the document with the filename US Coffee Labels Zip Code Merge to the drive and folder where your Data Files are located, print the labels, save and close all open files, then exit Word**

FIGURE H-15: US records sorted in zip code order

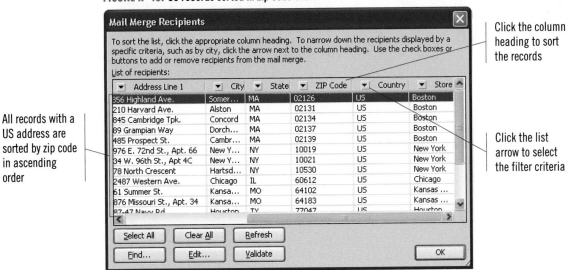

Click the column heading to sort the records

All records with a US address are sorted by zip code in ascending order

Click the list arrow to select the filter criteria

FIGURE H-16: Merged labels

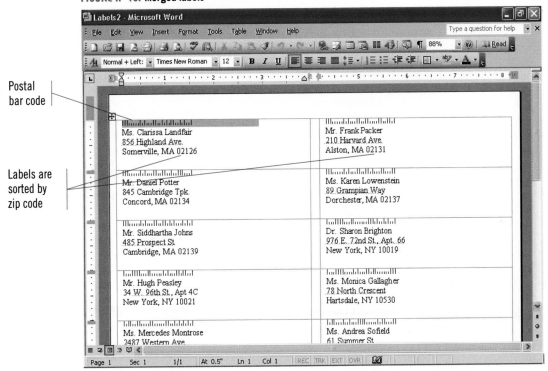

Postal bar code

Labels are sorted by zip code

Word 2003

Clues to Use

Inserting individual merge fields

You must include proper punctuation, spacing, and blank lines between the merge fields in a main document if you want punctuation, spaces, and blank lines to appear between the data in the merge documents. For example, to create an address line with a city, state, and zip code, you insert the City merge field, type a comma and a space, insert the State merge field, type a space, and then insert the Zip Code merge field: <<City>>, <<State>> <<Zip Code>>.

You can insert an individual merge field by selecting the field name in the Insert Merge Fields dialog box, clicking Insert, and then clicking Close. You can also insert several merge fields at once by clicking a field name in the Insert Merge Field dialog box, clicking Insert, clicking another field name, clicking Insert, and so on. When you have finished inserting the merge fields, click Close. You can then add spaces, punctuation, and lines between the merge fields you inserted in the main document.

Practice

▼ CONCEPTS REVIEW

Label each toolbar button shown in Figure H-17.

Figure H-17

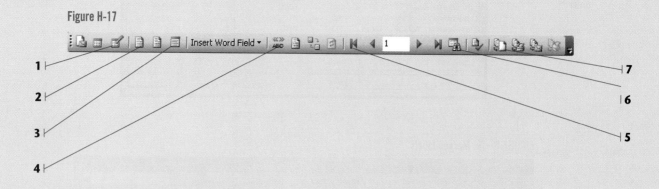

Match each term with the statement that best describes it.

8. Main document
9. Merge field
10. Data field
11. Boilerplate text
12. Data source
13. Data record
14. Filter
15. Sort

a. To organize records in a sequence
b. A file that contains customized information for each item or individual
c. To pull out records that meet certain criteria
d. A category of information in a data source
e. The standard text that appears in every version of a merged document
f. A complete set of information for one item or individual
g. A file that contains boilerplate text and merge fields
h. A placeholder for merged data in the main document

Select the best answer from the list of choices.

16. In a mail merge, which type of file contains the information that varies for each individual or item?
    a. Data source
    b. Main document
    c. Label document
    d. Merge document

17. Which of the following buttons can be used to insert a merge field for an inside address?
    a.
    b.
    c.
    d.

18. Which of the following buttons can be used to preview the merged data in the main document?
    a.
    b.
    c.
    d.

19. To change the font of merged data, which element should you format?
    a. Data record
    b. Merge field
    c. Field name
    d. Boilerplate text

20. Which of the following is included in a data source?
    a. Records
    b. Boilerplate text
    c. Labels
    d. Merge fields

▼ SKILLS REVIEW

1. Create a main document.

a. Start Word, then open the Mail Merge task pane.

b. Use the Mail Merge task pane to create a letter main document, click Next, then select the current (blank) document.

c. At the top of the blank document, press [Enter] four times, type today's date, press [Enter] five times, then type **We are delighted to receive your generous contribution of AMOUNT to the New England Humanities Council (NEHC).**

d. Press [Enter] twice, then type **Whether we are helping adult new readers learn to read or bringing humanities programs into our public schools, senior centers, and prisons, NEHC depends upon private contributions to ensure that free public humanities programs continue to flourish in CITY and throughout the REGION region. I hope we will see you at a humanities event soon.**

e. Press [Enter] twice, type **Sincerely**, and press [Enter] four times, type your name, press [Enter], then type **Executive Director**.

f. Save the main document as **Donor Thank You Main** to the drive and folder where your Data Files are located.

2. Design a data source.

a. Click Next, select the Type a new list option button in the Step 3 of 6 Mail Merge task pane, then click Create.

b. Click Customize in the New Address List dialog box, then remove these fields from the data source: Company Name, Address Line 2, Country, Home Phone, Work Phone, and E-mail Address.

c. Add an **Amount** field and a **Region** field to the data source. Be sure these fields follow the ZIP Code field.

d. Rename the Address Line 1 field **Street**, then click OK to close the Customize Address List dialog box.

3. Enter and edit records.

a. Add the following records to the data source:

Title	First Name	Last Name	Street	City	State	Zip Code	Amount	Region
Mr.	John	Conlin	34 Mill St.	Exeter	NH	03833	$250	Seacoast
Mr.	Bill	Webster	289 Sugar Hill Rd.	Franconia	NH	03632	$1000	Seacoast
Ms.	Susan	Janak	742 Main St.	Derby	VT	04634	$25	North Country
Mr.	Derek	Gray	987 Ocean Rd.	Portsmouth	NH	03828	$50	Seacoast
Ms.	Rita	Murphy	73 Bay Rd.	Durham	NH	03814	$500	Seacoast
Ms.	Amy	Hunt	67 Apple St.	Northfield	MA	01360	$75	Pioneer Valley
Ms.	Eliza	Perkins	287 Mountain Rd.	Dublin	NH	03436	$100	Pioneer Valley

b. Save the data source as **Donor Data** to the drive and folder where your Data Files are located.

c. Change the region for record 2 (Bill Webster) from Seacoast to **White Mountain**.

d. Click OK to close the Mail Merge Recipients dialog box.

4. Add merge fields.

a. Click Next, then in the blank line above the first body paragraph, insert an Address Block merge field.

b. In the Insert Address Block dialog box, click Match Fields.

c. Click the list arrow next to Address 1 in the Match Fields dialog box, click Street, then click OK.

d. In the Insert Address Block dialog box, select the Never include the country/region in the address option button, then click OK.

e. Press [Enter] twice, insert a Greeting Line merge field using the default greeting line format, then press [Enter].

f. In the first body paragraph, replace AMOUNT with the Amount merge field.

g. In the second body paragraph, replace CITY with the City merge field and REGION with the Region merge field. (*Note:* Make sure to insert a space before or after each merge field as needed.)

h. Save your changes to the main document.

5. Merge data.

    a. Click Next to preview the merged data, then scroll through each letter.

    b. Click the View Merged Data button on the Mail Merge toolbar, place the insertion point before "I hope" in the second sentence of the second body paragraph, then press [Enter] twice to create a new paragraph.

    c. Combine the first and second body paragraphs into a single paragraph.

    d. Make any other necessary adjustments to the letter, save your changes, then click the View Merged Data button to return to the preview of the document.

    e. Click Next, click Edit individual letters, then merge all the records to a new file.

    f. Save the merged document as **Donor Thank You Merge** to the drive and folder where your Data Files are located, print a copy of the first letter, then save and close all open files.

6. Create labels.

    a. Open a new blank document, then open the Mail Merge task pane.

    b. Create a label main document, click Next, then select the Change document layout option button if necessary in the Step 2 of 6 Mail Merge task pane.

    c. Open the Label Options dialog box, select Avery standard 5162 – Address labels, then click OK.

    d. Save the label main document as **Donor Labels Main** to the drive and folder where your Data Files are located, then click Next.

    e. Select the Use an existing list option button, click Browse, then open the Donor Data.mdb file you created.

7. Sort and filter records.

    a. Filter the records so that only the records with NH in the State field are included in the merge.

    b. Sort the records in zip code order, then click OK.

    c. If the Mail Merge toolbar is not open, point to Toolbars on the View menu, then click Mail Merge.

    d. Click Next, insert a Postal bar code merge field using the default settings, press [→], then press [Enter].

    e. Insert an Address Block merge field using the default settings, click the View Merged Data button on the Mail Merge toolbar, then notice that the street address is missing and the address block includes the region.

    f. Click the View Merged Data button again, click the Address Block merge field in the upper-left table cell to select it if necessary, then click Address block in the Mail Merge task pane.

    g. Click Match Fields in the Insert Address Block dialog box to open the Match Fields dialog box.

    h. Click the list arrow next to Address 1, click Street, scroll down, click the list arrow next to Country or Region, click (not matched), click OK, then click OK again.

    i. Click the View Merged Data button to preview the merged data, and notice that the address block now includes the street address and the region name is missing.

    j. Click Update all labels in the Mail Merge task pane, then click Next to move to Step 5.

    k. Examine the merged data for errors, then click Next to move to Step 6.

    l. Click Edit individual labels, merge all the records, then save the merged file as **NH Donor Labels Merge** to the drive and folder where your Data Files are located.

    m. In the first label, change Ms. Eliza Perkins to your name, save the document, then print it.

    n. Save and close all open Word files, then exit Word.

▼ INDEPENDENT CHALLENGE 1

You are the director of the Emerson Arts Center (EAC). The EAC is hosting an exhibit of ceramic art in the city of Cambridge, Massachusetts, and you want to send a letter advertising the exhibit to all EAC members with a Cambridge address. You'll use Mail Merge to create the letter. If you are performing the ACE steps and are able to print envelopes on your printer, you will also use Word to print an envelope for one letter.

a. Start Word, then use the Mail Merge task pane to create a letter main document using the file WD H-3.doc, found on the drive and folder where your Data Files are located.

b. Replace Your Name with your name in the signature block, then save the main document as **Member Letter Main** to the drive and folder where your Data Files are located.

c. Use the file WD H-4.mdb, found on the drive and folder where your Data Files are located, as the data source.

d. Sort the data source by last name, then filter the data so that only records with Cambridge as the city are included in the merge.

e. Insert an Address Block and a Greeting Line merge field in the main document, preview the merged letters, then make any necessary adjustments.

f. Merge all the records to a new document, then save it as **Member Letter Merge** to the drive and folder where your Data Files are located.

g. Print the first letter.

Advanced Challenge Exercise

- If you can print envelopes, select the inside address in the first merge letter, click Tools on the menu bar, point to Letters and Mailings, then click Envelopes and Labels.
- On the Envelopes tab, verify that no check mark appears in the check box next to Omit, type your name in the Return address text box, type **60 Crandall Street, Concord, MA 01742**, click Options, make sure the Envelope size is set to Size 10, then change the font of the Delivery address and the Return address to 12-point Times New Roman.
- On the Printing Options tab, select the appropriate Feed method for your printer, then click OK.
- Click Print, then click No to save the return address as the default.

h. Close all open Word files, saving changes, and then exit Word.

▼ INDEPENDENT CHALLENGE 2

One of your responsibilities at JDE Enterprises, a growing information technology company, is to create business cards for the staff. You use mail merge to create the cards so that you can easily produce standard business cards for future employees.

a. Start Word, then use the Mail Merge task pane to create labels using the current blank document as the main document.

b. Select Avery standard 3612 – Business Card labels.

c. Create a new data source that includes the following fields: Title, First Name, Last Name, Phone, Fax, E-mail, and Hire Date. Add the following records to the data source:

Title	First Name	Last Name	Phone	Fax	E-mail	Hire Date
President	Sandra	Bryson	(312) 555-3982	(312) 555-6654	sbryson@jde.com	1/12/01
Vice President	Philip	Holm	(312) 555-2323	(312) 555-4956	pholm@jde.com	1/12/01

d. Add six more records to the data source, including one with your name as the Administrative Assistant.

e. Save the data source with the filename **Employee Data** to the drive and folder where your Data Files are located, then sort the data by Title.

▼ INDEPENDENT CHALLENGE 2

f. In the first table cell, create the JDE Enterprises business card. Figure H-18 shows a sample JDE business card, but you should create your own design. Include the company name, a street address, and the Web site address www.jde.com. Also include a First Name, Last Name, Title, Phone, Fax, and E-mail merge fields. (*Hint:* If your design includes a graphic, insert the graphic before inserting the merge fields. Use the Insert Merge Field dialog box to insert each merge field, adjusting the spacing between merge fields as necessary.)

g. Format the business card with fonts, colors, and other formatting features. (*Note:* Use the Other Task Panes list arrow to reopen the Mail Merge task pane if necessary.)

FIGURE H-18

JDE Enterprises

Sandra Bryson
President

234 Walden Street, Dublin, PA 32183
Tel: (312) 555-3982; Fax: (312) 555-6654
E-mail: sbryson@jde.com
www.jde.com

h. Update all the labels, preview the data, make any necessary adjustments, then merge all the records to a new document.

i. Save the merge document with the filename **Business Cards Merge** to the drive and folder where your Data Files are located, print a copy, then close the file.

j. Save the main document with the filename **Business Cards Main** to the drive and folder where your Data Files are located, close the file, then exit Word.

▼ INDEPENDENT CHALLENGE 3

You need to create a team roster for the children's softball team you coach. You decide to use mail merge to create the team roster. If you are completing the ACE steps, you will also use mail merge to create mailing labels.

a. Start Word, then use the Mail Merge task pane to create a directory using the current blank document.

b. Create a new data source that includes the following fields: First Name, Last Name, Age, Position, Parent First Name, Parent Last Name, Address, City, State, Zip Code, and Home Phone.

c. Enter the following records in the data source:

First Name	Last Name	Age	Position	Parent First Name	Parent Last Name	Address	City	State	Zip Code	Home Phone
Sophie	Wright	8	Shortstop	Kerry	Wright	58 Main St.	Camillus	NY	13031	555-2345
Will	Jacob	7	Catcher	Bob	Jacob	32 North Way	Camillus	NY	13031	555-9827
Brett	Eliot	8	First base	Olivia	Eliot	289 Sylvan Way	Marcellus	NY	13032	555-9724
Abby	Herman	7	Pitcher	Sarah	Thomas	438 Lariat St.	Marcellus	NY	13032	555-8347

d. Add five additional records to the data source using the following last names and positions:
O'Keefe, Second base
George, Third base
Goleman, Left field
Siebert, Center field
Choy, Right field
Make up the remaining information for these five records.

e. Save the data source as **Softball Team Data** to the drive and folder where your Data Files are located.

f. Sort the records by last name, then click Next in the Mail Merge task pane.

g. Insert a table that includes five columns and one row in the main document.

h. In the first table cell, insert the First Name and Last Name merge fields, separated by a space.

i. In the second cell, insert the Position merge field.

j. In the third cell, insert the Address and City merge fields, separated by a comma and a space.

k. In the fourth cell, insert the Home Phone merge field.

l. In the fifth cell, insert the Parent First Name and Parent Last Name merge fields, separated by a space.

m. Preview the merged data and make any necessary adjustments. (*Hint*: Only one record is displayed at a time when you preview the data.)

n. Merge all the records to a new document, then save the document with the filename **Softball Roster Merge** to the drive and folder where your Data Files are located.

o. Press [Ctrl][Home], press [Enter], type **Wildcats Team Roster** at the top of the document, press [Enter], type **Coach:**, followed by your name, then press [Enter] twice.

p. Insert a new row at the top of the table, then type the following column headings in the new row: **Name, Position, Address, Phone, Parent Name**.

q. Format the roster to make it attractive and readable, save your changes, print a copy, then close the file.

r. Close the main document without saving changes.

Advanced Challenge Exercise

■ Open a new blank document, then use the Mail Merge task pane to create mailing labels using Avery standard 5162 – Address labels.

■ Use the Softball Team Data data source you created, and sort the records in zip code order.

■ In the first table cell, create your own address block using the Parent First Name, Parent Last Name, Address, City, State, and Zip Code merge fields. Be sure to include proper spacing and punctuation.

■ Update all the labels, preview the merged data, merge all the records to a new document, then type your name centered in the document header.

■ Save the document with the filename **Softball Labels Merge ACE** to the drive and folder where your Data Files are located, print a copy, close the file, then close the main document without saving changes.

s. Exit Word.

▼ INDEPENDENT CHALLENGE 4

Your boss has given you the task of purchasing mailing labels for a mass mailing of your company's annual report. The annual report will be sent to 55,000 people. Your company plans to use Avery standard 5160 white labels for a laser printer, or their equivalent, for the mailing. In this independent challenge, you will search for Web sites that sell Avery labels, compare the costs, and then write a memo to your boss detailing your purchasing recommendations.

a. Use your favorite search engine to search for Web sites that sell Avery labels or the equivalent. Use the keywords **Avery labels** to conduct your search.

b. Find at least three Web sites that sell Avery 5160 white labels for a laser printer, or their equivalent. Note the URL of the Web sites and the price and quantity of the labels. You need to purchase enough labels for a mailing of 55,000, plus enough extras in case you make mistakes.

c. Start Word, then use the Professional Memo template to create a memo to your boss. Save the memo as **5160 Labels Memo** to the drive and folder where your Data Files are located.

d. In the memo, make up information to replace the placeholder text in the memo header, be sure to include your name in the memo header, then type the body of your memo.

e. In the body, include a table that shows the URL of each Web site, the product name, the unit cost, the number of labels in each unit, the number of units you need to purchase, and the total cost of purchasing the labels. Also make a brief recommendation to your boss.

f. Format the memo so it is attractive and readable, save your changes, print a copy, close the file, then exit Word.

▼ VISUAL WORKSHOP

Using the Mail Merge task pane, create the post cards shown in Figure H-19. Use Avery standard 3611 – Post Card labels for the main document and create a data source that contains at least four records. Save the data source as **Party Data**, save the main document as **Party Card Main**, and save the merge document as **Party Card Merge**, all to the drive and folder where your Data Files are located. (*Hint:* Use a table to lay out the postcard; the clip art graphic uses the keywords "party cake balloon"; and the font is Comic Sans MS.) Print a copy of the postcards.

FIGURE H-19

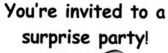

You're invited to a surprise party!

Grace Pappas
186 Buena Vista Terrace
Apt. 5C
San Francisco, CA 94117

For: Claudette Summer
When: August 3rd, 7:00 p.m.
Where: The Wharf Grill
Given by: Your Name

You're invited to a surprise party!

Mika Takeda
456 Parker Ave.
San Francisco, CA 94118

For: Claudette Summer
When: August 3rd, 7:00 p.m.
Where: The Wharf Grill
Given by: Your Name

Collaborating on Documents

OBJECTIVES

Track changes

Insert, view, and edit comments

Compare and merge documents

If you have a SAM user profile, you may have access to hands-on instruction, practice, and assessment of the skills covered in this unit. Log in to your SAM account and go to your assignments page to see what your instructor has assigned.

Several Word features make it easier to create and edit documents in cooperation with other people. The Track Changes, Comment, and Compare and Merge features in Word facilitate collaboration when two or more people are working on the same document. In this appendix, you learn how to track and review changes to a document, how to insert and work with comments, and how to compare and merge two documents. You have circulated a copy of the Chicago Marketing Report to two of your colleagues for feedback. You use the Track Changes, Comment, and Compare and Merge features to review their suggestions for changes and to combine their feedback into a final document.

Tracking Changes

A **tracked change** is a mark that shows where an insertion, deletion, or formatting change has been made in a document. When the Track Changes feature is turned on, each change that you or another reviewer makes to a document is tracked. In Print Layout view, text that is inserted in a document is displayed as colored, underlined text. Formatting changes and text that is deleted are shown in balloons in the right margin of the document. As you review the tracked changes in a document, you can choose to accept or reject each change. When you accept a change it becomes part of the document. When you reject a change, the text or formatting is restored to its original state. To turn tracked changes on and off, you use the Track Changes button on the Reviewing toolbar or the Track Changes command on the Tools menu. ░░░░ Your boss, Alice Wegman, has used Track Changes to suggest revisions to your draft report. You review Alice's tracked changes, accepting or rejecting them as you go, and then edit the document with your additional changes.

STEPS

TROUBLE

If the Reviewing toolbar is not already displayed, click View on the menu bar, point to Toolbars, then click Reviewing. If tracked changes and/or comments do not appear in your document, click the first list arrow on the Reviewing toolbar, then click Final Showing Markup.

1. **Start Word, open the file** WD AP-1.doc **from the drive and folder where your Data Files are located, then save it as** Chicago Draft 1

   The document, which contains tracked changes, opens in Print Layout view, as shown in Figure AP-1. Notice that the Track Changes button on the Reviewing toolbar is enabled, indicating that tracked changes are turned on in the document. Any change you make to the document will be marked as a tracked change.

2. **Click the** Next button 🔁 **on the Reviewing toolbar**

   The insertion point moves to the first tracked change in the document, in this case, a sentence inserted in the introductory paragraph.

3. **Click the** Accept Change button 🔲 **on the Reviewing toolbar, then click** 🔁

   The sentence becomes part of the document and the insertion point moves to a balloon containing a comment. You will work with comments in the next lesson, so you skip over the comment for now.

4. **Click** 🔁

   The insertion point moves to the balloon containing the deleted text "Half."

QUICK TIP

To quickly restore the text to its original state, select the entire line of text, and then click 🔲.

5. **Click the** Reject Change/Delete Comment button 🔲 **on the Reviewing toolbar, click** 🔁, **then click** 🔲

   The deleted word "Half" is restored to the document, the insertion point moves to the inserted word "Full," and then "Full" is removed from the document, returning the text to its original state, as shown in Figure AP-2.

6. **Click** 🔁 **to select the next tracked change, right-click the selected text, then click** Accept Insertion **on the shortcut menu**

   The sentence becomes part of the document text. You can accept or reject any tracked change by right-clicking it and then selecting the appropriate command on the shortcut menu.

QUICK TIP

To facilitate collaboration with several reviewers, the tracked changes made by each reviewer are displayed in a different color.

7. **Scroll down until the heading** Travel Writers & Photographers Conference **on page 2 is at the top of your screen, select** sixth **in the first sentence under the heading, type** seventh, **place the insertion point in front of** discussion **in the next line of text, then type** spirited **followed by a space**

   Your tracked changes are added to the document using a different color, as shown in Figure AP-3.

8. **Click the** Track Changes button 🔲 **on the Reviewing toolbar to turn off the Track Changes feature, press [Ctrl][Home], replace** Your Name **with your name at the top of the document, then click the** Save button 🔲 **on the Standard toolbar to save your changes**

FIGURE AP-1: Reviewing toolbar and tracked changes

Reviewing toolbar

Vertical bars indicate the adjacent line includes a tracked change

Track Changes button

Inserted text (your color might differ)

Comment in a balloon

Deleted text in a balloon

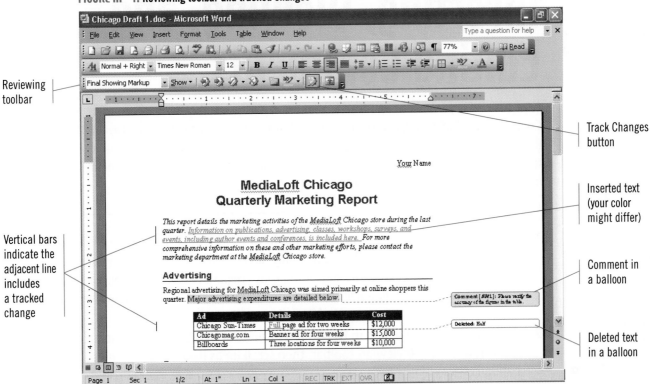

Word 2003

FIGURE AP-2: Text restored to its original state

Tracked change text becomes part of the document

Text is restored to the original state

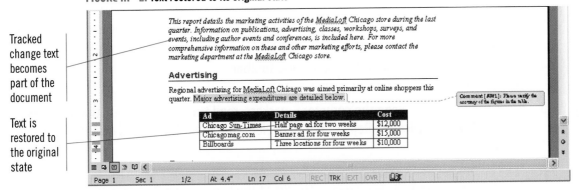

FIGURE AP-3: Tracked changes in the document

Deleted text

Your tracked changes appear in a color that is different than Alice's tracked changes (your color might differ)

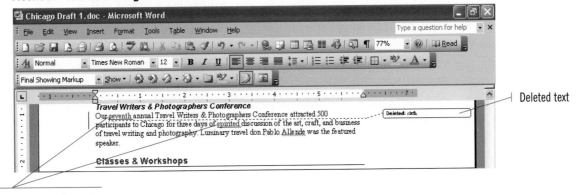

Inserting, Viewing, and Editing Comments

A **comment** is an embedded note or annotation that an author or reviewer adds to a document. Comments are displayed in a balloon in the right margin of a document in Print Layout, Web Layout, and Reading Layout views. To insert a comment, you can use the Insert Comment button on the Reviewing toolbar or the Comment command on the Insert menu. You review the comments in the document, responding to them or deleting them, and then add your own comments.

STEPS

1. **Click the** Track Changes button **on the Reviewing toolbar to turn on the Track Changes feature, then scroll down until the heading** Advertising **is at the top of your screen**

   The paragraph under the Advertising heading contains a comment. Notice that a comment mark appears in the document at the point the comment was inserted, and a dashed line leads from the comment mark to the comment balloon in the margin.

   QUICK TIP

   When you point to a comment in the document, a ScreenTip that contains the name of the comment author, the date and time the comment was inserted, and the comment text appears.

2. **Click the** comment balloon **in the right margin to select it, click the** Insert Comment button **on the Reviewing toolbar, then scroll up as needed to see the comment balloon**

   A blank comment balloon is inserted in the document using a different color (the same color as your tracked changes). You respond to a comment by selecting the comment and then inserting your own comment.

3. **Type** The numbers are correct., **then click outside the comment balloon to deselect the comment**

   The text is added to the comment balloon, as shown in Figure AP-4. You can edit comment text by placing the insertion point in a comment balloon and then typing.

4. **Click the** Next button **on the Reviewing toolbar**

   The next comment in the document is selected.

5. **Point to the text between the comment markers, read the comment text that appears in a ScreenTip, then click the** Reject Change/Delete Comment button **on the Reviewing toolbar**

   The comment is removed from the manuscript.

6. **Scroll down, select** Polly Flanagan **in the list at the top of page 2, then press** [Delete]

   Polly Flanagan is removed from the list and the list is renumbered.

7. **Click** , **then type** Polly Flanagan is the least likely to accept an invitation to speak.

   A new comment is inserted in the document, as shown in Figure AP-5.

8. **Click the** Reviewing Pane button **on the Reviewing toolbar**

   The comments and tracked changes in the document are listed in the Reviewing Pane at the bottom of the screen. It's useful to view comments and tracked changes in the Reviewing Pane when the full text of a comment or tracked change does not fit in the balloon.

9. **Click** **to close the Reviewing Pane, press** [Ctrl][Home], **save your changes to the document, then print a copy**

FIGURE AP-4: Response comment in the document

Comment marks surround the text at the location the comment was inserted

Alice Wegman's comment

Your response comment in a color that is different than Alice's (your color might differ)

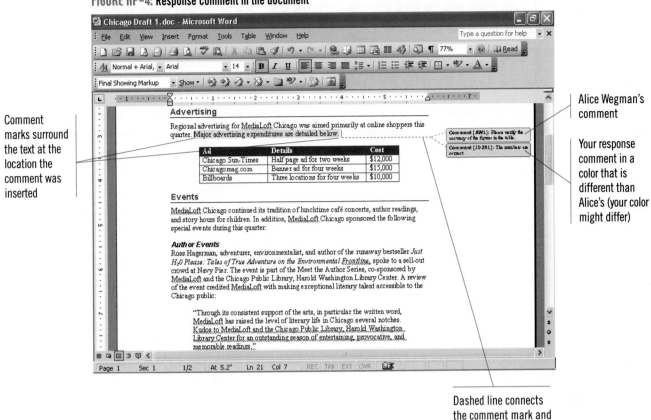

Dashed line connects the comment mark and the comment balloon

FIGURE AP-5: New comment in the document

New comment

Deleted text

Deleted formatting

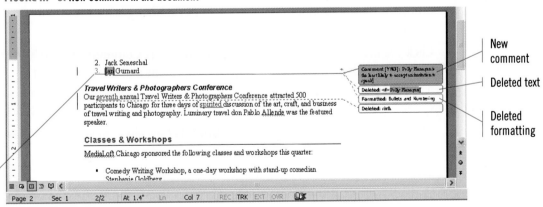

List is renumbered automatically

Word 2003

Comparing and Merging Documents

The Word Compare and Merge feature is used to compare any two documents to show the differences between the two. Compare and Merge is often used to show the differences between an original document and an edited copy of the original. It is also used to merge the changes and comments of multiple reviewers into a single document when each reviewer edits the document using a separate copy of the original. When you compare and merge two documents, you have the option of merging the changes into one of the documents or of merging the changes into a new third document. The differences between the two documents are shown in the merged document as tracked changes. You can then examine the merged document, edit it, and save it with a new filename. ▰▰▰▰ A second colleague, Nazila Sharif, returns her revisions to you in a separate copy of the document. You use the Compare and Merge feature to merge your document with Nazila's to create a new document that shows the differences between the two copies.

STEPS

1. **Click** Tools **on the menu bar, click** Compare and Merge Documents, **use the** Look in list arrow **to navigate to the drive and folder where your Data Files are located, then select the file** WD AP-2.doc **in the Compare and Merge Documents dialog box**
   The Compare and Merge Documents dialog box is shown in Figure AP-6. You use this dialog box to select the document that you want to merge with the current document. The file WD AP-2.doc is the file that contains Nazila's comments and tracked changes.

2. **Click the** Merge button list arrow **in the dialog box, then click** Merge into new document
   Your document is merged with Nazila's copy into a new document, as shown in Figure AP-7. Notice that each reviewer's comments and tracked changes are displayed in a different color in the merged document.

3. **Save the document as** Chicago Draft 2 **to the drive and folder where your Data Files are stored**
   The document is saved with a new filename.

4. **Read the document to review the tracked changes, click the** Accept Change list arrow 🖉▾ **on the Reviewing toolbar, then click** Accept All Changes in Document
   All the tracked changes are accepted and become part of the document.

5. **Click the** first comment **to select it, click the** Insert Comment button 🔲 **on the Reviewing toolbar, type** No., **then click outside the comment balloon to deselect it**
   A new comment is added to the document, as shown in Figure AP-8. After you have returned a copy of the file containing the comments to your colleagues, you will delete the comments and finalize the document.

6. **Save your changes to the document, print a copy, close all open files, then exit Word**

FIGURE AP-6: Compare and Merge Documents dialog box

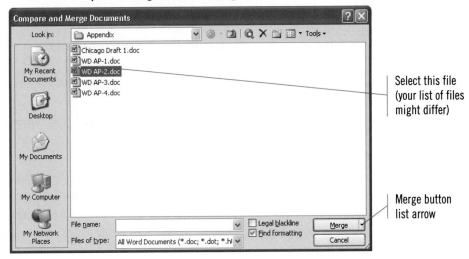

Select this file
(your list of files
might differ)

Merge button
list arrow

FIGURE AP-7: Merged document showing changes from each reviewer

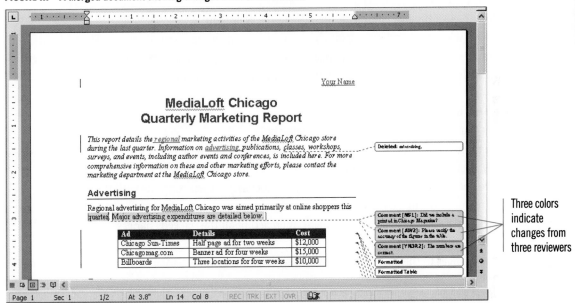

Three colors
indicate
changes from
three reviewers

FIGURE AP-8: New comment

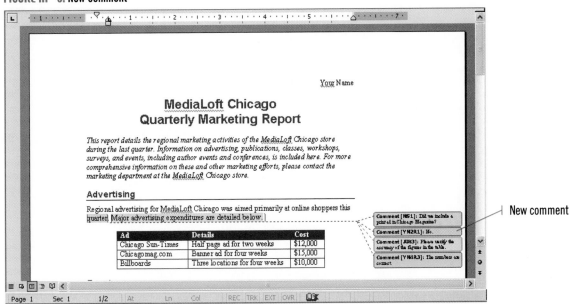

New comment

Word 2003

▼ SKILLS REVIEW

1. Track changes.

a. Start Word, open the file WD AP-3.doc from the drive and folder where your Data Files are located, then save it as **EDA Draft 1**.

b. Change the zoom level to Page Width, then open the Reviewing toolbar if it is not already displayed.

c. Using the Next button, review the tracked changes in the document.

d. Reject the first tracked change, then accept all remaining tracked changes in the document. Skip over the comments for now.

e. Make sure the Track Changes feature is turned on.

f. In the first sentence under the Guiding Principals heading, change Five to **Six**. Then, add the following sentence as point number six in the numbered list: **Open space in the rural district must be preserved.**

g. Under the Proposed Actions heading at the bottom of page 2, delete the sentence Sponsor an e-commerce workshop.

h. Turn off the Track Changes feature, press [Ctrl][Home], replace Your Name with your name at the top of the document, then save your changes.

2. Insert, view, and edit comments.

a. Scroll down, select the first comment, then delete the comment.

b. Scroll down, select 84% under the Issues heading, insert a new comment, then type **Should this be 86%?**

c. Scroll down, select the next comment, insert a new comment, then type **We can only estimate.**

d. Press [Ctrl][Home], save your changes to the document, then print a copy.

3. Compare and merge documents.

a. Open the Compare and Merge Documents dialog box.

b. Navigate to the drive and folder where your Data Files are located, select the file WD AP-4.doc, click the Merge button list arrow, then click Merge into new document.

c. Choose to keep the formatting changes from your document, then continue with the merge.

d. Save the merged document as **EDA Draft 2** to the drive and folder where your Data Files are located.

e. Review the tracked changes in the document, then accept all the tracked changes.

f. Delete all the comments.

g. Save your changes to the document, print a copy, close all open files, then exit Word.

Glossary

Adjustment handle The yellow diamond that appears when certain AutoShapes are selected; used to change the shape, but not the size, of an AutoShape.

Alignment The position of text in a document relative to the margins.

Anchored The state of a floating graphic that moves with a paragraph or other item if the item is moved; an anchor symbol appears with the floating graphic when formatting marks are displayed.

Application *See* Program.

Ascending order Lists data alphabetically or sequentially (from A to Z, 0 to 9, or earliest to latest).

AutoComplete A feature that automatically suggests text to insert.

AutoCorrect A feature that automatically detects and corrects typing errors, minor spelling errors, and capitalization, or inserts certain typographical symbols as you type.

Automatic page break A page break that is inserted automatically at the bottom of a page.

AutoShape A drawing object, such as a rectangle, oval, triangle, line, block arrow, or other shape that you create using the tools on the Drawing toolbar.

AutoText A feature that stores frequently used text and graphics so they can be easily inserted into a document.

Bitmap graphic A graphic that is composed of a series of small dots called "pixels."

Boilerplate text Text that appears in every version of a merged document.

Bold Formatting applied to text to make it thicker and darker.

Border A line that can be added above, below, or to the sides of a paragraph, text, or a table cell; a line that divides the columns and rows of a table.

Browser A software program used to access and display Web pages.

Bullet A small graphic symbol used to identify items in a list.

Cell The box formed by the intersection of a table row and table column.

Cell reference A code that identifies a cell's position in a table. Each cell reference contains a letter (A, B, C, and so on) to identify its column and a number (1, 2, 3, and so on) to identify its row.

Center Alignment in which an item is centered between the margins.

Character spacing Formatting that changes the width or scale of characters, expands or condenses the amount of space between characters, raises or lowers characters relative to the line of text, and adjusts kerning (the space between standard combinations of letters).

Character style A named set of character format settings that can be applied to text to format it all at once.

Chart A visual representation of numerical data, usually used to illustrate trends, patterns, or relationships.

Click and Type A feature that allows you to automatically apply the necessary paragraph formatting to a table, graphic, or text when you insert the item in a blank area of a document in Print Layout or Web Layout view.

Click and Type pointer A pointer used to move the insertion point and automatically apply the paragraph formatting necessary to insert text at that location in the document.

Clip A media file, such as a graphic, photograph, sound, movie, or animation, that can be inserted into a document.

Clip art A collection of graphic images that can be inserted into documents, presentations, Web pages, spreadsheets, and other Office files.

Clip Organizer A library of the clips that come with Word.

Clipboard A temporary storage area for items that are cut or copied from any Office file and are available for pasting. *See also* Office Clipboard and System Clipboard.

Column break A break that forces text following the break to begin at the top of the next column.

Comment An embedded note or annotation that an author or reviewer adds to a document.

Copy To place a copy of an item on the Clipboard without removing it from a document.

Crop To trim away part of a graphic.

Cut To remove an item from a document and place it on the Clipboard.

Cut and paste To move text or graphics using the Cut and Paste commands.

Data field A category of information, such as last name, first name, street address, city, or postal code.

Data record A complete set of related information for a person or an item, such as a person's name and address.

Data source In a mail merge, the file with the unique data for individual people or items.

Delete To permanently remove an item from a document.

Descending order Lists data in reverse alphabetical or sequential order (Z to A, 9 to 0, or latest to earliest).

Document The electronic file you create using Word.

Document properties Details about a file, such as author name or the date the file was created, that are used to organize and search for files.

Document window The workspace in the program window that displays the current document.

Drag and drop To move text or a graphic by dragging it to a new location using the mouse.

Drawing canvas A workspace for creating graphics.

Drop cap A large dropped initial capital letter that is often used to set off the first paragraph of an article.

Field A code that serves as a placeholder for data that changes in a document, such as a page number.

Field name The name of a data field.

File An electronic collection of information that has a unique name, distinguishing it from other files.

Filename The name given to a document when it is saved.

Filter In a mail merge, to pull out records that meet specific criteria and include only those records in the merge.

First line indent A type of indent in which the first line of a paragraph is indented more than the subsequent lines.

Floating graphic A graphic to which a text wrapping style has been applied, making the graphic independent of text and able to be moved anywhere on a page.

Font The typeface or design of a set of characters (letters, numbers, symbols, and punctuation marks).

Font effect Font formatting that applies a special effect to text, such as a shadow, an outline, small caps, or superscript.

Font size The size of characters, measured in points (pts).

Footer Information, such as text, a page number, or a graphic, that appears at the bottom of every page in a document or a section.

Format Painter A feature used to copy the format settings applied to the selected text to other text you want to format the same way.

Formatting marks Nonprinting characters that appear on screen to indicate the ends of paragraphs, tabs, and other formatting elements.

Formatting toolbar A toolbar that contains buttons for frequently used formatting commands.

Frame A section of a Web page window in which a separate Web page is displayed.

Full screen view A view that shows only the document window on screen.

Getting Started task pane A task pane that contains shortcuts for opening documents, for creating new documents, and for accessing information on the Microsoft Web site.

Gridlines Nonprinting lines that show the boundaries of table cells.

Gutter Extra space left for a binding at the top, left, or inside margin of a document.

Hanging indent A type of indent in which the second and subsequent lines of a paragraph are indented more than the first.

Hard page break *See* Manual page break.

Header Information, such as text, a page number, or a graphic, that appears at the top of every page in a document or a section.

Header row The first row of a table that contains the column headings.

Highlighting Transparent color that can be applied to text to call attention to it.

Home page The main page of a Web site and the first Web page viewers see when they visit a site.

Horizontal ruler A ruler that appears at the top of the document window in Print Layout, Normal, and Web Layout view.

HTML (Hypertext Markup Language) The programming language used to code how each element of a Web page should appear when viewed with a browser.

Hyperlink Text or a graphic that opens a file, Web page, or other item when clicked. Also known as a link.

I-beam pointer The pointer used to move the insertion point and select text.

Indent The space between the edge of a line of text or a paragraph and the margin.

Indent marker A marker on the horizontal ruler that shows the indent settings for the active paragraph.

Inline graphic A graphic that is part of a line of text in which it was inserted.

Insertion point The blinking vertical line that shows where text will appear when you type in a document.

Italic Formatting applied to text to make the characters slant to the right.

Justify Alignment in which an item is flush with both the left and right margins.

Keyboard shortcut A combination of keys or a function key that can be pressed to perform a command.

Landscape orientation Page orientation in which the page is wider than it is tall.

Left-align Alignment in which the item is flush with the left margin.

Left indent A type of indent in which the left edge of a paragraph is moved in from the left margin.

Line spacing The amount of space between lines of text.

List style A named set of format settings, such as indents and outline numbering, that can be applied to a list to format it all at once.

Main document In a mail merge, the document with the standard text.

Manual page break A page break inserted to force the text following the break to begin at the top of the next page.

Margin The blank area between the edge of the text and the edge of a page.

Menu bar The bar beneath the title bar that contains the names of menus; clicking a menu name opens a menu of program commands.

Merge To combine adjacent cells into a single larger cell.

Merge field A placeholder that you insert in the main document to indicate where the data from each record should be inserted when you perform a mail merge.

Mirror margins Margins used in documents with facing pages, where the inside and outside margins are mirror images of each other.

Negative indent A type of indent in which the left edge of a paragraph is moved to the left of the left margin.

Nested table A table inserted in a cell of another table.

Normal view A view that shows a document without margins, headers and footers, or graphics.

Nudge To move a graphic a small amount in one direction using the arrow keys.

Office Assistant An animated character offers tips and provides access to the program's Help system.

Office Clipboard A temporary storage area shared by all Office programs that can be used to cut, copy and paste multiple items within and between Office programs. The Office Clipboard can hold up to 24 items collected from any Office program. *See* Clipboard and System Clipboard.

Open To use one of the methods for opening a document to retrieve it and display it in the document window.

Outdent *See* Negative indent.

Outline view A view that shows the headings of a document organized as an outline.

Overtype mode A feature that allows you to overwrite existing text as you type.

Paragraph spacing The amount of space between paragraphs.

Paragraph style A named set of paragraph and character format settings that can be applied to a paragraph to format it all at once.

Paste To insert items stored on the Clipboard into a document.

Pixels Small dots that define color and intensity in a graphic.

Point The unit of measurement for text characters and the space between paragraphs and characters; ½ of an inch.

Portrait orientation Page orientation in which the page is taller than it is wide.

Print Layout view A view that shows a document as it will look on a printed page.

Print Preview A view of a file as it will appear when printed.

Program Task-oriented software (such as Excel or Word) that enables you to perform a certain type of task such as data calculation or word processing.

Reading Layout view A view that shows a document so that it is easy to read and annotate.

Right-align Alignment in which an item is flush with the right margin.

Right indent A type of indent in which the right edge of a paragraph is moved in from the right margin.

Sans serif font A font, such as Arial, whose characters do not include serifs, which are small strokes at the ends of letters.

Save To store a file permanently on a disk or to overwrite the copy of a file that is stored on a disk with the changes made to the file.

Save As Command used to save a file for the first time or to create a new file with a different filename, leaving the original file intact.

Scale To resize a graphic so that its height to width ratio remains the same.

ScreenTip A label that appears on the screen to identify a button or to provide information about a feature.

Scroll To use the scroll bars or the arrow keys to display different parts of a document in the document window.

Scroll arrows The arrows at the ends of the scroll bars that are clicked to scroll a document one line at a time.

Scroll bars The bars on the right edge (vertical scroll bar) and bottom edge (horizontal scroll bar) of the document window that are used to display different parts of the document in the document window.

Scroll box The box in a scroll bar that can be dragged to scroll a document.

Section A portion of a document that is separated from the rest of the document by section breaks.

Section break A formatting mark inserted to divide a document into sections.

Select To click or highlight an item in order to perform some action on it.

Serif font A font, such as Times New Roman, whose characters include serifs, which are small strokes at the ends of letters.

Shading A background color or pattern that can be applied to text, tables, or graphics.

Shortcut key *See* Keyboard shortcut.

Sizing handles The black squares or white circles that appear around a graphic when it is selected; used to change the size or shape of a graphic.

Smart tag A purple dotted line that appears under text that Word identifies as a date, name, address, or place.

Smart Tag Actions button The button that appears when you point to a smart tag.

Soft page break *See* Automatic page break.

Sort To organize data, such as table rows, items in a list, or records in a mail merge, in ascending or descending order.

Split To divide a cell into two or more cells.

Standard toolbar A toolbar that contains buttons for frequently used operating and editing commands.

Status bar The bar at the bottom of the Word program window that shows the vertical position, section, and page number of the insertion point, the total number of pages in a document, and the on/off status of several Word features.

Style A named collection of character and/or paragraph formats that are stored together and can be applied to text to format it quickly.

Subscript A font effect in which text is formatted in a smaller font size and placed below the line of text.

Superscript A font effect in which text is formatted in a smaller font size and placed above the line of text.

Symbols Special characters that can be inserted into a document using the Symbol command.

System Clipboard A clipboard that stores only the last item cut or copied from a document. *See* Clipboard and Office Clipboard.

Tab *See* Tab stop.

Tab leaders Lines that appear in front of tabbed text.

Tab stop A location on the horizontal ruler that indicates where to align text.

Table A grid made up of rows and columns of cells that you can fill with text and graphics.

Table style A named set of table format settings that can be applied to a table to format it all at once.

Tags HTML codes placed around the elements of a Web page to describe how each element should appear when viewed with a browser.

Task pane An area of the Word program window that contains shortcuts to Word formatting, editing, research, Help, clip art, mail merge, and other features.

Template A formatted document that contains placeholder text you can replace with your own text.

Text box A container that you can fill with text and graphics.

Theme A set of complementary design elements that you can apply to Web pages, e-mail messages, and other documents that are viewed on screen.

Title bar The bar at the top of the program window that indicates the program name and the name of the current file.

Toggle button A button that turns a feature on and off.

Toolbar A bar that contains buttons that you can click to perform commands.

Tracked change A mark that shows where an insertion, deletion, or formatting change has been made in a document.

Type a question for help box The list box at the right end of the menu bar that is used to query the Help system.

Undo To reverse a change by using the Undo button or command.

URL (Uniform Resource Locator) A Web address.

Vertex The point where two straight lines meet or the highest point in a curve.

Vertical alignment The position of text in a document relative to the top and bottom margins.

Vertical ruler A ruler that appears on the left side of the document window in Print Layout view.

View A way of displaying a document in the document window; each view provides features useful for editing and formatting different types of documents.

View buttons Buttons to the left of the horizontal scroll bar that are used to change views.

Web Layout view A view that shows a document as it will look when viewed with a Web browser.

Web page A document that can be stored on a computer called a Web server and viewed on the World Wide Web or on an intranet using a browser.

Web site A group of associated Web pages that are linked together with hyperlinks.

Wizard An interactive set of dialog boxes that guides you through a task.

WordArt A drawing object that contains text formatted with special shapes, patterns, and orientations.

Word processing program A software program that includes tools for entering, editing, and formatting text and graphics.

Word program window The window that contains the Word program elements, including the document window, toolbars, menu bar, and status bar.

Word-wrap A feature that automatically moves the insertion point to the next line as you type.

Index

Some of the exercises in this book require that you begin by opening a Data File. Follow one of the procedures below to obtain a copy of the Data Files you need.

Instructors

- A copy of the Data Files is on the Instructor Resources CD under the category Data Files for Students, which you can copy to your school's network for student use.

- Download the Data Files via the World Wide Web by following the instructions below.

- Contact us via e-mail at reply@course.com.

- Call Course Technology's Customer Service Department for fast and efficient delivery of the Data Files if you do not have access to a CD-ROM drive.

Students

- Check with your instructor to determine the best way to obtain a copy of the Data Files.

- Download the Data Files via the World Wide Web by following the instructions below.

Instructions for Downloading the Data Files from the World Wide Web

1. Start your browser and enter the URL www.course.com.

2. When the course.com Web site opens, click Student Downloads, and then search for your text by title or ISBN.

3. If necessary, from the Search results page, select the title of the text you are using.

4. When the textbook page opens, click the Download Student Files link, and then click the link of the compressed files you want to download.

5. If the File Download dialog box opens, make sure the Save this program to disk option button is selected, and then click the OK button. (NOTE: If the Save As dialog box opens, select a folder on your hard disk to download the file to. Write down the folder name listed in the Save in box and the filename listed in the File name box.)

6. The filename of the compressed file appears in the Save As dialog box (e.g., 3500-8.exe, 0361-1d.exe).

7. Click either the OK button or the Save button, whichever choice your browser gives you.

8. When a dialog box opens indicating the download is complete, click the OK button (or the Close button, depending on which operating system you are using). Close your browser.

9. Open Windows Explorer and display the contents of the folder to which you downloaded the file. Double-click the downloaded filename on the right side of the Windows Explorer window.

10. In the WinZip Self-Extractor window, specify the appropriate drive and a folder name to unzip the files to. Click Unzip.

11. When the WinZip Self-Extractor displays the number of files unzipped, click the OK button. Click the Close button in the WinZip Self-Extractor dialog box. Close Windows Explorer.

12. Refer to the Read This Before You Begin page(s) in this book for more details on the Data Files for your text. You are now ready to open the required files.

Macintosh users should use a program to expand WinZip or PKZip archives. Students, ask your instructors or lab coordinators for assistance.

Keep Your Skills Fresh with Quick Reference CourseCards!

Thomson Course Technology CourseCards allow you to easily learn the basics of new applications or quickly access tips and tricks long after your class is complete.

Each highly visual, four-color, six-sided CourseCard features:

- **Basic Topics** enable users to effectively utilize key content.

- **Tips and Solutions** reinforce key subject matter and provide solutions to common situations.

- **Menu Quick References** help users navigate through the most important menu tools using a simple table of contents model.

- **Keyboard Shortcuts** improve productivity and save time.

- **Screen Shots** effectively show what users see on their monitors.

- **Advanced Topics** provide advanced users with a clear reference guide to more challenging content.

Over 75 CourseCards are available on a variety of topics! To order, please visit *www.courseilt.com/ilt_cards.cfm*

IF THIS BOOK DOES NOT HAVE A COURSECARD ATTACHED TO THE BACK COVER, YOU ARE NOT GETTING THE FULL VALUE OF YOUR PURCHASE.